D1389412

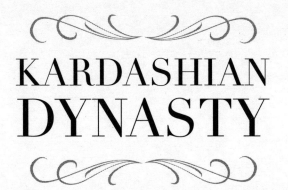

KARDASHIAN
DYNASTY

KARDASHIAN DYNASTY

IAN HALPERIN

**SIMON &
SCHUSTER**

London · New York · Sydney · Toronto · New Delhi

A CBS COMPANY

First published in Great Britain by Simon & Schuster UK Ltd, 2016
A CBS COMPANY

1 3 5 7 9 10 8 6 4 2

Simon & Schuster UK Ltd
1st Floor
222 Gray's Inn Road
London WC1X 8HB

www.simonandschuster.co.uk

Simon & Schuster Australia, Sydney
Simon & Schuster India, New Delhi

A CIP catalogue record for this book
is available from the British Library

Hardback ISBN: 978-1-4711-5519-2
Trade paperback ISBN: 978-1-4711-5520-8
eBook ISBN: 978-1-4711-5522-2

Interior design by Jaime Putorti

Printed and bound by CPI Group (UK) Ltd, Croydon, CR0 4YY

MIX
Paper from
responsible sources
FSC
www.fsc.org   FSC® C020471

Simon & Schuster UK Ltd are committed to sourcing paper
that is made from wood grown in sustainable forests and support the Forest
Stewardship Council, the leading international forest certification organisation.
Our books displaying the FSC logo are printed on FSC certified paper.

To Jackie Collins,
The most noble, selfless, whip-smart,
do-gooder author ever. One runaway bestseller after
another. You dared to define another side of Hollywood.
There will never be another you. RIP!!!

KARDASHIAN
DYNASTY

Shortly after 5:00 p.m. on June 17, 1994, an unknown businessman with bushy eyebrows and salt-and-pepper hair stepped to the microphone before a throng of reporters and a TV audience of millions to read a prepared statement on behalf of his longtime friend and former roommate O. J. Simpson.

As the man read O.J.'s statement—interpreted by most observers as a suicide note—his name flashed on the screen. It was the first time most people had heard the name Kardashian.

Five days earlier, Simpson's ex-wife Nicole Brown Simpson and a waiter named Ronald Goldman were found brutally murdered outside her Brentwood condominium. Suspicion immediately focused on former football star Simpson, whose on-again, off-again relationship with Nicole had been tumultuous.

Robert Kardashian first heard about the murders on the morning of June 13 from a friend, who had heard about them from her hairdresser. Stunned, he immediately drove to Simpson's Rockingham estate. During the ten-minute drive, he placed a call to his ex-wife Kris Jenner.

"Did you hear Nicole was killed?" he asked.

Kris told him she had heard the news from Nicole's mother.

"I was supposed to have lunch with Nicole today," she informed him, still reeling from the shock.

In the days to come, O.J. would quietly move into Kardashian's home to escape the media circus. Together, they put together a legal team and planned a strategy. It was from Kardashian's Encino home, in fact, that O.J. took off in a white Bronco SUV with his friend Al Cowlings, beginning the most famous police chase in history.

Simpson had been scheduled to surrender himself to authorities that morning at 11:00 a.m. but had failed to appear, prompting Los Angeles police to declare him a fugitive. Shortly after Kardashian read his friend's statement, law enforcement authorities zeroed in on Simpson's Bronco on Interstate 5, setting off a worldwide frenzy that ended hours later in O.J.'s arrest for the murders of Nicole and Goldman.

For the duration of the subsequent nine-month trial, Kardashian would sit silently next to O.J. on the defense bench every day as a member of his vaunted Dream Team. In the process, he became a household name. For almost a year, the world was riveted by the trial, while a large segment of the population obsessed over the minute details of the case and the personalities of its many players. After the verdict, the media and the public eventually turned their attention to other matters.

Few could have predicted that two decades later, the case would inadvertently give rise to a celebrity phenomenon that would eventually occupy more column inches and magazine covers than even the Trial of the Century.

When Robert Kardashian was born in 1944, America was still fighting a world war. And while the war heralded an economic recovery from the Great Depression, which had ravaged the economy, most

Americans were waiting until the war ended to start families because of lingering economic uncertainties. The Allied victory in 1945 eventually gave rise to the country's largest ever baby boom. However, unlike most Americans who had suffered through the Depression, Robert's parents, Helen and Arthur Kardashian, didn't need to worry about their financial future.

By the time Robert came along, Arthur was one of the wealthiest businessmen in Los Angeles. His vast fortune, however, wasn't a result of the Horatio Alger, rags-to-riches, immigrant-made-good story that the American public liked to feast on. Arthur hadn't pulled himself up by his own bootstraps. It was his father, Tatos, who had arrived in America three decades earlier and started a garbage-collection business that would eventually see Robert Kardashian born into the lifestyle that would come to be associated with his family name.

For his part, Tatos Kardashian owed his success as much to superstition as to hard work—and to a mystical prophet that helped his family escape genocide.

In the mid-nineteenth century, a group of Protestant Armenian religious rebels known as the Molokans were given permission by Tsar Nicholas II to escape religious persecution in Armenia and move to the Russian village of Karakale, which is today a part of Turkey. The Molokans—roughly translated as "milk lovers"—earned the title because they often ate and drank milk and other banned foods on religious feast days. Their defiance of Eastern Orthodox customs earned them the scorn of their fellow Armenians, who would often shun them or violently attack them as heretics. A smaller sect of Molokan religious zealots were known as "Jumpers" because of their tendency to leap in the air and raise their fists in worship during church services, in a religious fervor similar to that displayed by Pentecostalists.

One such Jumper family was Sam and Hurom Kardaschoff—the Russian version of *Kardashian*—who gave birth in Karakale to a boy named Tatos in 1896.

Four decades earlier, another boy from Karakale named Efim Klubiniken—an illiterate twelve-year-old—was said to have issued an apocalyptic prophecy:

> *Those who believe in this will go on a journey to a far land, while the unbelievers will remain in place. Our people will go on a long journey over the great and deep waters. People from all countries will go there. There will be a great war. All kings will shed blood like great rivers. Two steamships will leave to cross the impassable ocean.*

The prophecy was ignored. But in the early years of the twentieth century, Klubiniken—now a respected village elder—called a meeting of church leaders from the region and reminded them of his boyhood prediction. He warned them that the time was coming for them to escape Russia and that soon they would be barred from leaving. He pointed to a map of the West Coast of the United States and declared that his people should settle in America—"the land of the living"—before it was too late.

"He prophesied this was the time for them to leave Russia as there were terrible times coming, especially for the Armenians," researcher Joyce Keosababian-Bivin later told the London *Daily Mail*.

Over the next ten years, more than two thousand ethnic Armenians heeded the warning and fled to California, even as their friends and neighbors taunted them for believing such superstitious nonsense.

In 1913, Tatos's parents made their way to Bremen and boarded the SS *Brandenburg* to Philadelphia. A month later, seventeen-year-old Tatos followed on the SS *Köln*. On board the cramped ship, he met another fleeing Jumper, Hamas Shakarian, whom he would later marry.

Four years later, as the First World War raged and Russia became engulfed in revolution, Turkish forces stormed the region, massacring Armenians, including virtually every inhabitant of Karakale. Eventually more than 1.5 million Armenians would perish in a genocide that was said to have inspired Hitler's Final Solution. Today, Armenians refer to the slaughter as the Great Calamity. If the Kardashians hadn't heeded the warnings of the prophet Efim Klubiniken, they would almost certainly have been counted among its victims.

Instead, Tatos and many of his fellow Armenians thrived in their new home, Southern California. Los Angeles was still a sleepy desert town full of orange groves and silent-movie studios that would not truly explode into a metropolis for decades. The arrival of the Kardashian family in 1913 coincided with the opening of the Los Angeles Aqueduct, which would guarantee the drought-stressed city an ample water supply and pave the way for its eventual exponential growth.

Tatos, now known as Tom, opened a small garbage-collection business that would later grow into a thriving enterprise and make him a small fortune.

In 1917, Hamas gave birth to a boy, Arthur, followed by two more children later. In 1938, Arthur would wed another Armenian émigré, Helen Arkenian. By that time, he had started a thriving meatpacking business. When America entered the Second World War in December 1941, military contracts to keep the troops fed made Arthur Kardashian's company the most successful meat supplier on the West Coast.

By the time Robert was born in February 1944, the family were multimillionaires and neither Robert nor his older brother, Tommy, wanted for anything. The family lived in a Spanish-colonial mansion in the tony LA suburb of Windsor Hills, where Robert would graduate from Dorsey High in 1962. From there he attended the University of Southern California (USC), where he was the student manager of the football team. He graduated in 1966 and eventually earned a law degree from the University of San Diego in 1969.

Shortly after graduation, Robert joined the small boutique law firm Eamer Bedrosian, which was run by two Armenians. As the firm was too small for its associates to specialize, Robert practiced a combination of corporate and entertainment law but was occasionally called on to represent clients on criminal matters such as DUI. A profile in *Los Angeles* magazine would later describe Kardashian as "bright but no genius . . . the 'let's do lunch guy' rather than the idea man." Indeed, the young attorney was known for cultivating a growing circle of friends, many of whom would eventually become clients. His talent for turning three-hour business lunches into new revenue would earn Robert a partnership in the firm in less than three years.

One of those clients was an oil executive named Harry Rothschild, who invited Robert for a gathering and a round of tennis at his Benedict Canyon estate in the summer of 1970. It was on the tennis court that day that Robert Kardashian first met O.J. Simpson.

O.J. had been a star running back at USC shortly after Kardashian graduated and had been drafted by the Buffalo Bills. He had played professionally for a year by the time the two met but had registered unimpressive stats. The two men hit it off almost immediately and became fast friends.

Before long, O.J. would often crash during the off-season at the Beverly Hills house that Robert shared with his older brother, Tommy. O.J. and Robert had something in common—an entrepreneurial spirit that found them sitting around the pool hatching get-rich-quick schemes.

As O.J.'s growing prowess on the football field eventually turned him into a superstar, the two men attempted to cash in on his fame by opening up a clothing store on the USC campus called J-A-G. It didn't last long. They followed that up with a frozen yogurt shop— one of the first in the nation—in Brentwood called JOY (under the business name Juice Inc.). They sold it two years later at a loss.

Recalling their unsuccessful business ventures, Kardashian would later tell Larry King, "We have been in business deals together and we have lost a lot of money together. And that's when you tell what a person is like."

Kardashian's business mentor, George Mason of Bear Stearns, would later describe Kardashian's business enterprises to the *Los Angeles Times*.

"Some click, some don't," he said. "I think he's more entrepreneurial. He's not the kind who wants to be chained to a desk and take a briefcase full of work home with him every night."

With Mason's guidance, one of Kardashian's ventures without Simpson—a trade magazine he founded with his brother in 1973 called *Radio & Records*—would eventually make him a very rich man when he sold his shares in 1979 for more than $12 million. With the profits from the sale, Kardashian started another business with Simpson called Concert Cinema, screening music videos in theaters before featured movies, but it too was a bust. Despite their many failed ventures, Kardashian would later describe O.J.'s integrity in business as "excellent," even if he didn't feel the same way about his friend's personal life. By the time Kardashian was named president of MCA's radio network in the mid-1980s, he had already stopped practicing law and was a full-time businessman. Throughout the '80s, the two bachelors were often inseparable. At one point, O.J. even stayed at Kardashian's Deep Canyon home for more than six months.

While his partners attended to the business of the firm, Robert would often disappear for hours at a time on what he would claim were business lunches. More often than not, he could be found at one of the many racetracks in and around Southern California, betting on the horses. One afternoon, he was pondering his next bet at the legendary seaside track known as Del Mar, long frequented by celebrities since its being built in the '30s by a consortium that included Bing Crosby and Gary Cooper. Looking up from the racing guide, he spotted a stunning eighteen-year-old girl leaning against a pillar, waiting for her friend to bet. Around her neck was a gaudy necklace that belied her otherwise elegant attire. Its letters spelled out OH SHIT.

Undeterred by the crude accessory, he made his move. "Is your name Janet?" he inquired. Recognizing a line when she heard one, the young woman played it coy. But she also found the slick mustachioed stranger attractive and somewhat intriguing, despite the fact that he was eleven years her senior. He reminded her a little of Tony Orlando.

Yet when he asked if he could call her, she demurred. "I'm not giving you my phone number," she replied, walking off. But when Robert Kardashian set his sights on something, he did not usually give up easily. Around the time that he laid eyes on her necklace, Robert decided this was the woman for him.

Kristen Mary Houghton wasn't necessarily born with a silver spoon in her mouth. A silver candlestick, perhaps. Growing up in the privileged environs of Point Loma, California, on the outskirts of San Diego, Kris often told people that she came from "the candle family." When she was eight years old, her maternal grandparents, Louise and Jim, had opened one of California's first candle emporiums along with her mother, Mary Jo, in La Jolla, not far from the hillside house where Dr. Seuss penned most of his children's classics.

A year earlier, her mother had divorced her father, Robert—an engineer at the Convair plant—after a stormy marriage. Kris and her younger sister, Karen, were devastated. Divorce still wasn't that commonplace and parents didn't yet know how to explain to young children that they weren't responsible for breaking up a happy home. It weighed heavily on young Kris, who desperately hoped her parents would get back together.

Leaving the palatial white house where she had spent her early, happy years, Kris moved to nearby Clairemont with her mother and sister to be near Mary Jo's parents. As a single mother, Mary Jo laid down a series of strict rules and chores that she hoped would keep her daughters from becoming spoiled like a lot of their privileged schoolmates. Kris remembers her mother as "the most classy lady who always had the most beautiful outfits on." She credits Mary Jo's style for inspiring her own love of fashion.

Despite the divorce, as a child, Kris later recalled, she lived a "real-life Gidget, dream-come-true" story, spending every waking moment at the beach. When she was eight, however, her idyllic routine hit a snag—a scare that would stay with her for many years. One day, on the way home from school, she banged her shin on a post and had to have it x-rayed. The results showed a bone tumor. Fearing cancer, her parents authorized surgery to amputate her leg at the hip if necessary. Terrified by the ordeal, Kris woke in the recovery room with her leg intact and cancer-free.

Kris idolized her grandmother Lou, who had grown up in Arkansas but had come west with Mary Jo after she discovered that her first husband had cheated on her. For a time, she raised her daughters as a single mother, until she met a San Diego naval-base accountant named Jim.

Lou had always dreamed of starting a business. Who'd ever heard of a store devoted solely to candles, one of her lifelong passions? Nobody thought the business stood a chance, but to everybody's surprise, the Candelabra was a roaring success.

Like her grandmother, Kris loved the beeswax and paraffin candles that glowed from every shelf. But her favorite items were the Gloomchaser holders, fashioned from crushed glass of every color. These housed the votive candles that became the store's signature merchandise. Every day after school, Kris would rush to the store to help out, wrapping gifts or stocking shelves.

The store proved so successful that the profits helped Mary Jo set up a shop of her own, a children's clothing boutique not far from the Candelabra. Soon Kris was racing from store to store. All the while, she watched and absorbed as her mother and grandmother strategized over marketing and business. And because the store's success allowed her to once again live the expensive lifestyle she had enjoyed before her parents' divorce, she liked it a lot. She never minded that the path to their success was paved with a lot of hard work, long hours, and exhausting attention to detail. She was willing to work hard if it led the way to what she called the "2 die 4" life.

Her mother and grandmother, she later recalled, liked beautiful things, and she inherited those tastes. For her, she wrote in her memoir, the definition of a perfect world was "hard work, beautiful candles and a lot of love." Years later, as her family became fashion icons, Kris would cite her experience working in the store as formative.

In the late '60s, her mother met a man named Harry Shannon. Kris liked to compare him to the Rat Pack, who had made cocktail parties and skirt chasing fashionable during that era. Shannon, she recalled, was an alcoholic who loved to party. A successful yacht broker, he flashed wads of cash and reeked of style, like something out of a Ralph Lauren ad, she remembered. But his drinking caused scenes that scared the girls, and eventually Mary Jo gave him an ultimatum: Quit drinking or he was gone from their lives. Sure enough, he hopped on the wagon, and the two were married in Mexico when Kris was thirteen. She rarely saw her own father after the divorce, and she took to her new stepfather almost from the day he quit drinking and became a new man. Soon she was calling him Dad.

Like Kris's grandmother, Harry possessed the entrepreneurial spirit. One day he announced that he was out of the yacht business. They were moving to Oxnard, California, where he had invested in a company harvesting abalone—an edible sea snail considered a delicacy and an aphrodisiac in many parts of the world.

On Kris's sixteenth birthday, Harry presented her with a red convertible Mazda RX-2, in which she would cruise the highway and plot her life plan. While other kids were planning what they would wear to the prom, she thought further ahead. "Fuck the prom," she recalled thinking to herself. "I want to get married and have six kids." To that end, her mother's pleas for her to go to college fell on deaf ears. She was eager to escape her sheltered, privileged life and see the world.

She didn't have long to wait. The mother of her best friend, Debbie Mungle, happened to be the manager of a pro golfer named Phil Rodgers, who had won five PGA tournaments and was considered one of the best in the game during the '60s, when he was often overshadowed by his peers Jack Nicklaus and Arnold Palmer. To celebrate their high school graduation in 1972, Mrs. Mungle bought Kris and Debbie tickets to Hawaii, to accompany Rodgers to the Hawaiian Open.

On that trip, Kris was introduced to one of Rodgers's friends, a PGA golfer named Cesar Sanudo, who at twenty-nine was twelve years older than she. They hit it off immediately.

"He made all the boys I'd hung out with in high school seem like, well, boys," she later recalled in her memoir about their courtship, although in the book she refers to him as "Anthony."

Sanudo had won only one event in his tour career, though he had come close to winning the US Open shortly before he met Kris— leading for two rounds before finishing tied for ninth. Her mother didn't approve of the age difference but thought that her daughter should make her own decisions. For almost a year, Kris followed Sanudo on the tour, traveling to Japan, Scotland, and Mexico, cheering him on.

Sanudo died in 2011, but his brother Carlos vividly remembers his relationship with Kris, whom he describes as "an absolute knockout" back then. He credits his brother with introducing Kris to the lifestyle that she would come to crave.

"Cesar introduced her to a lot of showbiz big shots, and he'd take her to big parties at mansions and on yachts," Carlos recalled. "In fact, you could say that Kris would never have made her family as big as it is today without the connections Cesar began making for her years ago."

He would later tell *Radar* that even as a seventeen-year-old Kris wasn't a stickler for monogamy.

"Whenever a bunch of us would be partying over at Cesar's condo while he was out on the road, Kris would hit on any number of guys," he recalled. "She even made a move on me! Of course, I would never do anything to hurt my brother. And I never understood how Kris could do something so lousy."

Kris, along with her friend Debbie, was living with Cesar when the two girls ran into another older man, Robert Kardashian, at the Del Mar racetrack in the summer of 1973.

After Kris snubbed him that day, she received a call a few days later on the private line she and Debbie had installed at Cesar's house. It was Robert, who claimed to have gotten her unlisted number from a friend who worked at the phone company. He used all his powers of persuasion to get her to agree to a date but Kris resisted, even after he called twice a week for the next six months. During these calls, he would tell her about his tight-knit Armenian family and the fancy Beverly Hills house he shared with his brother, Tommy, but she was involved with another man and it was getting serious.

In February, Cesar was playing in the Los Angeles Open at the Riviera Country Club. Kris would follow him around with a folding chair as he played. Midway through the round, as she was following the gallery down the fairway to the next hole, Kris felt a tap on her shoulder from behind. It was Bob Kardashian. Was he stalking her? she wondered. Indeed, he had come to the Riviera to seek her out after she informed him during one of their frequent phone calls that she would be there. She didn't tell him that Cesar had recently proposed and that she had said yes. At some point, she recalls, she realized that it wasn't Cesar whom she loved but the glamorous lifestyle that surrounded him. That's when she finally relented and agreed to go out on a movie date with Bob.

When the film ended, they headed back to her place. While they were going at it in her bedroom, Kris recalled in her memoir, they heard Cesar arrive home. Bob grabbed his clothes and raced downstairs, where he encountered Kris's angry fiancé demanding to know what he was doing there.

Carlos Sanudo had heard a similar version from his brother. He recalled, "Cesar was at a tournament in the South, and he had become so suspicious of Kris that he missed the cut because he was such a mess. He hurried back to San Diego, got home around midnight, went upstairs—and found Kris in the bedroom with Kardashian! Cesar yelled, 'You son of a bitch!' and Kardashian started to cry. Cesar grabbed him and threw him out of the house."

Although Kris and Cesar continued seeing each other for a time, Carlos says the incident marked "the beginning of the end of their relationship."

Not long afterward, news came that Kris's father, Robert Houghton, had been killed in a collision with a truck in Mexico while vacationing with his girlfriend. He was only forty-two. In recent months, Kris had re-established contact with her father, who had gotten to know Cesar and was looking forward to giving Kris away at the wedding, for which the couple had not yet set a date. The news hit her hard. He had invited her for dinner just a few days earlier, but she'd blown him off, claiming she was tired. When the news came, she remembered thinking that she would have loved for her father to have met Bob. They would have hit it off, she suspected. Yet despite Bob's increasing persistence, she was still engaged to Cesar and had planned to accompany him to the British Open in July, where he had rented a house adjacent to the course with Tom Watson.

She was determined to end the relationship, but she didn't have the guts to tell Cesar it was over. Even after she told Bob that she would fly back from the UK to attend a housewarming party at his new place in Beverly Hills, she chickened out at the last minute and was a no-show. Embarrassed because he had planned the party to introduce Kris to his friends and family and kick off their relationship, Bob was furious.

In the end, Cesar made the decision easy for her when Kris discovered that he had been cheating on her with a new girlfriend he had met in Carmel. She called Bob to tell him she and Cesar were finally done. Thrilled with the news, he invited her to spend the weekend in LA.

When she arrived at LAX the next day, Bob was waiting for her out front with somebody in a green Mercedes convertible. He introduced her to his companion.

"This is O.J., my best friend."

CHAPTER TWO

Things were moving fast. By the end of their first weekend together, Bob had brought Kris back to the new Deep Canyon Drive house he shared with Tommy and O.J., who was staying with them for a while during the off-season. On Sunday, he brought her to his mother's house, where she met the entire family. She loved everything about them—from the Armenian breakfast pastries to the family values to their adherence to the cultural traditions that they had retained from the Old Country, even though all of them had been born in the United States.

Every weekend after that, Kris would take the short flight from San Diego to visit Bob, who introduced her to everybody he knew. He had told his friends that she looked exactly like Natalie Wood, and everybody wanted to meet the young beauty and see what he saw in her. For her part, she was smitten.

"I was attracted to him right off the bat," she would recall. "He had the greatest personality."

By the end of their first weekend together, he had vowed to marry her. After their third, he decided to pop the question.

"I knew, I think, from right around the first time I met him that I wanted to marry him and make a life together," she later told a documentary film crew. Yet the relationship was simply happening too fast. Bob was devastated, she recalled, when she declined, explaining that she had other plans.

Kris had applied right out of high school for a job as a stewardess. What better way to fulfill her dream of seeing the world? She had recently received word that American Airlines had an opening. She was invited to fly to Texas for the six-week flight-attendant training program. She hoped Bob would wait for her, but she wasn't willing to give up the opportunity. For his part, he took it as a humiliating rebuff. Kris hadn't even finished her training program when he met Priscilla Presley through his brother, Tommy; she was dating one of the "Memphis Mafia," Joe Esposito. Priscilla had split from Elvis three years earlier, though the two remained friends and bonded over their seven-year-old daughter, Lisa Marie, who lived with Priscilla most of the time.

Reading about Bob's dalliance with Priscilla, Kris began to question whether she had done the right thing. She was "bummed, not devastated," she recalled, at the prospect that he would end up with Elvis's gorgeous ex. Deep in her heart, she confessed, she still hoped Bob would end up with her. Ensconced in the American Airlines dorm in Fort Worth, Kris would talk to him on the pay phone every night. Probably to make her jealous, Bob even asked her advice on what to get Priscilla as a birthday present. Shortly before she graduated, he shared the news that the couple had broken up. Kris was hopeful. Still, she was determined to begin her exciting new job.

When she told him that she would be stationed in New York City, Bob informed her that he was planning to accompany O.J. to New York right after they got back from the Olympics in Montreal, where O.J. would be working as a commentator. When they met up in New York, they were both excited to tell her about the highlight of the Olympics—Bruce Jenner's gold medal for the United States in the decathlon.

"Who's Bruce Jenner?" Kris responded.

O.J. had been married for almost a decade to Marguerite Whitley, with whom he had two children and another on the way. So Kris was a little surprised that he had brought along Maud Adams, the Swedish supermodel who was well known as a Bond Girl for her appearance in *The Man with the Golden Gun* a couple of years earlier. Still, it was a thrill to be around the handsome football star who was mobbed by autograph seekers wherever they went. Who was she to moralize about his personal life? "We were having too much fun to dwell on it, and, after all, I wasn't his babysitter," she recalled.

The life of a flight attendant wasn't as glamorous as she had imagined. Instead of Fiji and Hawaii or Europe, she would often end up spending the night in Cleveland or Cincinnati, on one of the short-hop routes that junior flight attendants were usually assigned. More often that not, she was forced to smile as she fought off the advances of drunken men who believed that groping pretty stewardesses was one of the perks of their mundane business trips. In her memoir, she recalled that she had a secret strategy for fending off this unwanted attention—holding a pot of coffee over the offender's crotch. In those days, however, sexual harassment was part of the job and she wouldn't have lasted long had she employed this tactic. But it makes for an empowering anecdote.

Before long, on the advice of a friend, she had signed up as an "extra," often filling in on the LA–New York route for the senior flight attendants when they booked vacation time. It allowed her to see Bob for a few hours, or sometimes overnight, whenever she landed at LAX. Their relationship, she recalled, had been escalating. Still, what hope could it have for success when she spent most of her time three thousand miles away from him, with no reprieve in the immediate future, and he was back in Southern California, forever tempted by the California girls who surrounded him and his famous friends?

It was this dilemma that Kris would later claim caused her to find religion. Convinced that the only hope for her and Robert was the almost impossible prospect of a transfer to LA, she would head to New York's St. Patrick's Cathedral to light candles and pray. Only veterans with ten years or more of experience get transferred to LA, her colleagues told her. Within a year, however, her prayers were answered when she received a call from corporate headquarters informing her that her transfer request had been approved. When Bob picked her up in his Rolls Royce after she arrived back in LA, this time to live, Kris claims she finally knew that he was the one for her.

She shared an apartment with two other flight attendants near the airport, but she was spending most of her nights at Bob's place in Beverly Hills, where he still lived with Tommy and occasionally O.J., during the football star's increasingly frequent separations from Marguerite. Later that year, Tommy announced that he had bought his own place, across the street from Sammy Davis Jr. Now Kris was free to move in. But although she spent the night more often than not, "living in sin" was a whole other kettle of fish. For, as she quickly discovered, Bob had become a born-again Christian, and his religion was finding itself at odds with his lifestyle. At first, she was impressed that Bob was a "spiritual" man. It gave him a depth that she hadn't noticed in the fun-loving playboy.

The first clue that he paid more than lip service to his faith was when she realized that he kept a Bible on his desk and beside his bed. His whole family, it seemed, was deeply religious, though they were not adherents of the Orthodox faith of most Armenians. Soon she was accompanying him to Bible studies at the house of pop singer Pat Boone, who had been one of the earliest Christian fundamentalist celebrities. He was also deeply right-wing, a staunch Republican, and a fierce critic of any number of liberal causes, from the pro-choice to the gay-rights movements. In later years, Boone would be caricatured as a buffoon after he joined the "birthers," claiming Barack Obama was born in Kenya, and then blamed the 2015 Charleston massacre of eight black churchgoers by a white supremacist on Obama, who he claimed empowered the minions of Satan, such as Dylann Roof. But in 1977, Boone was still a darling of the small minority of show-business Republicans that included the likes of Doris Day and Zsa Zsa Gabor.

Every week, Bob would join Boone and his assorted follow-ers for an hour-long prayer session. Some weeks Boone would lead the sessions, but more often they would be led by a pastor named Kenn Gullicksen, who had been instrumental in founding the Vine-yard Churches, a neo-charismatic evangelical Christian movement in which worshippers were encouraged to connect with the Holy Spirit—similar in some ways to the fundamentalist Protestant Molo-kan movement that had led Bob's Armenian ancestors away from the traditional Eastern Orthodox Church. This may explain some of the appeal of Boone's prayer sessions. Gullicksen—who used a full band at his church services—appeared to have a special resonance with musicians and would become the pastor most associated with the burgeoning Christian-rock movement. A few years after Bob and Kris started attending his sessions, in fact, he would burst into the public eye as the minister who converted Bob Dylan to Christianity.

Whatever went on in those weekly sessions, Kris was clearly pulled in almost immediately. She and her family were Presbyterian, but they had attended church only on holidays, and none of them considered themselves particularly devout. Now Kris decided that she had accepted Christ as her savior and began calling herself a born-again Christian. Although she had virtually moved in with Bob, their sessions with Boone convinced them that "it was against God's plan" for them to live together. Indeed, their new faith decreed that they shouldn't even be having sex outside marriage, and Bob decided that they must stop sleeping together until they got married because it was "not God's will." Kris has never been shy about her feelings on sex and, although she too had embraced Bob's fundamentalist Christian beliefs, this may have been taking things a little too far for her. "What the hell is going on here?" she remembers wondering to herself as she moved from his palatial home into a tiny apartment in Sherman Oaks.

On top of the enforced celibacy, Bob had appeared to distance himself from their relationship. When Elvis died in August 1977 and Bob called to offer condolences to Priscilla and Lisa Marie, Kris wondered whether he would get back together with his old flame now that she was free of the emotional ties to her ex-husband. For months, Bob had proposed at least two or three times a week, but at that time Kris hadn't been ready. Now that she desperately wanted to embark on her dream of being a wife and mother, she wanted nothing more than to get married. By the winter of 1978, Kris had vowed that if Bob didn't propose soon, she would move on. On Easter Sunday that year, she spent the night at his house—in separate beds—so that they could get up early to go to church. Before they left for the service, Bob finally popped the question.

The wedding was scheduled for July. A couple of weeks before the big day, Kris arrived at Bob's house to find O.J. Simpson in the den. He asked her for a favor. While having drinks with Robert and some friends at the Rodeo Drive nightclub the Daisy recently, he had fallen for the beautiful eighteen-year-old waitress named Nicole Brown who had served them. They were already dating, but she still lived with her parents and he needed a woman to call her for him just in case her mother answered the phone. Kris later claimed she disapproved because he was still married to Marguerite at the time, but she made the call.

And, like O.J., Kris was instantly infatuated with the shy, stunningly beautiful California girl. "We were destined to become best friends," she later wrote.

The wedding took place on July 8, with O.J. acting as a groomsman and A. J. Cowlings—the man who later drove the infamous Bronco—serving as the ring bearer. The ceremony was a lavish affair, with no expense spared, more than three hundred guests, and a reception afterward at the swanky Bel-Air Country Club.

A European honeymoon followed, during which American Airlines repeatedly called to find out when Kris was planning to return to her route. Bob was unequivocal and old-fashioned. "Tell them you're retiring," he informed her. Kris was all too glad to oblige and eager to pursue her stated dream of being a full-time wife and mother. It didn't take long to accomplish the latter, especially after the months of religious celibacy that had preceded their nuptials. On April 18, 1979, Kris gave birth to Kourtney Mary Kardashian.

"I gave birth to Kourtney when I had been married nine months, two weeks and two days to the day that I got married," she later recalled. "And I know that because all the Armenian women were counting. Trust me."

The new parents doted on their little princess, but it wasn't long before Kris discovered she was pregnant again. Kimberly Noel Kardashian came along on October 21, 1980, when Kourtney was only eighteen months old. Kris later admitted she was "overwhelmed."

"Here I am 24 years old with these two little babies thinking 'Oh my gosh,'" she recalled. Bob could have easily afforded a nanny to help ease the burden, but in Armenian families that's not the way things are done. He would often tell his young wife that he didn't want her to get "spoiled." He finally relented when he saw the emotional toll motherhood was taking on Kris, and after Kim was born a nanny was hired to give her a break and to allow the couple to spend more time with friends.

O.J. retired from football shortly before Kim came along, and he had always wanted to take up skiing, a sport strictly forbidden during his playing career because of the potential for injury. Now he took it up with a passion, and it became a tradition for Kris and Bob to join him and his new full-time girlfriend, Nicole, on Aspen ski retreats while O.J.'s wife remained behind at their Rockingham house.

Kris and Nicole were becoming fast friends, but Kris also loved spending time with O.J., who was much more fun loving than her serious husband. He also doted on little Kourtney, which helped endear him to the new mother. "I absolutely loved O.J.," she later wrote. "He was like a brother to me."

With a nanny to look after the children, Kris was finally able to balance her role as a mother with an active social life. She and Bob became regular fixtures on the LA party circuit, and Kris became known as something of a socialite, often crossing paths with Kathy Hilton, who also had young children, including a new baby named Paris, but still managed to find time for an active social schedule. Kathy's parties were legendary in Beverly Hills, as were the lavish wedding and baby showers she would host for her friends.

By that time, Kris's two toddlers were quite a handful. And despite the fact that Kim was younger, you wouldn't have known it from the way they interacted.

"Kim had always been the one to take over and sort of boss Kourtney around because Kourtney was the quiet one," Kris later recalled. "For a while Kimberly kind of ran the house."

Bob doted on his two girls, but his Armenian family was wondering what was wrong with him. When was he going to produce a boy to carry on the proud Kardashian name? His best friend, O.J., also teased him mercilessly about his macho shortcomings. The pressure on Kris was becoming so intense that she later confided to friends that she felt like Anne Boleyn who was beheaded by Henry VIII because she failed to bear him a son. She read every book she could find on the best way to conceive a boy and started to collect old wives' tales from her friends and family, all of whom were eager to give her tips on the most conducive sexual positions or time of day.

Their sex life, she later confessed, had slowed considerably after the kids came along, but now they were determined to have as much sex as possible if it would speed the conception of a boy. "It was wham

bam thank you ma'am," she wrote in her memoir about their sex sessions, describing the "crazy sex positions" they tried, including upside
down or with her feet in the air.

Finally, in the summer of 1986, Kris announced she was pregnant again. The whole family prayed for one thing, and finally their
prayers were answered. In March 1987, Robert Arthur Kardashian
was born. His parents and grandparents were thrilled; his big sisters,
not so much. Kourtney, Kim, and Khloé—the third sister who came
along in 1984—did not take well to being upstaged by what the family called their "little prince."

"My sisters abused the hell out of me," Rob would later recall.
"They would beat me up until I would cry. They gave me wedgies
nonstop. They tortured me as a kid." His sisters loved to dress him up
as a girl and put lipstick on him.

"We thought it was so funny," Kim later recalled. "My dad would
come home and go crazy."

A year earlier, O.J. and Nicole had married, and the two couples
were still inseparable, frequently vacationing together and socializing
two or three times a week, including at the scavenger-hunt parties that
Nicole loved to throw at their Rockingham Drive house. In his deposition for O.J.'s civil trial years later, Bob claimed that he no longer hung
out separately with O.J., only with O.J. and Nicole as a couple.

"It was almost always as couples. We did not spend time alone. I
mean, I'm sure we'd go to lunch or something. But it was rare that
O.J. and I would do something alone."

Kris's devout Christianity never waned during these years. The
family went to church every Sunday, and she would attend a community Bible study every Tuesday in Santa Monica—sessions that were
somewhat more traditional than the ones hosted by Pat Boone, which
they rarely attended anymore. These Tuesday sessions were attended
mostly by women, and it is in Bible study that Kris would meet many
of her closest friends, including Candace Garvey, the wife of baseball

star Steve Garvey. It was the '80s, and when the women weren't talking about the Bible, they were talking about the latest rage in Beverly
Hills, breast-augmentation surgery.

All her friends, Kris recalled, were having boob jobs, so she decided
that she had to have one, too. But when she awoke after her first surgery and got a look in the mirror at her new breasts, Kris decided
that she still didn't look like a *Playboy* centerfold. That was the look
she was seeking. By then, Nicole had given birth to two children and
she was looking to perk up her own breasts. She went to the world-
renowned Beverly Hills plastic surgeon to the stars, Harry Glassman,
for her procedure. When Kris saw the result—"her boobs were 2die4,"
she observed—she decided she wanted to try again. During the '80s,
"Everyone wanted to have big, enormous boobs," she recalled. Glassman was all too glad to oblige, and once again Kris went under the
knife. The Bible, after all, didn't say anything about boob jobs. It did,
however, frown on infidelity.

Before O.J. married Nicole, Bob and Kris and some of his other
friends—well aware that he had cheated openly on Marguerite
throughout their marriage—had arranged for him to take a marriage
Bible-study course to cure him of what Kris described as his "wandering eye." Alas, it appears that Kris never took such a class herself.

To outsiders, they seemed like the ideal family, and at first they
were. "Kris and Robert, they had it all," their friend Lisa Miles told an
E! documentary crew. "Robert would be on the tennis court and Kris
would be in the kitchen cooking and baking and there was food, then
parties and entertainment."

It was around 1989, Kris later claimed, that she knew something was wrong. She had everything she had always wanted: a large
family and a loving husband. But like many of the women of her
mother's generation, she realized that this wasn't enough. She was
feeling unfulfilled. "I was selfish, restless and bored," she would later
recall. Yet she couldn't figure out what was wrong or why she was

depressed. She knew that her feelings for Bob weren't what they used to be. Nor was the sex. She was craving passion, she later explained, and she wasn't getting it from her husband.

Her friend Nicole was also unhappy, having confided that O.J. was cheating on her. Kris had noticed her becoming morose and withdrawn. Now the two spent much of their time complaining about their husbands and their lives. The two couples still got together as a foursome on occasion, but the fun gatherings were a thing of the past. Nicole had begun to broach the idea of separating from O.J., and Kris claimed that this inspired her to bring up the idea of a separation with Bob. He would not even entertain the possibility. Armenians don't do that, he declared. "It's either marriage or divorce," she recalls him telling her.

A divorce was out of the question, if only for the sake of the kids, and she soon discarded the idea of a separation. If she couldn't find fulfillment with Bob, however, she wasn't averse to looking elsewhere, despite her still-devout Christian beliefs. In her 2011 memoir, *Kris Jenner . . . and All Things Kardashian*, Kris provides a candid account of what happened after she encountered a producer named "Ryan" at the home of a friend and felt an instant attraction. She remembers him as the spitting image of Rob Lowe, and when she went upstairs to get a music player, she claims he followed her and kissed her. That kiss, she recalls, was like an "awakening" from a long, deep sleep. She had not felt such emotion with Robert for many years, and it was what she had been craving. Yet she was married to "one of the best guys in the entire world" and she was a good Christian woman. How could she give that all up for passion?

Before long, she met Ryan at his Studio City apartment, and she was "in his bed with the sheets flying."

Knowing what we do now about Kris and her proclivities, her description of the affair is hardly a shock. But at the time, she was still known as a devout Christian housewife and respected socialite, with the perfect family and a profound respect for family values.

Draw the curtain back on many so-called respectable citizens and find a very different picture. Kris is all too happy to paint that picture, describing the relationship as "all about sex."

Right after she dropped the children at school, she recalls, she would race to her new lover's apartment and have "crazy, fabulous sex for hours in the middle of the day. . . . Wild crazy sex all the time. We had sex in cars, sex on the tennis court, sex in the pool house, sex in the garage when we got home, sex up and down the stairs, sex everywhere, all the time."

To explain her whereabouts, she confesses to constantly lying to her husband as well as her friends. Bob seemed to know something was wrong and tried desperately "to be a better husband," but she explains that she was obsessed. "I was out of control and selfish," she would later write about the affair. "I just didn't care anymore."

It all came to a head when Bob hired a private detective to follow her and finally decided to confront the couple when he received a call from the PI, who had followed them to a Beverly Hills restaurant one morning. When Bob entered the restaurant and found them together, he shouted, "I caught you. Now I know where you spend your time."

When Bob confided in O.J., Kris recalls, Simpson demanded Ryan's phone number. "You just fucked Snow White," he shouted into the phone, loudly enough for Kris to overhear. "You got that? You just fucked Snow White. Do you know what you've done to this entire universe, you asshole? You motherfucker. Now you're going to have to deal with me." He was hardly one to judge. By this time, Nicole had discovered evidence of multiple affairs. But this was about loyalty. His best friend had been cuckolded.

"All you need to do is get a vibrator," he chided Kris. "What'd you need this guy for?"

Years later, an award-winning Hollywood animator named Todd Waterman revealed that he was in fact the man Kris described in her memoir as "Ryan." At the time their affair began, he explained, he was a twenty-three-year-old professional soccer player on contract with the LA Heat. "I was attracted to Kris," he told the *Sunday Mail*, claiming that the two had met at a nightclub. "I'm sure we danced and had a good time in the club," he recalled. "We came back to her friend's home in Beverly Hills. And our first time [we had sex] was in her friend's closet. We found a little place in the house and consummated the relationship. It was a magical night, surreal. I think it was two people who were both open to experiencing something in their life at that time. It was fate, we invited it and we just ran with it and from that point on, we didn't hold back."

Although Kris described his place in Studio City as a "tiny, dumpy apartment," Waterman claimed that it was in fact Kris who had found the apartment, because she wanted a place where they could get together. There they would have sex for hours at a time, just as she described.

"The love swept us away," he explained. "We made our own different reality. It was special, it was a little crazy, a little wild—we didn't exercise caution or self-restraint. I think we were both very much in love."

He remembers that they took a lot of risks during the affair. "We did some crazy things. I remember playing tennis at her home with my friend the soccer player Justin Fashanu. And Robert was watching us play. We're in the affair now and I'm sure he suspected at this point. He was trying to throw me off my game actually. He was just calling out foot fault while I served."

He doesn't recall all the details about their sexual escapades but claims that he is "sure" they had sex in Kris's house when Bob was out. Eventually, he quit soccer because it paid so poorly, but when they were together, Kris paid for everything. "She was generous," he stated. "I didn't have the money for the lifestyle she was leading. She was paying a lot, or it was Robert I guess," he recalled. One of the details Kris left out about the affair in her memoir is that once they were outed, she openly flaunted the relationship for some time.

"I just remember good times, barbecues, pool parties—it was fun," he said. "I would go to events as her boyfriend. I met celebrities at parties. Magic Johnson and the LA Lakers were at a pool party. I remember going from a George Michael concert to that house party and dancing in the backyard with George Michael there and Billy Idol."

Although Kris described the time Bob caught them in the Beverly Hills restaurant and wrote that he caught them three more times, she neglected to describe what happened during the other encounters. Waterman fills in the gaps. "When he hired the private investigators I would say that's when it started going bad. It was the midway point of the affair," he recalled.

"I remember he turned up at our apartment and he got into the complex," he told the *Mail*. "I said we'd call the police, let a little time go by and then I decided to drive Kris back to wherever she had to go. I was driving in an open Jeep at the time. As I pulled out of my garage, it was about 5 pm and a sunny day, he comes charging out with a golf club in his 450 SL convertible. He took a swing and whacked the back of my car. I said, 'Holy shit, Kris, can I pull over and confront him? What do you want to do?' She screamed out, 'No, no keep driving he might have a gun in the car. I know he keeps a gun.' So we've got this little high speed chase going on at rush hour and I'm in a Jeep and he's trailing me and he's trying to overtake us. I did a couple of spin out moves and he just kept going, luckily—maybe he got his composure again or something."

Waterman remembers fearing for his life and wondering if Kris's husband might try to have him "wiped out," because he was known to be a very powerful man.

He confirmed Kris's account of getting a call from O.J. at one point. "O.J. said he wanted to talk and he invited me to the house to talk. I said, 'No thank you.' I said, 'If you want to talk I have no problem meeting you in a public place but I have no desire to go to your home.'"

Bob never did pull a gun, but he was clearly apoplectic with rage and utterly humiliated at the very public manner in which Kris flaunted her new boyfriend. Kris claims that the affair finally came to an end when she walked in on "Ryan" at his apartment one night and caught him naked with another woman. Suddenly the shoe was on the other foot, she recalls.

"I had just ruined my entire life and my whole family and given everything I knew and loved for this guy, thinking I was going to be with him." She had even thought of marrying him. Waterman confirms the incident.

"I think I got busted," he recalled. "I don't remember if that's exactly how it happened. I'm not justifying the action, I was young, not only that I also allowed myself certain safeguards. Because in my mind she was still going home to her husband and still getting in his bed at night." Still, he claims he was devastated when he and Kris finally ended it but assumed it was inevitable given his financial situation.

"There was no way I could support her or help maintain what she was accustomed to financially, and with the age difference as well I didn't see that working out in the future. I was heartbroken. Sometimes you stop something not because you stop caring but because it isn't practical."

And yet, despite the awkward encounter and the realization that Waterman was cheating on her, Kris still couldn't bring herself to end it. "That's how crazy I was," she later confessed.

For his part, however, Bob had finally had enough of the humiliation. He had been determined to make the marriage work for the sake of the children and to avoid disappointing his deeply religious family. And he likely would have continued his silent suffering if only

Kris had remained discreet. The final straw, in fact, may have been discovering that Kris would often bring the kids along on her dates with Waterman. It was certainly a surprise to Todd's mother, Ilza, who assumed that Kris was already separated from her husband.

"She wouldn't talk about her husband with me," Ilza later recalled about the affair. "If she did I would have said, 'What are you doing here with my son? What are you doing coming after my young son with all of these kids?' They went skiing, went to games. That's why I thought she was separated because [the kids] went everywhere."

Waterman later claimed he formed a special bond with Khloé in particular. "Khloé would go out with us," he said. "She'd be in the back seat of the car if we were going to lunch. I had a special relationship with her more than the other children. She just was the cutest. She was a smart kid and when talking to her sisters, she would say, 'You don't like him do you?' She was funny."

When Bob finally filed for divorce in 1990, things got very ugly. And as revenge for the humiliation he had been suffering for months, he took the one measure that he knew would cause Kris the most suffering possible: He cut off her credit cards. There is no question that in her list of priorities, her children came first. But a very close second was definitely her Platinum card. Kris liked to shop. The first time her card was declined, she was beside herself with rage. She immediately contacted one of LA's top divorce attorneys, Dennis Wasser, and demanded that he safeguard the lavish lifestyle to which she had most certainly become accustomed. The couple were at war.

CHAPTER THREE

Cut off from virtually all funds, Kris was forced to borrow money from her mother and grandparents just to make ends meet. After Bob's eventual death in 2003 from esophageal cancer, his widow, Ellen Kardashian, made public his journals from this period, which provide a telling glimpse of the turmoil the family was enduring in this difficult period. Many of the entries reflect his chagrin over Kris's cavalier attitude toward their four young children as she continued to openly carry on her affair with Todd Waterman.

On December 15, 1989, Bob wrote,

> Todd drove up to the main gate + parked. He went in the house and slept in my bed till? Khloé and Robert were in the house. She doesn't care! Only about herself . . . she was at TODD'S house from 10:00–11:15 She left kids + screwed all nite. Great state of caring.

On Christmas day, he penned another entry:

> I was home alone with 4 kids. I put them to bed & played w/them.

The most unsettling entries, however, concern what he describes as Kris's "neglect" or "abuse" of the children. In an entry dated August 23, 1989, he writes,

> Kris was kicking and beating her and said she was going to kill [Kim]! Kim was hysterical.

In another entry, he claims that when Kim was sick with the flu, Kris made her stay at a friend's house even though she had been throwing up.

> She knew Kim was sick and still sent her away . . . All the while Kris was screwing Todd in my bed!

On March 20, 1990, he wrote,

> Kourtney started crying . . . She was sad because Mommy wasn't home at all. Kourtney wanted her to cook dinner for them. How sad that a child has to beg her mother to cook her dinner and be home with her.

He also describes hearing Kris say,

> "I love Todd more than anything in this world."

On April 23, 1990, he wrote,

> [Kris] doesn't really care about the kids at all.

The cancellation of her credit cards was bad enough, but in early 1990, Bob also cancelled her charge card at Gelson's grocery store. She remembers being so broke that she took the kids out one night for pizza and realized that she didn't have enough money to pay the bill. This, she later described, was the "lowest moment." In June 1990, Kris's lawyer finally filed a court petition for emergency relief as well as spousal and child support. The document sheds considerable light on the style to which she had become accustomed while married to the millionaire Beverly Hills lawyer. It is a style she claimed in the court documents that she "deserved."

"The petitioner and I shared a luxury lifestyle," Kris declared. "Nothing was too good for our family. Even our children's clothing was purchased at exclusive boutiques." This lifestyle, she explained, included frequent, expensive European holidays, regular dinners at fancy restaurants, and fancy parties. She described one such occasion.

"The New Year's Eve party alone cost between $10,000 and $12,000. Since January 1990 the petitioner has essentially cut me off from all funds." She was so broke, she claimed, that she had been forced to take her first job since quitting as a flight attendant at American Airlines a decade earlier.

"In order to have some cash at my disposal to meet the basic needs of myself and my children, I have taken a job offered to me by my friend who has just gone through a divorce. [But] I am earning less money than our paid household help."

In her petition, Kris demanded an allowance for her and the children's monthly expenses, which she claimed added up to $37,189. For his part, Bob—who had taken some time off from his law firm to deal with the personal issues brought on by the messy separation— claimed that he was "unemployed" and was earning only $2,000 a month. Kris argued that his unemployment was "voluntary" and demanded he be ordered back to work so he could earn enough to restore her lavish lifestyle and spending habits.

Among the expenses she detailed in the documents was a monthly mortgage on their home of $15,000, and the salaries of their household staff, including a gardener, a maid, and a housekeeper, as well as clothing costs that included $800 a month for the children and $2,000 for her own wardrobe.

The petition also demanded that Bob pay the outstanding credit-card bills of more than $21,000 that had accumulated before he cut off her cards, including hefty charges at luxury department stores such as Neiman Marcus and Saks Fifth Avenue.

For his part, Bob claimed in his journal that many of these bills and others were lavish gifts that Kris had bestowed on her lover. When he found a $1,200 Sears bill for a new refrigerator on his personal store credit card, for example, he called Sears to claim the company had made a mistake. He had not ordered a fridge, nor had one been delivered.

"They informed me that my wife had purchased this refrigerator for Todd Waterman," he wrote. In his response to her court petition, he claimed that Kris had kept a gun and silverware, worth more than $35,000, that they had received as wedding presents.

In response to her financial claims, the court eventually awarded Kris a monthly allowance, but her petition had demanded more than just money. She also demanded that Bob be barred from entering the home in which she had been living since he stormed out months earlier.

"As a result of [Robert's] and my irreconcilable differences, there is a tremendous amount of discord at the family residence," she wrote. "Every time [Robert] and I speak, [Robert] emotionally abuses me to the point that I am unable to handle the simplest tasks for hours after our conversation. In every conversation [Robert] and I have, [Robert] calls me a whore, a bitch, a slut and other names I can not repeat. On May 3, 1990 Kimberly found me crying after a brutal conversation with [Robert] and she became so upset I had a difficult time getting her to her carpool on time. Kimberly called my office twice that afternoon crying hysterically, begging me to come home."

Bob responded by complaining about the fact that Kris had allowed her boyfriend to move into the home.

"I believe this situation is inappropriate for several reasons," he declared in his own petition. "Firstly my children are exposed to another man living with their mother. I believe that is inappropriate and I ask the court to enjoin and restrain [Kris] from living with any member of the opposite sex in or about the presence of our children. As a matter of fact, my son Robert said he slept on the couch in [Kris's] bedroom when [Kris] and her boyfriend were in bed together in the bedroom. In my opinion this situation is detrimental to the children."

In response to these claims, the court ordered both parties to undergo a psychiatric evaluation. The court-appointed professional suggested Bob start by sending Kris a letter to help process his feelings.

"Once I filed for divorce almost all communication ceased and our anger just built up," he wrote her in 1990. "Imagine what effect this behavior ultimately will have on the children's future morals, life and general outlook . . . A real nightmare, isn't it?"

The eventual evaluation didn't spare either side. Kris, concluded the report,

> is currently experiencing considerable situational stress which is resulting in increased impulsivity and disorganization in her thinking, affects and behaviors. She also has an immature need for gratification in relationships. Her emotions effect her decision-making process in a very inconstant manner sometimes having a strong impact and other times very little impact in similar situations.

The psychiatrist administered a test called the Minnesota Multiphasic Personality Inventory (MMPI), which is a controversial clinical assessment tool developed in the 1930s, frequently used by mental health professionals to determine adult personality and psychopathology disorders, and often employed in family custody disputes. Kris scored a "spike 4" on the test, which, the psychiatrist noted, is associated with women who are "immature, impulsive, high risk takers who do things others do not approve of just for the personal enjoyment of doing so. The results indicate that Kristen may occasionally show bad judgment and that she tends to be somewhat selfish, pleasure orientated, narcissistic, and manipulative, she doesn't tend to be anxious and shows no neurotic or psychotic symptoms."

Bob had accused his wife of being "reckless and non-motherly" to her children. The psychiatrist noted that Kris believed she was a loving mother to her children, but that "her sense of self is based much more on fantasy than realistic considerations."

The report also had harsh judgment for Bob's behavior during this period, concluding that he was "impulsive when overwhelmed" and, more troubling, was given to episodes of "situational anger." It may have been one of these episodes that caused Kris to seek a restraining order, which barred either party from "molesting, attacking, striking, threatening, sexually assaulting, battering, or otherwise disturbing the peace of the other party."

In the end, it is this anger—characterized by frequent, almost violent, shouting episodes in front of the children—that caused the court to award Kris custody. To the court, Bob acknowledged his anger.

"This is true," he said. "It was true that I was very upset when I found out the respondent was having an affair and I wanted a divorce."

Kris too later acknowledged that her behavior during this period was out of control and admitted that she deeply regretted it. In her memoir, she wrote that she felt ashamed and deeply disgusted with herself. She claimed that the affair with Waterman was a "deeply horrific" situation that had taken over her life. She had always imagined herself as someone who was strongly committed to family values, Christian morality, and her children. Yet her behavior had broken up her marriage and hurt "the greatest guy in the world," Bob.

Watching her young kids play in the pool, she reflected, made her realize that it wasn't fair to subject her kids to the "battlefield" they had been forced to live on for these many months.

Then one day, she claims, she had an epiphany. She decided it was time to get her life back on track and "be a woman who always tries to live the truth." Days later, she would meet the man whom the world still knew as Bruce.

CHAPTER FOUR

The affair with Waterman was over, or so Kris would claim. She writes that she had vowed to forget about dating and devote herself to being a mother. "I had destroyed my marriage," she later wrote, "but I didn't want to lose my kids."

Then one day she received a call from her close friend Candace Garvey. She was in Alaska with her Dodgers superstar husband, Steve, shooting an outdoor adventure show. While there, Steve had been invited to a celebrity fishing tournament in Ketchikan, where he played with the former Olympic decathlon champion Bruce Jenner and invited him to be a guest on their TV show.

Candace wondered if Kris knew who he was. She had noticed that Bruce wore sweatpants every day and could use someone to help him improve his style. She happened to know a soon-to-be-divorced woman who knew how to dress and, especially, how to shop. Jenner wasn't particularly interested in dating a professional shopper, but Candace insisted that Kris would be perfect for him. She was determined to set them up on a blind date when they returned to LA.

Kris responded by insisting that she never wanted to look at another man; she just wanted to be a mom. But her friend persisted, and she finally agreed to meet Bruce.

Steve happened to be scheduled to play in Michael Jordan's charity golf tournament at the Riviera country club the following month. When Kris got her first look at Bruce, coming out of the clubhouse, she was immediately enamored of his long shaggy hair and boyish smile. "He looked adorable," she recalled. "The minute I saw him, I said, 'This guy's great. He's fabulous. He was funny, really good looking, but the sweetest guy I have ever met in my life."

When he laid eyes on her, he immediately picked her up and gave her a bear hug. Years later, he would remember the moment. Candace had told him about Kris's large brood. It just so happened that Bruce also had four kids.

"I thought, 'She has four kids. Hmmm.' That to me was intriguing," Jenner later recalled. "I threw my arms around her and because she had four kids, I said, 'At last in the arms of a real woman. Four kids, huh?' And that kind of did it right there."

A couple weeks later, Bruce came by the house to take Kris to a cocktail party in honor of Ronald and Nancy Reagan. Bruce happened to be a staunch Republican, and these were the social circles he was comfortable in. Kris had never been particularly political but, as a devout Christian, she had twice voted for Reagan and considered him somebody who epitomized her values. His extreme right-wing views and demonization of gays and minorities were not deal breakers for a woman who had grown up in the conservative confines of San Diego and had long worshipped at the altar of far-right evangelicals. The opportunity to hobnob with the beloved ex-president—who famously feared his son Ronald Jr. was gay after he became a ballet dancer and who had done virtually nothing to combat the new AIDS epidemic when he was president because of the homophobia of the Republican base—only endeared Bruce to her.

Kris would claim that they fell in love on that first date. "I was surprised that I would fall for somebody that quick. I fell hard," she said. Ten-year-old Kim also took to her mother's new man almost immediately.

"We had to do a school project," she later recalled, "and Bruce said, 'Why don't [you] do it on [me]?' And I said, 'Who are you?' We had no idea who he was. 'Why would I do a project on you?' and he said, 'Let me tell you' and he explained to me about the Olympics and the decathlon and he came in and did the project with me and my teacher had the biggest crush on him so of course I got an A."

But not all members of the family were won over. "Kourtney hated Bruce to begin with," Kris told E!. "She just resented the fact that this person was going to perhaps take her dad's place."

Kim remembers that her older sister would wear only black when Bruce was around and that she and her mom's new boyfriend were constantly at each other's throats. Bruce would later describe their initial conflict as a "learning process" for all of them.

In the 2010 book she wrote with her sisters, *Kardashian Konfidential*, Kourtney recalled that she never saw her parents fighting or arguing until they announced they were getting a divorce. When she heard the news, she remembers that she took it very badly and started acting out. She immediately blamed the split on Kris, with whom she got into "screaming, hair-pulling fights." She remembers that her mother would grab her arm, forcing her to dig in her nails to break free. At one point, she even ran away, taking refuge at a friend's house down the block until her father came to get her.

She acknowledges that she hated Bruce at first, because she felt she would be betraying her father if she was nice to her mom's new boyfriend. They frequently battled, with Kourtney bellowing "You're not my dad!" whenever he asked her to do anything.

But neither Kourtney nor the rest of the kids had a lot of time to process the significance of their mother's new relationship. Suddenly Bruce and Kris were inseparable, going everywhere together. She claims that she knew she was falling in love with him almost from the beginning. "He was magnetic," she reminisced later. "Physically, sexually, emotionally. He was the best friend, best lover, best dad, best pal."

But if the relationship was going to have any chance of success, there was still a major obstacle to overcome. Bob and Kris were still locked in a toxic battle over their divorce, money, house, and custody of the kids. It was at that point, Bruce later recalled, that he decided to "take charge."

The battle had by that point been raging for more than eighteen months. "I said, 'Maybe I should take Robert out to dinner,'" Bruce told E!. He then called Bob and they arranged to meet at Hamburger Hamlet on Sunset Boulevard.

"I said, 'Okay, you don't have to pay her anything,'" Bruce claimed. "'Just sign the papers and get it over with.' So Kris basically got nothing out of the divorce. And I said, 'I'll pick up the pieces. No hard feelings. Let's keep a good relationship.'"

Kris shared a similar version in her memoir. "You know what," she claims she told Bruce, "I came into the marriage with nothing. I'll leave with nothing."

She writes that she called her lawyer, Dennis Wasser, and told him that the whole thing had been worked out. She was letting Bob keep the house. That's the version that Kris and Bruce peddled for years. But what neither of them revealed was that the eventual settlement actually called for Bob to pay Kris $5,000 a month. If, as Bruce claimed, Bob wouldn't have to pay Kris anything, Bruce would have had a difficult time supporting Kris and eight children. As a longtime friend of his recently shared with me, "When he met Kris Kardashian, Bruce didn't have a pot to piss in."

Indeed, when he began dating Kris in the fall of 1990, Jenner was renting a tiny one-bedroom bungalow and could barely afford it. By

that point, the golden boy of the Montreal Olympics had fallen on
hard times.

I still remember the day that Bruce Jenner crossed the finish line in
the 1,500 meters to win the decathlon at the 1976 Olympics in my
hometown of Montreal. I happened to be in the Olympic Stadium
that day with my family, and as a twelve-year-old sports fanatic, I
knew that I had witnessed something special. A few minutes later, I
was less thrilled when Bruce trotted around the track in a victory lap
carrying an American flag. As a Canadian, I didn't have a lot to cheer
for during those games. Canada had won no more than a pathetic
silver medal in track and field. Maybe that's why I couldn't appreciate the patriotic fervor that erupted in the United States as millions
watched the moment on television and relished Jenner's besting the
defending Soviet champion while the Cold War still raged even in
the world of sports. But from the moment he completed that lap, it
seemed, the incredible athletic accomplishment that I had witnessed
was eclipsed by the orgy of marketing that followed. By the time he
crossed the line that day, in fact, Jenner's sports career had come to an
end and he was no longer "the world's greatest athlete"—he was now
simply the world's most hyped commercial pitchman.

Within weeks, he was everywhere—on the Wheaties box, hawking Coca-Cola. He was America's new golden boy. There were even a
Bruce Jenner doll and a lunch box being sold to kids within weeks of
the 1976 Closing Ceremonies and a board game not long afterward.
And while he was making millions in endorsements, I had already
turned my attention to the upcoming hockey season and all but forgotten that I had witnessed an incredible sporting feat.

It turns out I wasn't the only who was put off by the sudden
Bruce Jenner marketing onslaught. When Eric Heiden won five
speed-skating gold medals at the Lake Placid Olympics four years

later, he immediately made it clear that he had no desire to cash in on his success the way Mark Spitz and Bruce Jenner had after being crowned golden boys at the 1972 and 1976 Games.

"I felt embarrassed for them sometimes," he said. "As an athlete I saw sports as a recreation and not as a tool to completely sell yourself commercially. I guess they were doing what they felt was right for them."

Years later, Jenner would reflect back on the criticism and tell *Sports Illustrated*, "If there was a time when it seemed that I was too visible, you've got to remember that it wasn't so much me capitalizing on the Games—but that I needed a job. People offered me work at a nice salary. It was more like other people trying to capitalize on what I had done. They called me, I didn't call them. And that first year I did basically what everybody asked me to do."

In a 1977 profile of Jenner, a year after he won at the Olympics, the *Washington Post*'s Kenneth Turan attempted to refute the growing accusations that Jenner had capitalized on his Olympics success in an unseemly manner and that he was a little too arrogant in media interviews, in which he always seemed to revel in the attention.

"He simply is a real-life version of the American dream, fairly bursting with honest vitality, infectious health and cheerful good humor," Turan wrote. "Is it his fault that he's direct, self-assured, sincere? The type of person we'd all like to be when we grow up?"

And, while he had amassed plenty of detractors, Jenner's numerous defenders argued that he had worked hard for his success and had earned the accolades and fortune that followed.

William Bruce Jenner was born at the height of the baby boom on October 28, 1949, in the sleepy village of Mt. Kisco, New York, less than an hour's drive from Manhattan. And although the town is now populated with sprawling multimillion-dollar estates, it was at the time more of a middle-class commuter community. His father, William, was an arborist, although when Bruce was born, these professionals were still referred to as tree surgeons. Three years before Bruce came along, Bill Jenner had competed in the US Army Olympics in Nuremberg, Germany, where he won a silver medal in the hundred-yard dash. His mother, Esther, was a housewife who occasionally took secretarial work to bring in extra money.

Bruce would later say that his defining moment came when he failed second grade. "I was a dyslexic kid," he recalled. "I always thought everybody else was better than me." He remembered that he used to scream and cry when he had to go to school, which he described as a "trauma." The problem was reading. While his sister was getting straight A's, Bruce just couldn't learn to read. Dyslexia was a mostly undiagnosed disorder at the time, so Bruce was labeled "slow." Eventually a doctor figured it out, but since there was no cure, Bruce continued to struggle in school, feeling like a failure.

That all changed in fifth-grade gym class, when his coach set up a course for running and Bruce achieved the best time of any of his classmates. Suddenly there was something he was better at than all those kids who could read.

"My greatest gift in life was being dyslexic," he later told *Esquire*. "It made me special. It made me different. If I had not been dyslexic, I wouldn't have needed sports. I would have been like every other kid. Instead, I found my one thing, and I was never going to let go of it. That little dyslexic kid is always in the back of your head."

That became the cliché that many Americans could recite from memory two decades later: Dyslexia was the bane of Bruce Jenner's childhood and athletics the panacea. But a longtime friend and confidant of Bruce's suggested to me there may have been darker factors plaguing the youngster than simply a learning disability.

"Bruce told me that he was [physically] abused as a child, but he never told me who was the abuser," said the friend. "I know it haunted him."

In his 1996 memoir, *Finding the Champion Within*, Bruce provided what may be a telling clue. He claimed that when he was young, his parents fenced in their yard to curb his "wanderlust."

"When that didn't help," he recalled, "they strapped me in a harness tied with a clothesline to a stake planted in the middle of the yard."

By high school, still plagued by dyslexia, Bruce excelled in football, baseball, and track, and his athletic prowess made him determined to survive the grueling school curriculum. He needed at least a C to stay eligible for sports. It was becoming clear that track was the sport that might even win him an improbable college scholarship, especially after he won the state championships in high jump and pole vault. It's not that he craved a degree. He knew college would be hell. But America was caught up in the Vietnam War, he was approaching draft age, and a student deferment was his best hope of avoiding the army. When the offer finally came, it was not for track and field but for football. Tiny Graceland College—a Mormon institute in Laumania, Iowa—was offering him $500 off the school's $2,500 annual tuition, plus free room and board, to play quarterback for them.

When he arrived at Graceland, he immediately attracted the attention of the school's track coach, L. D. Wheldon, who had heard that there was a new kid who was versatile in numerous field events. Wheldon had become obsessed with the decathlon and immediately knew what he called a "multiventor" when he saw one—a kid who might have the ability to take on the most grueling of all athletic disciplines.

When Bruce blew out his knee as a linebacker during his freshman year, it appeared that his fledgling college athletic career was over almost as soon as it had begun. His season ended when his knee went under the knife. The good news was that even if he flunked out of Graceland, the injury likely left him ineligible for military service. His football career, however, was definitely over. But when he returned for his sophomore year, Wheldon was waiting. The knee might not have fully healed, but he could start training for other events such as javelin and shot put, in what Bruce called the "mythical decathlon" that Wheldon saw him competing in—and which Bruce was sure would never happen outside the coach's imagination.

But Wheldon persisted, and before long Bruce Jenner was one of the top college decathletes in the country. At the 1972 US Olympic Trials, he placed third, good enough for a spot on the team heading to Munich for the Summer Games.

"Nobody was more shocked than I was when I made it to Munich in 1972," he later told *Vogue*.

> *I'd only been doing the decathlon for two years, and I snuck on the team. My only goal was to see if I could make it into the top ten. I came in tenth, so I was very happy with my first Olympic experience. After the competition was over, I remember sitting on the side of the stadium, kind of in the shadows, and watching for the first time, in person, a gold medal ceremony. The Soviet Union's Nikolai Avilov had won the decathlon and broken the world record. It was right then that I decided to take the next four years of my life and see how good I could become. I couldn't sleep I was so excited—I went for a run at 1:00 a.m. on the streets of Munich and began my training for Montreal in 1976.*

It turned out the decathlon wasn't his only passion at Graceland. He fell hard for a seventeen-year-old classmate named Chrystie Crownover.

"When we were first getting to know each other," she later recalled, "he was telling me about a football game he played with such enthusiasm and it meant so much to him, he started crying and I was just getting to know him and I thought, 'My God. This guy is so passionate about his sports.'"

Chrystie also fell hard and was determined to help Bruce succeed, coming to the track, clocking his runs, and pushing him to his limits.

"We both just went full speed ahead towards whatever it would take to get there," Chrystie remembered. The couple married in December 1972. A few months later, they graduated and immediately moved to San Jose, where Bruce took a short-lived part-time job selling insurance in between training six to eight hours a day for the 1976 Games. He even installed a hurdle in the hallway of their cramped apartment so he could practice one of his weaker events. He soon abandoned the insurance job when it got in the way of his primary goal.

"I basically made the decision from that point on that I would take the next four years of my life, give up everything, concentrate on this one little area called sports," he reflected on his intense, driven schedule. "I realized that I had something special that I could dig down deeper than anybody else and come up with a performance when I needed it."

Meanwhile, Chrystie took a job as a flight attendant to pay the bills.

"When I realized that this was the man that I wanted to spend the rest of my life with, I wanted to be part of this commitment. To me it meant I'll work, you don't work, you train all day and I'll be the breadwinner."

It paid off when he stepped to the podium on July 30, 1976, to accept the gold medal and the unofficial title of "world's greatest athlete" that comes with winning the Olympic decathlon. He later recalled the immediate aftermath of his world-record-shattering victory.

"I got out of the stadium, walked out the back door, and there were literally five hundred people outside the stadium door all cramming to get your autograph and I go, 'Whoa, nobody was doing that before.'" Before he left the stadium that afternoon, he knew he was through with the decathlon for good.

"It was a very bittersweet moment, though, because I knew I was going to retire. I left my vaulting poles in the stadium. I was done. I was missing out on everything in life. It was time to move on. For me, there's more to life than running and jumping."

Crownover later recalled her husband's immediate post-Games euphoria. "He didn't sleep all night," she told the *Boston Herald*. "He would get up and walk around naked with the medal around his neck, beaming and flexing."

Before the Games, in which he was the odds-on favorite going in, Bruce had signed with an agent-manager named George Wallach. Before the Olympic torch had dimmed, Wallach had signed a slew of lucrative endorsement deals and motivational speaking gigs worth millions of dollars. Even his golden Labrador, Bertha, landed a sponsorship deal for General Mills.

The euphoria was short-lived, however, because Bruce got word in November that his eighteen-year-old brother, Burt, had been killed in a car crash while joyriding with his sixteen-year-old girlfriend, whom he had persuaded to skip school that day. The tragedy haunts Bruce and his family to this day. When he and Chrystie discovered that she was pregnant, they decided to name their son after Bruce's late brother. On September 9, 1978, Burt Jenner was born, but Bruce was too busy fulfilling his hectic schedule of celebrity endorsements and motivational speaking to devote much time to fatherhood.

Deep down, Chrystie resented being a virtual single mother. She had worked hard to support her husband as he spent every waking hour training for his dream. Now she barely saw him as he capitalized on every marketing opportunity that Wallach landed for him. Shortly before Burt was born, Bruce had even auditioned for the role of Superman that eventually went to Christopher Reeve. Although resentful of his misplaced priorities, she publicly defended what many saw as crass commercialism. "After all the work Bruce has put in, he's entitled to make a few bucks," she told the *New York Times*.

Billed as the clean-cut all-American boy, Jenner largely stayed away from controversy during these years. The only hiccup concerned his most famous endorsement, in which he declared that Wheaties—"the breakfast of champions"—had been an integral part of his success.

"I worked out a lot and ate a lot of Wheaties," he shilled, "because a complete breakfast with Wheaties is good-tasting and good for you." Not everybody was buying it. In 1977, the San Francisco consumer-fraud unit sued General Mills—manufacturer of the cereal—alleging false advertising over Jenner's claims. "It is difficult to believe that an Olympic-caliber athlete such as Bruce Jenner actually used Wheaties as an important nutrial source in training for the 1976 Olympics," the city's consumer-fraud attorney, David Moon, charged. But Jenner supplied affidavits and firsthand sources attesting to the veracity of his training regimen, and the suit was eventually dropped. John Belushi would mock the controversy on an episode of *Saturday Night Live*, in which he wore a USA tank top over his pot belly and trained by gorging on chocolate doughnuts.

By then, Bruce's marriage was already in deep trouble. When Chrystie found out she was expecting another child in 1979, Bruce later admitted to *Playboy*, he suggested an abortion. He claims he "rejected the idea in 30 seconds," but Chrystie later told a different story. "When I found out I was pregnant Bruce raised the issue of an abortion," she told a magazine reporter.

> *And I went along with him just as I always did. I had all the tests and had even paid for the operation. But one night I was out to dinner and my friend asked me why I wanted an abortion. I told him, "I don't want the abortion." He said, "Why are you having it?" And I said, "Because Bruce wants it." He said, "You are having the abortion because the man that you are not going to be living with wants you to have it?" I thought, what an idiot*

*I am. I wanted the child very, very much. But I was conditioned
to make decisions that were best for him. It was totally my choice
to have the baby.*

Before Cassandra Jenner was born on June 10, 1980, Bruce had
moved out of the house. He was not even present for his daughter's birth. In retrospect, we know that Bruce was harboring a secret.
Chrystie would talk candidly about it after he came out as Caitlyn. At
the time, however, she put on a brave face in an interview with *People*
magazine, blaming their troubles on his newfound success:

*I think Bruce probably takes more responsibility for our mar-
riage failing than he needs to. He doesn't really say it, but that's
my intuition. I am sorry because I don't want him carrying that
burden. His real moment of truth came when he told me he
wanted out of the marriage. It was painful for him—and for me
too. It was such a feeling of rejection. He told me it was not me, it
was self-imposed. The pressures of his career, the public, his being
away from his family. This led to guilt, especially about the family.
So the best way to eliminate the guilt was to eliminate the source
of the guilt. Had it not been for the demands of our new wealth
and our concern over what people were thinking, our marriage
might have had a better chance. But I am not totally convinced
we'd still be together because we're such different people. Bruce
was the first to admit it. He'd say, "I am treating you terribly and
I don't know why." So that was when we decided to live apart.
Now he has achieved a certain public status and has a power
with other people that is very alluring. You don't get money and
fame without paying for it, with time or with your soul.*

She would also cite the fortune her husband made following
the 1976 Games as a factor in their marital troubles. "The power of

money is so damned destructive," she said. "When people are making as much money as Bruce, they just think they can do what they
want. I was making the money for a long time in our relationship, but
I didn't use money as a source of power against him. After Burt was
born I used to tell Bruce how powerless and undignified I felt having
no earning power. I hated that feeling. Prior to the Olympics it was
'our money'; then afterwards it became 'his' money."

The divorce was finalized in 1981. By then, Bruce had met and
fallen for an actress and former beauty queen named Linda Thompson, who had lived with Elvis Presley for four years during the 1970s.
Other than the Elvis connection, Thompson was best known as a
regular on the variety show *Hee Haw*. Within days of his divorce from
Chrystie, Bruce married Thompson. Soon afterward, he fired his longtime agent, Wallach, announcing that Thompson would take over the
management of his career. "There wasn't a place for me anymore,"
Wallach told the *Washington Post*. "I was not happy about it."

Wallach's fate may have been sealed when he landed Jenner—
who had already been rejected for *Superman* because of his acting
skills—a role in the putrefying 1980 Village People biopic *Can't Stop
the Music*, playing a lawyer named Ron White. It was hard for critics
to decide which was worse—the film or Jenner's performance. "The
Village People, along with ex-Olympic decathlon champion Bruce
Jenner, have a long way to go in the acting stakes," opined *Variety*.

The film—which was a huge critical and box-office flop—was
named the worst picture of the year at the inaugural Golden Rasp-
berry Awards that year and Jenner received a "Razzie" nomination
for Worst Actor. In Razzie founder John Wilson's book, *The Official
Razzie Movie Guide*, however, he names the film as one of "The 100
Most Enjoyably Bad Movies Ever Made." Bruce later claimed he had
seen the writing on the wall even before the film was released.

"I knew we were in trouble with the movie," he wrote, "when
disco was pronounced dead and young people were blowing up disco

records in stadiums before baseball games across America just before our film's opening weekend."

By the time of the movie's release, Jenner was so ubiquitous that he had become a punch line. Wallach had accepted a guest-starring role for him in the season finale of the hit Fox TV series *Married . . . With Children*. But when Jenner saw the script, he backed out of the commitment. His reticence undoubtedly stemmed from a particular scene in which Jenner, playing himself, meets the series's main character, Al Bundy, who engages him in dialogue that Jenner found demeaning:

> JENNER: Hi, I'm Bruce Jenner.
>
> AL BUNDY: You mean exercise bike, infomercial pitchman Bruce Jenner? Costar in the Village People classic *Can't Stop the Music* Bruce Jenner?
>
> JENNER: I prefer to think of myself as decathlon gold medal winner Bruce Jenner.
>
> BUNDY: And I prefer to think of myself as high school football hero Al Bundy, but we all have to live in the present.

Linda Thompson would later recall the first time she set eyes on Bruce. She was lying in bed with Elvis at Graceland in July 1976 when they switched on the television to watch Jenner take the final lap in the 1,500 meters—the last event in the decathlon. Linda remembers that she and Elvis both found him to be an amazing "specimen" of a man.

She said, "Elvis remarked, 'Damn if that guy is not handsome! I'm not gay, but damn, he's good-looking!' I quite agreed and teasingly said, 'Wow! He is gorgeous! I'm going to marry that guy someday!' Elvis replied, 'Yeah, sure, honey, over my dead body.'"

Three years later, she was playing in a celebrity tennis tournament to raise money for deaf children, held at the Playboy mansion. At the invitation of Hugh Hefner, Bruce had been living at the mansion since separating from Chrystie. Bruce won the tournament that day, and Linda had been designated to hand him his trophy.

He asked her whether she came to the mansion often. Anxious to convince him that she was no bimbo, Linda protested that it was actually her first time. When he became flirty, she brought up the fact that he was married. She had seen his wife on TV at the Olympics.

"No, I'm separated, and it's really not a lot of fun," he responded. One thing led to another, and the two were soon dating seriously. Linda even accompanied him to Australia to promote *Can't Stop the Music*. Returning from the trip, she discovered that she was pregnant. This was Linda's first pregnancy and she was thrilled, though it soon became apparent that, as before, Bruce was not particularly looking forward to becoming a father.

"I found myself pregnant for the first time in my life," she later recalled in an essay for the *Huffington Post* about her time with Bruce. "When the doctor's office called me to tell me the results of the pregnancy test, I fell to my knees with joy and prayed that I would be worthy of carrying that precious life. It is a feeling I'll never forget. I really felt in that moment that whatever had transpired in my life of any negative nature, any transgression I had ever perpetrated, had somehow been cleansed away from my being."

Bruce's divorce still had not been finalized, but he immediately proposed. On January 5, 1981, the two were married in a small ceremony in Oahu, Hawaii, with two-year-old Burt serving as best man. Brandon Thompson Jenner came along five months later on June 4.

The newlyweds, billed as the new "glamor couple," would often be photographed on red carpets and at social events. They also hosted a number of charitable fund-raisers. Having dated Elvis for four years, Linda was no stranger to the celebrity circuit, and she was pleasantly surprised to learn that Bruce appeared to have less baggage than the King.

"The Bruce I knew back then was an easygoing, down-to-earth, casual, romantic, good and loving man," she recalled years later. "I was extremely happy to have found such a remarkable partner with whom to share my life. I found him to be honorable and, well, just too good to be true. Just too good to be true indeed."

It had been five years since his triumph in Montreal, and his cachet was definitely starting to wane, especially after the Village People movie made him a punch line. But Linda was determined to keep the Jenner brand alive. She helped negotiate a six-part arc for Bruce on the hit TV series *CHiPs*, as motorcycle officer Steve McLeish, and a TV biopic starring Bruce as football player Jim Gregory—the first white quarterback to play for the black Louisiana college—called *Grambling's White Tiger*. His performances were not much better received than the Village People movie.

In 1982, Linda found herself pregnant once again. On August 21, 1983, Brody Jenner came along, and now Bruce was the father of four children. Again, the prospect didn't thrill him and, as Linda and the kids later revealed, he spent very little time fulfilling his fatherly duties.

He had embarked on a series of dubious financial ventures, including a company called Bruce Jenner Aviation that sold aircraft supplies to corporations. Bruce had learned to fly and had purchased a Beechcraft Bonanza in order to pilot himself to his myriad appearances. He had also licensed his name to a chain of fitness centers that eventually went bust.

By 1984, the marriage was clearly on the rocks. The couple separated that year and later attempted therapy. Three decades later, Linda would finally disclose the source of the problems, but at the time, she explained their estrangement and 1986 divorce as resulting from Bruce's hectic travel schedule and the fact that they had no time to spend together. The terms of the divorce were never made public, but Linda would later reveal, "I may be the only woman in the state of California to have waived child support and alimony."

The fact is that by the time the divorce was finalized in 1986, Bruce had no money to give her. His career was on the wane and his business ventures had gone bust. He later described his bleak life after the separation from Linda. "I had been beaten by the system. In my career, in my two failed marriages, in my association with others."

When he moved out, he rented a small house in Malibu. With the endorsements dried up and only the occasional speaking gig—barely enough to pay the rent—the next six years would not be kind. "If you would have looked into my living room anytime between 1984 and 1990, you would have seen failure personified," he wrote in his memoir. "Look at that shabby one-room rented house. Who could live there, absolutely alone, with only a television set for company?"

By the time Candace Garvey told him about her friend Kris, he claims he had only $200 in the bank and was more than $300,000 in debt. But until he met Kris, he would later claim, his biggest deficiency was his "bankrupt soul." On their first date, Bruce recalls, he poured out that soul to her. "I told her I'd been miserable for umpteen years. That I'd spent the last six years in a Southern California version of solitary confinement."

As part of the divorce agreement, Bob was allowing Kris to stay in the Beverly Hills house for six months, but Bruce didn't feel comfortable living with her in her ex-husband's place, nor bringing his four children to stay there. Within months of their first date, on February 10, 1991, they took Bob's settlement money and leased a house in Malibu. At dinner with the Garveys the same night, Bruce proposed.

One of the benefits of their new union was the fact that each had four kids. But it was also a potential stumbling block. Would these disparate families be able to get along? From the beginning, Kourtney had been the only holdout. But after Bruce managed to negotiate a detente between her parents, she began to warm to him.

"It was absolutely like a modern-day *Brady Bunch*," Kris would later tell E!, "and everybody got along." Kourtney also remembers the merging of the families fondly. "It was cool how he had three boys and a girl and my mom had three girls and a boy," she recalled. "It was so meant to be." Khloé remembered one particular dynamic that presented itself early on. "I think at times that Kourtney and Kim had crushes on one of the boys but they would never really say anything because it was, like, gross."

There was at least one member of the new clan whose memories differ slightly from the harmonious picture painted by his sisters. At first, Rob recalls, "I was relieved to have brothers but now I was still getting picked on even more." He especially remembers a game of hide-and-seek when he had to go the bathroom. As he was peeing on the side of the house, his siblings caught him. He was so startled that he turned around, spraying them in the process. From that day forward, they called him "pee boy." Kim too recalls that Rob was frequently "beaten up" by Brandon, Brody, and Burt.

It wasn't long after she married Bruce in April 1991 that Kris finally managed to put her long and toxic feud with her ex-husband behind her. It helped that they both had new people in their lives. Bob had begun dating a woman named Denice Halicki, who bonded immediately with the four Kardashian kids. Denice was the widow of the Hollywood personality H. B. Halicki, who had been killed in an accident on the set of the sequel to his film *Gone in 60 Seconds*. His 1989 death had left Denice with a considerable fortune. With Bruce playing peacemaker, Bob and Kris had once again become friends and frequently dined with Bruce and Denice, along with their old friends O.J. and Nicole, who had largely kept their distance during the bitter divorce battle.

Kris now had a project. She was determined to revive her new husband's long-dormant career, and she set about the task in earnest. Like Linda before her, she appointed herself his manager, but unlike his ex-wife, she appeared to have the magic touch. She would later claim that she took Bruce's Olympic gold medal from his sock drawer where he kept it and had it framed. The medal would become their motivation.

"We wanted to be champions again," she wrote. Her only real job had been a two-year stint as a flight attendant, but she had grown up working in her grandparents' candle shop and had watched very carefully. It soon became apparent that she had inherited her family's flair for business. Almost immediately, she envisioned a Bruce Jenner clothing line, Jenner fitness equipment, vitamin supplements, a new round of endorsements. She was determined to put him back on the map.

She hired Bob's former assistant, set up an office, bought a computer system, and set about the task of reviving the Jenner brand. Within weeks, she had assembled a professional press kit and sent it out to speakers' bureaus. Suddenly, Bruce was hot again, and the money rolled in.

"We just had to get him out there in front of the world again," she wrote. "That became my primary focus eighteen hours a day." Soon Bruce burst back into the American consciousness with an ubiquitous infomercial Kris had developed called "Superfit with Kris and Bruce Jenner." It proved lucrative.

The producer of the infomercial, Jack Kirby, later recalled working with Kris on the project. "I lovingly refer to her as the Velvet Hammer," he told the *Hollywood Reporter*. "A lot of time women in this business are unfairly categorized as bitchy. Kris was a smart woman and recognized that, so she would go on a charm offensive and make you love her."

With a new source of income, the couple leased a house in the Benedict area near Beverly Hills so the Kardashian kids could be near their dad. They also employed a nanny named Pam Behan to look after the brood of eight growing children. Behan had previously worked for Bruce, taking care of his four kids. Years later, Behan would detail her experience working for the Jenners in a memoir, *Malibu Nanny*.

She revealed that, although she had always gotten along with Bruce and loved him like a brother, her relationship with Kris didn't start off famously. In the memoir, she hints at the legendary control freak that millions would eventually come to know.

Each week I made one big trip to the store to purchase all of the food for the week. Occasionally, as on this particular day, she would ask me to make a quick run to the store for a few special items. When I got home, Kris, who was in the kitchen, looked at the groceries I had just purchased, and let out a torrent of expletives. "$#&%! $#&%! $#&%! I can't believe you forgot the $#&%ing broccoli!" Broccoli was not on the short list she had given me that day, although it was a regular item on the weekly list. I did not know, shame on me, that keeping broccoli stocked in the refrigerator was so critical.

Note to self: although not obvious to the average person, myself included, broccoli is a staple as important as milk and butter, and must be kept in the fridge at all times. The tension in the room was so thick you could almost see it. I thought to myself, Oh my gosh, what have I done? Why am I here? This lady really doesn't like me. I was raised in the conservative Midwest with a prim and proper mother, and I had never heard a lady cuss like that before. I was quite certain at the moment that I had made a huge mistake in coming to work for Kris, and mentally started packing my bags. However, I had four kids who were depending on me, and it was important for me to be a stable force in their lives.

The next day, Kris apologized for her tantrum, though she believed she had acted "rationally." "If I knew then what I know now," Behan recalled, "I would have realized, 'That's just Kris.'" After Behan got used to the routine, she soon realized that Kris's bark was worse than her bite, and she eventually came to respect her employer, who would occasionally give her expensive hand-me-down clothing and other items. She also had fond memories of the children, describing Kourtney as "a serious child" who "spoke her mind" while Kim was "always very sweet and friendly." She describes Khloé as "a pistol, full of energy," and Rob as "mostly sweet and precious." Apart from her nanny duties, Behan was also expected to function as Kris's "personal assistant," and she was frequently run ragged while Kris focused on her growing business empire.

It was around this time that Nicole finally decided to end her tumultuous marriage to O.J. To hear Kris tell it, she had no idea "until it was too late" that her best friend was being brutally and physically abused. Although Kris wasn't as close to O.J. as she had once been, she received a call from him shortly after she started dating Bruce, who was also a good friend of Simpson's. "What's going on, Kris? Why didn't you tell me you were dating Bruce Jenner?" she reports him asking. It was a significant phone call, she later wrote. "O.J. was like a big brother to me."

She recalls that Nicole had been angry with her for throwing away her relationship with Bob, but soon they were all hanging out again, just like old times. Nicole, she claims, was very "private" about what she had been going through with O.J. Kris knew they were having trouble, but she believed this stemmed from O.J.'s infidelities.

In 1992, Nicole decided to end the marriage and had moved into her own place. The couple had always had a "volatile" relationship, Kris says, but she just couldn't understand why Nicole would make a decision that seemed so "final." She does remember something Nicole told her a number of times, which she said was later forever seared into her memory: "He's going to kill me and he's going to get away with it." Yet after they divorced and Nicole informed her that she and O.J. had started "dating again," Kris wrote that she was "excited" for her friends. Soon, it was again like old times, with the couple throwing parties and entertaining as in the early days. Bruce and Kris would come over to O.J.'s place and they would all play the Newlywed Game.

On one occasion, Nicole's house key went missing, and she became convinced that O.J. or someone sent by him had taken it and was spying on her. She confided all this to Kris. And yet, "I didn't really realize that abuse was going on at the time or how bad it was," she later wrote. "She didn't share the abusive side of him with anybody for a really long time."

I recently met a woman named Monica Levy who claims to have been part of the LA social set when Kris and Bruce were friendly with O.J. and Nicole. She is convinced that Kris's version of the story is "revisionist history" and that she couldn't possibly have been unaware of O.J.'s abusive side.

"I wouldn't say I was friends of theirs exactly, but I was on the periphery of their circle. I'd often see them at parties or at fundraisers," she recalls.

> It was known that Kris was close friends with both O.J. and Nicole. Everybody in the early '90s knew that O.J. beat the crap out of Nicole. That's why she left him. It was kind of common knowledge. Come on—it was in the papers long before the murders, long before. If I knew, I can guarantee her very good friend Kris knew. But she was charmed by O.J. and loved basking in his celebrity. Everybody was. I have to say he could turn on the charm, especially around the ladies. If she didn't see it, she didn't want to see it, but believe me, she knew. I wouldn't be too hard on her, though, or single her out as some kind of villain. For fuck's sake, [Nicole's] own sister knew and didn't do anything. She was also charmed by the guy. And then she had the audacity to whore her sister's name on behalf of battered women. She has more to answer for than Kris Jenner, believe you me.

Indeed, on May 23, 1989, the *Los Angeles Times* reported that O.J. had pleaded no contest to a charge that he beat his wife at their Brentwood home on January 1 of that year. He had been accused of "slapping, kicking and threatening to kill" Nicole during an argument on New Year's Day.

I wasn't an avid O.J.-trial watcher, but I still vividly remember when photos of Nicole with a severely beaten face were produced. I also remember being dumbfounded by the sheer number of black Americans, especially women, who continued to defend O.J. after that. I could understand why so many African Americans were convinced of his innocence and believed he had been framed, especially after it was revealed that Detective Mark Fuhrman—later convicted of perjury—was an inveterate racist who had frequently used the word *nigger*. But I couldn't understand how people could have witnessed those sickening photos and continued to defend O.J.

Nor could I fathom how, as Levy alluded to, Nicole's sister Denise could assert after Nicole's murder that her sister was "not a battered woman. My definition of a battered woman is somebody who gets beat up all the time. I don't want people to think it was like that. I know Nicole. She was a very strong-willed person. If she was beaten up, she wouldn't have stayed with him. That wasn't her. Everybody knows about 1989. Does anybody know about any other time?"

It later emerged that Denise herself was well aware of at least one other time that Nicole had been abused. When she was called to the stand during the subsequent trial, she recalled an incident during the early '80s, when she had been at the couple's house after dinner with friends at a Mexican restaurant. When Denise suggested to O.J. that he had been taking her sister for granted, "He started yelling at me, 'I don't take her for granted. I do everything for her. I give her everything.' A whole fight broke out. Pictures started flying off the wall; clothes started flying down the stairs. He grabbed Nicole and told her to get out of the house. He picked her up and threw her against the wall. He picked her up and threw her out of the house. She ended up falling on her elbows and her butt. We were all sitting there screaming and crying, and then he grabbed me and threw me out." Brown also admitted that she had taken photos of Nicole's battered face following the New Year's Day argument, which Nicole later filed away in a safe-deposit box. Nicole's father also saw the photos but, according to what a close family friend told *People* magazine, "he dismissed it." In a 1995 cover feature on the Brown family and their failure to intervene to help Nicole, *People* reporter Shelley Levitt paints a devastating portrait of the enablers around her—friends, family, and police—who failed to come to her aid.

"Some say the Browns were dazzled by O.J.'s stardom and seduced by his wealth," writes Levitt. "He had secured a Hertz dealership for Nicole's father, Louis, and he paid the college tuition for her younger sisters Dominique and Tanya."

She also quotes friends and neighbors who were aware of the abuse. Nicole's close friend Faye Resnick later even suggested that some of Nicole's family members had tried to talk her out of divorcing O.J. in 1992. "It's just like everything else, Faye," she claims Nicole told her. "O.J. always controls everyone and everything around him."

Like Levy, I find it impossible to believe that Kris was unaware of the abuse. Her retroactive and disingenuous explanation that she didn't know rings hollow, especially since she admits that Nicole had told her of her fears that O.J. would kill her.

But hindsight is better than foresight, and I'm not sure how fair it is to blame Kris and Nicole's other friends for their collective failure to intervene. The guilt they are likely feeling to this day is worse than any judgment that the public could bestow, and the cautionary tale may very well help countless women in similar situations.

Whatever Kris knew, by March 1994 Nicole and O.J. were back together. At the time, Kris had been trying very hard to conceive a baby with Bruce, and had so far been unsuccessful. She had recently suffered a miscarriage and was visibly depressed. To cheer her up, Nicole suggested that she take Bruce and all the kids on a Mexican vacation. Nicole rented a villa, and the whole clan jetted to their favorite vacation spot, Cabo. Nicole brought O.J. and their kids along. And although Nicole had definitely confided a number of troubling revelations about the dark side of her relationship by that point, Kris writes that "at the time I was happy to see her with him." If she had known then what she knows now, she admits, she would never have encouraged her "to return to that kind of hell."

It was on this trip that Kris claims to have confronted O.J. for the first time, when she saw him flirting with two girls at the bar after Nicole had gone to the bathroom. "Stop it," she told him. "Cut it out, O.J. What's wrong with you? We're on vacation as a family, your kids are sitting right over there."

On June 12, 1994, Kris received an urgent call from Nicole saying she had something "really really important" to talk about. She had to be at her daughter Sydney's rehearsal in two hours, but she needed to talk urgently. Kris begged off, explaining that she had to go to the market, but they arranged to meet for lunch the following day. Blowing off her friend that day, Kris later recalled, is a decision that would haunt her forever.

CHAPTER FIVE

W hen Bob reached her on the phone on his way to O.J.'s on the morning of June 13, Kris was just about to call him to share the same news. After she told him that she had been scheduled to have lunch with Nicole that very morning, her ex-husband uttered the words that would stay with her:

"I hope O.J. didn't do it."

When he arrived at the gates of his friend's Rockingham home minutes later, he informed a cop that he was a friend of O.J.'s, "one of his closest friends." He was told that Simpson had not yet arrived. Bob could not enter. Moments later, O.J.'s longtime attorney, Howard Weitzman—the man who had won an acquittal for auto magnate John De Lorean on drug-dealing charges ten years earlier—drove up. He was also the lawyer who had represented O.J. when he was accused of assaulting Nicole in 1989. But Weitzman was all business, and Bob was left standing at the gate until O.J. arrived in the black Cadillac of his business adviser Skip Taft. He got out of the car carrying a duffel bag but ignored Bob, who was still standing there. Next, Bob's former assistant Cathy Randa got out of the car carrying a Louis Vuitton garment bag that belonged to O.J. He offered to take the bag from her. Slinging it over his shoulder, he approached the police guard and told him that he had O.J.'s luggage, believing this would be his entree.

In the deposition he later gave for the Goldman family's civil suit against O.J., Bob described what happened next. "The bag was sitting at our feet. I walked over to the police officer, and I said, 'Mr. Simpson's bag is sitting here. You should take it. It's his luggage.' And he says, 'You can't bring it in.' I said, 'But it's his luggage. You should take it.' And he said, 'No, you can't come in.'"

Meanwhile, he looked over and saw that O.J. had been handcuffed by police.

He realized that he wasn't getting through the gate. So Bob threw the bag into the trunk of his Mercedes and gave Randa a lift to O.J.'s office, Orenthal Enterprises, two miles away.

There, he spent the afternoon answering phone calls from well-wishers and business associates, all clamoring to find out what was going on. Meanwhile, O.J. had gone downtown to police headquarters to answer questions. Around 4:00 p.m., he returned to the office. Upon arriving, he hugged Bob but was noncommittal about what he had told the police and sat down to watch the TV news coverage. Just after 6:00 p.m., he asked Bob to drive him home. When they arrived, they found police tearing the place apart. When O.J. took Bob upstairs to find out if anything was missing, he told Bob that he had eight thousand dollars in gambling winnings in his closet. There was no sign of the money, but O.J.'s gun collection—nine weapons in all, including an Uzi—was still there.

The place was chaos. At one point Bob saw O.J.'s surfer house-guest, Kato Kaelin, wandering around, and then he saw O.J.'s sister Shirley. He confided that he was worried about his friend's state of mind. "Stay near your brother tonight," he told her. "Don't leave him." Then he went home.

The next morning, he headed back to the house in his Rolls Royce. Before he left, he remembered O.J.'s garment bag from the day before and switched it from the trunk of the Mercedes to the trunk of the Rolls. Finding a swarm of media plaguing his beleaguered friend, he suggested that O.J. stay at his house for a couple of days until the frenzy "blows over." But it would be almost impossible to leave undetected. The media would simply follow. He suggested that O.J. cut through the tennis court of his neighbor's adjoining property and Bob would swing around and pick him up down the street.

Minutes later, with the press none the wiser, the two men headed to O.J.'s office. On the ride over, the decision was made to shelve Weitzman as the lead attorney and bring on Robert Shapiro to head the defense team. Shapiro had been suggested by O.J.'s friend Roger King, the owner of the TV conglomerate Kingworld Productions, which owned *Inside Edition*. King insisted that O.J. needed the best criminal defense attorney that money could buy and offered to bankroll Shapiro, whose legal bill would almost certainly run into the millions.

When Shapiro arrived at the office less than an hour later, one of the first things he did was take Bob aside and confess that he needed his help with the case. He didn't know O.J., and he needed someone on board that the former football star could trust. Bob had stopped practicing law two years earlier to devote himself full-time to his various business enterprises. Now Shapiro was asking him to reactivate his license and join the defense team. Ron Goldman's family and others would later openly speculate that Kardashian was merely added to the defense team so that he couldn't be called as a witness, because attorneys are governed by lawyer-client privilege.

The whole time that Shapiro was there, he was surprised to find O.J. repeatedly bringing up the subject of his golf clubs. He had apparently left them at LAX when he returned from a tournament in Chicago, and he seemed obsessed with getting them back. It seemed strange to everybody that O.J. was a prime suspect in the murder of his ex-wife but all he wanted to talk about was his golf clubs.

After Shapiro left, O.J. asked Bob to drive him to the airport to retrieve the clubs. After a twenty-minute ride, they left the Rolls curbside at the Arrivals area and headed to the American Airlines office. A customer-service rep informed them that the clubs could be found at the next carousel over. There, an attendant handed O.J. the black golf bag with a red Swiss Army insignia emblazoned on the carrying case. Finding the car, they tossed the clubs in the trunk alongside the Louis Vuitton garment bag and drove back to Bob's house.

As they returned along San Vincente Boulevard in Brentwood, they just happened to stop at a red light next to Kris Jenner, who was driving with Bob's cousin Cici. Kris recalled that they both looked at her through the window but there was no acknowledgment. They just sped off. That night, she says, she called Bob to ask him what that was about. Bob told her the story about the golf tournament and that O.J. needed to retrieve his clubs. Why couldn't he have simply had them delivered to the house? she asked. Bob assured her that he "really needed his clubs."

Kris exploded. "His wife is fucking dead! Why did O.J. need his golf clubs?" She was very suspicious and would remain so long afterward. Arriving home from the airport, Bob removed the clubs from the trunk and placed them in the garage, where they remained, seemingly unopened, for some time.

Asked during the civil deposition whether he ever saw O.J. remove anything from the bag, Bob recalled that the next day he had seen him remove a single club—an iron—from the bag. He then walked around the block, swinging the club. As for the garment bag, O.J. eventually brought it with him when he returned home. Bob saw it lying open in his bedroom. Both bags would end up playing a starring role in the events to follow and in the frequently leveled charge that Bob had helped his old friend cover up a murder.

O.J.'s kids Sydney and Justin had been brought to Bob's house by Al Cowlings, also unbeknownst to the media, which were still camped out at the Rockingham estate assuming O.J. was inside. Upon his return to the house, O.J. spent hours with the children. At one point, Bob overheard him tell them that their mommy was in heaven and that he might join her there. He'd later testify that he saw his friend crying.

It had been suggested by Shapiro that O.J. submit to a polygraph test. It would be inadmissible in court, but if he passed, they could release it to the press and the DA and show that O.J. had nothing to do with the murders. Bob liked the idea. O.J. insisted he would pass the test because he had nothing to do with the slayings. They contacted the office of Dr. Edward Gelb, one of the top polygraph experts in the country, who had taught the advanced polygraph course for the FBI. But Gelb was overseas. His assistant Dennis Nellany would instead administer the test.

In 1996, Lawrence Schiller published a book about the case entitled *American Tragedy*—reportedly with the full cooperation of Robert Kardashian, who was rumored to have shared in the royalties. According to Schiller, Nellany reported that Simpson had scored a "minus 22" on the test, which is about the lowest score possible and indicates a strong probability that he had lied in answer to all the key questions surrounding the slayings. Hearing the results, Bob was stunned. He claims that he was still completely convinced of his friend's innocence.

Schiller reports O.J.'s response: "What I said about Nicole, you know? Every time he said her name, my heart would beat like crazy. You guys have got to understand. I didn't do this!" On the drive back, he kept insisting to Bob that he was "nervous." Bob believed him. Besides, he had been on heavy anti-anxiety medication since the murders, which might have skewed the results. He offered to take the test again, but his lawyers suggested he wait a week.

When word eventually leaked out that O.J. had made a special trip to the airport to retrieve the golf bag, media speculation reached a frenzy around the idea that this was where O.J. had hidden the murder weapon—the so-called bloody knife used to kill the victims—which was never found. The bag was still in the garage, so Bob summoned Al Cowlings.

"I wanted to know if it was true," he recalled. "I wanted to know if there was anything in there and if there was I was going to turn it in." Together, he and Cowlings examined every square inch of the bag but failed to find either a knife or any bloodstains. The bag, however, wasn't the only potential location where O.J. could have stashed the weapon. Media photographers had snapped numerous photos of the still-unknown Kardashian with O.J.'s Louis Vuitton bag slung over his shoulder. Once he took a prominent place on the defense team, many pundits speculated that Bob had helped his client hide the evidence. Both Kim and Fred Goldman, the sister and father of murder victim Ron, would later publicly muse about his involvement.

"I have always wondered what was in his luggage bag, and if it did indeed hold the murder weapon that was used to kill my brother and Nicole," Kim told Radar Online. "That evidence would have convicted 'the killer,' " Fred Goldman later told the London *Mail on Sunday*.

Years later, Bob continued to deny that he had anything to do with a cover-up. "The police could have taken [the bag] at any time," he said. "They never sought to do so, in fact when we turned it in to the court nine months later, they still never did any tests to see if there was blood. I don't believe they really wanted to know the answer. I think it was better to leave speculation and to let the public think there was something sinister about these bags!"

Kris also counted herself among the most skeptical. In her memoir, she recalls arriving at Bob's to pick up the kids the week of the killings. She knew O.J. had been staying there following the murders. When she found nobody home, she claims she went to the room where O.J. had been sleeping. One thought, she remembered, consumed her. She needed to search the place. She found the Louis Vuitton bag and decided to examine it. "I went through it with a fine tooth comb, trying to satisfy my own curiosity, my own doubts," she recalled. "If there was a piece of incriminating evidence anywhere, I was determined to find it and turn it over to the prosecution. It was torturing me that there had to be something somewhere and I was determined to find it." After ransacking the room, she had come up empty.

It's a good story but is almost certainly apocryphal. The kids hadn't been staying with Bob that week and definitely not while O.J. was hiding at his house. They didn't even see their father again until after O.J. was arrested. By that time, the Louis Vuitton bag was long gone from the premises. On the other hand, Bob's story about searching the golf bag with Al Cowlings also doesn't ring true. It is almost impossible to believe that he would have turned over evidence against his own client, let alone a close friend.

After the trial, the most prominent O.J. watcher, Dominick Dunne of *Vanity Fair*, would address the increasing speculation that Bob had participated in a cover-up. "Simpson's friend Robert Kardashian," he wrote,

> will always be remembered as the person who walked off Simpson's property the day after the murders carrying a Louis Vuitton bag that many people believed held the bloody clothes worn by the killer. I have never felt that that was so. I don't believe that Simpson would have brought bloody clothes back to Los Angeles from Chicago, where he had gone after the murders to play in a golf tournament, knowing that he would have been met by police. I do wonder, however, if Kardashian could have played a part in the removal of the murder weapon from the golf bag that arrived at LAX the day after Simpson's return from Chicago, when he and Simpson, in the midst of his mourning, went to the airport to pick up Simpson's golf clubs. A knife in a golf bag might have gone through security undetected.

By June 17, police had collected enough evidence to conclude that O.J. had almost certainly killed Nicole and Ron Goldman. Shapiro called Bob at 8:30 a.m. to inform him that an arrest warrant had been issued. He had convinced authorities to allow his client to surrender himself at 11:00 that morning. The two decided to tell O.J. the news together. When Denice Halicki overheard, she suggested that they let A. J. Cowlings know. As his best friend and someone even larger than O.J., Al could stop him if he were to do "something crazy." She also suggested that the guns be removed from Bob's house before they gave him the bad news.

They found O.J. still in bed. They told him he was about to be charged with double homicide. Shapiro, according to Schiller, asked him if he had anything he wanted to tell them. It would be his last chance to be alone with his lawyers with no possibility of anyone eavesdropping.

"Basically, I've told you everything that's transpired," he replied. "I've got nothing to hide." He asked why the police aren't looking for other people. It's a "setup," he protested. His team needed to take some medical samples, including blood, urine, and skin, to prepare for his defense. A doctor and nurse were waiting to conduct the testing. Afterward, O.J. retired to his bedroom. When Bob informed him that it was time to go to police headquarters, O.J. remained motionless. "Why should I hurry? What can they do to me?" he asked. It was clear he had no intention of surrendering on schedule. O.J. was busy writing letters on a yellow legal pad to his children and to his mother. At one point, he handed Bob a sealed envelope labeled with the words *To Whom It May Concern, press or public.*

When Shapiro finally called at noon to explain that they were trying to get their client to the station, the authorities demanded the address where he was staying.

A while later, Bob got on his knees and took his friend's hand, suggesting that they pray together. According to Schiller's account, after a short prayer beseeching God for understanding and compassion, O.J. declared, "I'm gonna kill myself. I just can't live with the pain. I just can't go on." Bob warned him that if he pulled the trigger he would "go to hell." But O.J. appeared to have made up his mind.

For the next fifteen minutes, the conversation centered not on talking him out of the drastic act but on where it would take place. O.J. had been staying in the room where Kourtney stayed whenever she was with her father. When he announced that he intended to kill himself where he stood, Bob protested that it was his daughter's room. "I have my little girl in this room and every time I come in here, I'll see your body lying there. You can't do that." After much discussion about other possible rooms, Bob suggested he go outside to commit the act.

Years later, Bob shared with Barbara Walters what happened next: "I said, 'Why don't you do it right here?,' knowing for some reason that he probably wouldn't. And he said—looked up at the sun and said, 'I can't do it here, I'll be baking in the sun.' I said, 'O.J., you're not going to be here; your spirit's going to be gone. What do you care?'"

Eventually, Bob left him alone with Cowlings to talk him out of it and joined Shapiro and the doctors. The police were expected to arrive any time.

When police finally arrived to arrest the fugitive, Bob told Shapiro that he had left O.J. in a room with Cowlings. "O.J., it's time to go!" he yelled upstairs. He led police upstairs to the room, not knowing whether he'd find a body. The room was empty.

As police scrambled to search the house, Bob's assistant told him he was wanted on the phone. "Not now," he barked. When she told him it was his sister calling, he took the call. The voice on the other end of the line sounded familiar. It was O.J., telling him he had shot himself in the head but "didn't die." He had fired his pistol, but it had malfunctioned. He claimed to be at the Bel Air Church. Bob assumed he had chosen this location to kill himself, but O.J. informed his old friend that he was headed "over to Nicole's."

The police never asked Bob who he had been talking to, and he was under no obligation to reveal it. Meanwhile, nobody except Bob had any idea where O.J. might be. When word leaked out, more than a thousand reporters jostled for position outside the police station. When he failed to appear by 2:00 p.m., the LAPD issued an APB and a warrant for his arrest. Nobody was sure where he was.

Shapiro suggested that Bob open the letter that O.J. had given him, in case it contained a clue to his whereabouts. They opened it. Bob told him about the earlier suicide threats. "I think he's dead," he told his colleague. When they read the contents of the letter, Shapiro insisted that Bob be the one to inform the media. He called a press conference for 5:00 p.m. at the downtown conference room of the Twentieth Century Fox Tower, where Bob would read O.J.'s final letter.

At the appointed time, Shapiro stepped to the microphone and introduced his colleague. "This letter was written by O.J. today," Bob began.

To Whom It May Concern:

First, everyone understand. I have nothing to do with Nicole's murder. I loved her; always have and always will. If we had a problem, it's because I loved her so much.

Recently, we came to the understanding that for now we were not right for each other, at least for now. Despite our love, we were different and that's why we mutually agreed to go our separate ways.

It was tough splitting for a second time, but we both knew it was for the best. Inside, I had no doubt that in the future we would be close friends or more. Unlike what has been written

*in the press, Nicole and I had a great relationship for most of
our lives together. Like all long-term relationships, we had a few
downs and ups.*

*I took the heat New Year's 1989 because that's what I was
supposed to do. I did not plead no contest for any other reason
but to protect our privacy and was advised it would end the press
hype.*

*I don't want to belabor knocking the press, but I can't believe
what is being said. Most of it is totally made up. I know you have
a job to do, but as a last wish, please, please, please, leave my
children in peace. Their lives will be tough enough.*

*I want to send my love and thanks to all my friends. I'm
sorry I can't name every one of you, especially A.C. Man, thanks
for being in my life. The support and friendship I received from
so many: Wayne Hughes, Lewis Marks, Frank Olson, Mark
Packer, Bender, Bobby Kardashian. I wish we had spent more
time together in recent years. My golfing buddies: Hoss, Alan
Austin, Mike, Craig, Bender, Wyler, Sandy, Jay, Donnie, thanks
for the fun.*

*All my teammates over the years: Reggie, you were the soul
of my pro career. Ahmad, I never stopped being proud of you.
Marcus, you've got a great lady in Catherine, don't mess it up.
Bobby Chandler, thanks for always being there. Skip and Kathy,
I love you guys. Without you, I never would have made it through
this far.*

*Marguerite, thanks for the early years. We had some fun.
Paula, what can I say? You are special. I'm sorry I'm not going
to have, we're not going to have, our chance. God brought you to
me, I now see. As I leave, you'll be in my thoughts.*

*I think of my life and feel I've done most of the right things.
So why do I end up like this? I can't go on. No matter what the
outcome, people will look and point. I can't take that. I can't*

subject my children to that. This way, they can move on and go on with their lives.

Please, if I've done anything worthwhile in my life, let my kids live in peace from you, the press.

I've had a good life. I'm proud of how I lived. My mama taught me to do unto others. I treated people the way I wanted to be treated. I've always tried to be up and helpful. So why is this happening?

I'm sorry for the Goldman family. I know how much it hurts.

Nicole and I had a good life together. All this press talk about a rocky relationship was no more than what every long-term relationship experiences. All her friends will confirm that I have been totally loving and understanding of what she's been going through.

At times, I have felt like a battered husband or boyfriend, but I loved her; make that clear to everyone. And I would take whatever it took to make it work.

Don't feel sorry for me. I've had a great life, great friends. Please think of the real O.J. and not this lost person.

Thanks for making my life special. I hope I helped yours.

Peace and love, O.J.

By the time Bob finished reading the letter, a frenzy had erupted. The assembled reporters were shouting their queries. Many of them demanded to know how *Kardashian* was spelled. But Bob wasn't taking any questions. Security helped him off the stage and out of the packed room. He had failed to inform the throng that the O in the note's closing signature had been drawn in the form of a happy face. By the time the press conference ended, Bob and the defense team claimed that they still believed that O.J. was dead. They had even been debating who would be designated to tell his children the news.

But an hour later, around 6:20 p.m., a driver called the police to say he had spotted O.J. on an Orange County freeway, in a white Bronco being driven by a black man. Twenty-five minutes later, a police cruiser spotted the vehicle driving north on Interstate 405. Cowlings, at the wheel, shouted for the police to back off. O.J. was in the backseat, holding a gun to his head. Before long, more than twenty police cars were following the Bronco, in a low-speed chase that was soon picked up by TV news helicopters and beamed live into millions of households.

After the press conference, Bob had immediately headed to the Rockingham estate, where O.J.'s kids Jason and Arnelle were staying. To talk his way in, he lied to the police officer at the gate and claimed to be O.J.'s doctor. When he saw the kids, he immediately told them of his fear that their father had killed himself, because he loved his children more than anything and wanted to spare them a lengthy and costly trial that would deplete their financial futures.

As tears poured down Arnelle's face, somebody turned on the TV, showing the Bronco chase under way. Bob dialed the cell number he knew by heart. O.J. answered and filled him in. He had been headed to Nicole's grave, where he was going to kill himself, but there was a police cruiser blocking the entrance to the cemetery, he explained. "I've got this gun to my head," he told his old friend. "I just want to be with Nicole. How did I get into this, Bobby?"

When the police realized whom Bob was talking to, they demanded to speak to the famous fugitive. Bob refused. A SWAT team was dispatched to the house. O.J. informed Bob that he wanted to come home and kill himself there. But Bob counseled against this, informing him of the massive police presence.

The police tried to snatch the phone from Bob's hand, but he refused to let go. "I am talking to O.J. on the phone!" he screamed. "I am trying to bring him in."

Finally, the Bronco approached the gates just before 8:00 p.m., with O.J. still holding a gun to his head. Surrounded by a virtual army of police, with negotiators trying to talk him out of the vehicle, he and Cowlings remained in the driveway for more than an hour as surrender negotiations proceeded. "I'm not coming out unless I have three things," he told the police negotiator Peter Weireter. First, he demanded to speak to his mother. He wanted to talk privately with Bob Kardashian. And he insisted that the arrest happen inside the house, away from the cameras.

The negotiator accepted all three conditions, provided that O.J. agree to leave his gun inside the Bronco. All the while, his son Jason stood in the driveway pleading for his father to come out. When O.J. finally staggered out of the vehicle, he collapsed into Bob's arms, nearly knocking the smaller man to the ground.

"Juice, thank God you're alive," Bob said. "It's going to be okay." O.J. told his friend that he just couldn't bring himself to end it. Then he turned to the assembled police and apologized for putting them through the long drama. As agreed, O.J. was permitted to talk on the phone to his seventy-three-year-old mother, Eunice, who was in a San Francisco hospital. Then he was handcuffed and brought to headquarters to be booked. One drama had ended; the other had just begun.

It would be a full four months before the trial got under way, but even before O.J. set foot in the courtroom for the first time, it was clear that the case had the potential to shatter the tenuous peace between Kris and Bob that had taken hold over the previous two years.

"We ended up being really, really good friends," Kris told E!. It even became a family tradition for Bob to come over for dinner with Kris, Bruce, and the kids, a near miracle considering the animosity that had existed only a couple of years earlier. The real challenge, however, became ensuring that the case didn't tear apart the family.

"Right before the trial started," Kris later recalled, "Robert sat us down and wrote us a handwritten letter and said, 'I know you don't agree but this is what I have to do for my friend.' It was very stressful

on Robert. He believed in what he was doing and he was asking us
for his support."

But Kris had already privately made it clear to her ex-husband
that he would not have her support. Things came to a head when
a report surfaced that Kris and Nicole's close friend Faye Resnick
had signed a book contract, agreeing to reveal that she and Nicole
had been lovers. Khloé Kardashian happened to be good friends with
Resnick's twelve-year-old daughter. Faye would later cite this friendship after O.J.'s defense attorney suggested that Nicole might have
accidentally been killed by drug dealers stalking Resnick.

"If they're so worried about Colombian drug dealers," she asked,
"do you think one member of the defense team would let his daughter stay at my house?"

When O.J. heard the news of the supposed affair, he reportedly
phoned Kris from jail twice in one day to ask if she knew about the
alleged encounters.

When Bob heard about these calls, he showed up at Kris's house,
saying they needed to talk privately. Outside, she later revealed, Bob
asked her if the rumors about Resnick were true. Kris denied any
knowledge of her friends' purported lesbianism and then warned Bob
not to get "too deep" into this case. He hadn't been close to O.J. in the
past three years since the divorce and didn't know "what O.J. does."
Bob protested that his friend was innocent.

Police investigators had found O.J.'s blood outside of Nicole's
town house and traces of Nicole's blood inside the Bronco. When Kris
asked Bob about the blood evidence at the crime scene, he assured
her it was "old blood. He could have been there weeks ago." When
Kris wanted to know why he would have been bleeding at Nicole's
house, he speculated that perhaps O.J. cut himself. What about the
Bronco? she demanded. He explained that Nicole had been in the
Bronco many times.

But Kris later told prosecutors of at least one significant admission on Bob's part. "We're going to have a problem when Goldman's blood is found inside the Bronco," he reportedly told her, according to *Los Angeles* magazine.

When the trial finally got under way in January, the couple's four children were deeply conflicted, especially the ones who were old enough to understand what had happened. At the time of the murders, Kim was thirteen and Kourtney had just turned fifteen.

"Kourtney and I would go to the trial with our dad and we'd sit on one side and I remember looking over and my mom was on the other side sitting next to Nicole's parents and there was so much tension," Kim recalled. "If we're siding with this one, then my mom and Bruce were upset and if we sit here then my dad is upset."

Khloé was not quite ten, but she too remembers being deeply conflicted. "O.J. was always my 'Uncle O.J.' and Nicole was always 'Aunt Nicole,'" she stated. "You don't really know what to believe or how to perceive it."

Later, in their book *Kardashian Konfidential*, the older girls admitted that they "kind of believed O.J. at the time." Kim would tell *Rolling Stone*, "I definitely took my dad's side. We just always thought my dad was the smartest person in the world, and he really believed in his friend." The girls also revealed that it was a very scary period, with bomb threats and people camped outside the house, shouting. At one point, a police officer even threatened to "hurt" Bob's kids. Another time they remember being thrown out of a restaurant because the establishment didn't want to serve the lawyer who was defending O.J.

Exactly one week after the murders, Bob had got together with his kids for the first time since the tragedy. It was Father's Day, and they made plans to go for dinner at their favorite Chinese restaurant, Chin Chin, in Brentwood.

The kids wanted to know how Uncle O.J. was and were eager to write him a letter, which Bob promised to deliver. "Mommy says he's guilty," Khloé blurted out. "Mommy and Bruce both say it."

Livid, Bob proceeded to give his kids a civics lesson, explaining that in America a person is innocent until proven guilty. He urged them to wait until the trial was over to make up their minds. The subsequent nine-month trial would end up costing Bob more than just family harmony. To many of his friends and associates, he seemed obsessed with the case and with clearing his old friend.

Around the time of the murders, Kris and Bruce had been starring in an infomercial for a thigh-exercising device. A Kardashian associate told Jeffrey Toobin of *The New Yorker* that he believed Bob was devoting so much time to the case to show up his ex-wife and her new husband. "It bothered him that she was on TV all the time with the Thighmaster," said the source. "This case was his way to step over them. This was better than infomercials."

At one point in the trial, he even placed a full-page ad in a music trade magazine with the caption JUSTICE FOR JUICE. The ad was one of the reasons his Movie Tunes executive vice president, Michael Ameen—whose name was used in the ad—resigned from the company, explaining that Kardashian had lost perspective and allowed the case to "overwhelm" him.

Once a week throughout the trial, Bob would visit O.J. in jail, and the experience was said to be taking its toll.

"I've never been to a jail before. It's extremely depressing," he told the *Los Angeles Times*. "It makes me sick every time I go down there. We can't have any physical contact. I want to hug him, I want to show him that I care. It's very difficult. We're going 20 hours a day on this. But he's going through worse hell than I am. I can't complain. I sleep in a real bed at night. Look where he's sleeping . . . he's in a cage."

For her part, Kris was anxious to testify about what she knew of the conflicts between Nicole and O.J. She had met more than once with Marcia Clark and other prosecutors, who had taken the details as well as the accounts of other friends who had witnessed Nicole being treated badly by her ex. In the end, however, Kris was never called to testify. Clark had decided that the jury wouldn't be "receptive" to the domestic-violence angle. Kris was shocked by the decision. "Why aren't I and Nicole's other friends going to testify?" she recalls asking the lead prosecutor. "We have such valuable information."

It was just one more staggering miscalculation on the part of the badly outgunned prosecution team, which had botched its case from start to finish. Meanwhile, Kris recalls confronting Bob numerous times during the trial and trying to drill sense into him about his unwavering belief in his client's innocence. "Are you crazy?" she asked him more than once. He hadn't been spending time socially with O.J. and Nicole together toward the end. He hadn't witnessed what she had seen of their volatile relationship.

Kris remembers in vivid detail one of the pivotal moments in the trial: when prosecutor Christopher Darden had O.J. try on the bloody glove. Although she and Bruce often attended the trial in person, she was at home watching it on TV that day. She remembers screaming at the TV at the idiocy of the decision. Anybody who knows leather knows that if it gets wet it shrinks, she thought. The gloves had been soaked in blood. Of course they wouldn't fit. As she saw the gloves on the screen, she claims she flashed back to the day that she was shopping at Bloomingdales with Nicole and her friend bought those gloves for O.J. as "a treat." Again, it makes for a good anecdote, but one can't help but wonder why Kris didn't volunteer to testify to that little nugget at the trial.

On October 3, Kris received a call informing her that the jury had reached a verdict after a remarkably short four-hour deliberation. After months of trying, she and Bruce had finally conceived a child, and she was eight months' pregnant. Both Marcia Clark and Chris Darden counseled her against being in the courtroom during the reading of the verdict because they feared chaos would erupt and the baby might be at risk. Instead, Clark suggested she watch the proceedings in her office, along with Nicole's sisters.

The short deliberations, Kris believed, boded well for the prosecution. How could any jury seeing the evidence not come to the obvious
and inescapable conclusion that O.J. had committed the murders?

At 10:00 a.m., Judge Lance Ito brought in the jurors and asked
O.J. to stand. The clerk proceeded to read the verdict:

> *In the matter of the People of the State of California v. Oren-*
> *thal James Simpson, case number BA097211. We, the jury . . .*
> *find the defendant, Orenthal James Simpson, not guilty of the*
> *crime of murder in violation of Penal Code Section 187A, a fel-*
> *ony, upon Nicole Brown Simpson, a human being . . .*
>
> *In the matter of the People of the State of California v. Orenthal*
> *James Simpson. We, the jury . . . find the defendant, Orenthal*
> *James Simpson, not guilty of the crime of murder, in violation of*
> *Penal Code Section 187A, a felony, upon Ronald Lyle Goldman,*
> *a human being . . .*

Kris recalls that upon hearing these words, the whole courtroom
was in shock. But none more so than herself. She watched a grin break
out on O.J.'s face, followed by his leaning toward her ex-husband for
a hug, while sobbing emanated from Nicole's side of the courtroom.

The whole time, she remembered the words that Nicole had
said to her more than once: "He's going to kill me and he's going to
get away with it." Following the dramatic verdict, and the pandemo-
nium that ensued, the defense headed back to O.J.'s Rockingham
estate for a celebration that lasted most of the day. Riding to Rockingham with Bob in a white van, O.J. took his first car trip since the
Bronco chase.

As they headed down the freeway, thousands of people cheered
and held victory signs from overpasses as they passed. "It was very
exciting," Bob told Barbara Walters later. Exhausted by the nine-
month trial and the climactic verdict, Bob slipped out of the victory

party early. But rather than head home, he made a detour. Kris recalls him arriving at her house in the early evening, saying that he needed to talk to her.

He knew she was upset at the acquittal but he felt it important to "put this behind us"—at least for the sake of the kids. He didn't want the polarizing case and his role in winning an acquittal to get in the way of their friendship, because he feared it might destroy the family. Kris agreed. The encounter ended with both crying.

Bruce had been equally furious at the verdict, even though he had been closer to O.J. than to Nicole before the killings. He later shared his frustration with the *Los Angeles Times*.

"To see this guy walk away, you know? As soon as the verdict came down, the first thing my wife said to me was, 'Nicole was right. Because the bonehead told her he's going to kill her someday and get away with it, because he's O.J. Simpson. And he did.' She was absolutely right. The guy got away with it. He'll pay for it some day, some way."

But Kris was determined to move on. "We weren't going to let O.J. Simpson eat away at us anymore," she later wrote. Bob had successfully mended fences with his ex-wife, and he left that night confident that his family would recover from the polarizing trial. But Robert Kardashian knew as well as anybody that most of white America, despite the acquittal, was unwavering in the belief that O.J. had gotten away with murder. It wasn't just the fact that the jurors who sat in judgment were widely considered to be twelve people too stupid to get out of jury duty. It was also the fact that the jurors who rendered the verdict hadn't seen a lot of the evidence that the tens of millions of Americans following the case had seen—evidence that led to only one inescapable conclusion. And now, returning to the real world and having to face business associates, colleagues, and friends, Bob would have to explain the central role he had played in helping a vicious wife killer get away with the heinous crime.

Rather than make excuses or try to paint his participation as an act of loyalty to an old friend, he had decided to stick to the same story he had been peddling for the past year. In an op-ed piece published in the *Los Angeles Times* on the day following the verdict, he explained: "O.J. Simpson never lied to me. He has told me that he did not commit these horrible crimes and I have no reason not to believe him. It was from that perspective that I came to stand by his side during his trial." He saw the problem, not in how he had helped a killer escape but in the reaction he faced. "Who wants their life and everything they have done for the past 25 years dragged in front of the American public? Within a week, the assault began . . . The recent trend of the press to intrude into the private lives of innocent individuals in the name of 'getting the story' demonstrates the dwindling interest in the equally valid constitutional right to privacy. So great is society's demand for information that we can no longer say that all the news gathered is worthy of airing. Much of it is not. In such an environment, it's not hard to see why old family values like trust and friendship are increasingly rare. The price is too high in a society that tears apart anyone who dares to take a public stand in the midst of controversy."

Two years after the verdict, Kardashian would give a candid interview to Barbara Walters for a *20/20* special on the eve of the civil trial, in which he indicated for the first time that he had "doubts" about his friend's innocence.

"The blood evidence is the biggest thorn in my side," he told her. "That causes me the greatest problems. So I struggle with the blood evidence." However, he would still vote "not guilty" in the civil trial, he assured her.

In the same interview, he revealed that Bob Shapiro had believed O.J. to be guilty. "I overheard Mr. Shapiro at one point in the courtroom—during a break, say to Mr. Simpson, 'We should plea bargain; you would get twelve years' or whatever it was; and Robert Kardashian would get so much time as an accessory . . . my jaw dropped . . . I was astounded! And I was shaking! I was so mad, so upset . . . He knew that I knew nothing about any of this!"

Following Bob's death in 2003, Kim Goldman revealed that she had been told about a mystery bag that Kardashian wished for her to have, but that she never ended up getting. "We were notified by either a lawyer or someone from the Kardashian family that they had come across this bag among Robert Kardashian's things," she recalled. "Robert wanted the bag to be given to me after his death. This wasn't the Louis Vuitton garment bag that Robert took from the house the day after the murders."

The O. J. Simpson trial is now just a remnant of history, and Robert Kardashian's true role in the century's greatest miscarriage of justice will likely never be resolved. The notoriety of his name, however, would eventually give rise to the ubiquitous family that would eventually, in some circles, become nearly as controversial as the verdict.

CHAPTER SIX

Exactly one month after O.J. was found not guilty, Kris gave birth to a baby girl. Her first three girls had *K* names, and Bruce had agreed to continue the tradition. Eventually, with the help of her godmother, Kathie Lee Gifford, and after tossing out many options, they settled on Kendall. Kris already knew what her middle name would be. It seemed like a fitting tribute. Kendall Nicole Jenner was born on November 3, 1995.

With the trial finally over, Kris could return to devoting herself full-time to Bruce's career. It was once again thriving. Corporate endorsements and speaking engagements were paying handsomely. The couple were now regularly starring together in infomercials for a whole series of fitness equipment including the SuperStep, Power-Trainer, and other health products.

Bruce had finally returned to the pinnacle he had once occupied but had long since abandoned through a series of bad decisions and poor management. He fully credited Kris's business acumen for the turnaround.

"The reason today I am working as hard as I am is Kris," he told the *Los Angeles Times*. "I got rid of all agents, all managers, all the outsiders who prey on you. She knows how to keep all the percentages everyone else is always taking from you, until there's nothing left for ol' Bruce. She remade me from head to toe."

As part of the concerted effort to rebrand Jenner and revive his career, both Kris and Bruce frequently gave interviews about their idyllic relationship. When the *Los Angeles Times* asked Bruce about his previous marriages, he was dismissive.

"I've had one marriage, and that was six years ago," he responded. "The other ones? Contracts. That's all they were. Contracts. Not good experiences. I've had one marriage and I'm married to her right now."

But while they publicly professed that they had each finally found their soul mates, it seemed that Kris's self-professed weaknesses may have still been playing a role in her life. Her former lover Todd Waterman would claim that he and Kris were still carrying on even after she took up with Bruce.

A friend confirmed the affair to *In Touch Weekly*. "He was always around, and Bruce was completely in the dark. He was the Camilla in the Charles-Diana relationship."

Whether or not their marriage was the perfect match that the couple portrayed publicly in those days, there is no question that it was a financial success. They could finally afford to move out of the house they had been leasing since the divorce and get a place of their own. They settled on a beautiful gated community in the San Fernando Valley about fifteen miles from downtown LA called Hidden Hills, ranked as the twenty-seventh-wealthiest community in the United States and home to numerous celebrities, including Melissa Etheridge and Ozzy Osbourne. Kris's friend Lisa Miles had moved there from Beverly Hills and had gushed about it. When Kris visited for the first time and saw its wide-open spaces and lush gardens, she was sold.

"It was heaven," she recalled. In June 2006, they finally settled on a massive four-thousand-square-foot property that Kris termed "the monstrosity" because of its sheer size. Its $2.8 million selling price illustrated just how far Bruce's career had progressed since marrying Kris. Only a few short years earlier, he could barely afford his rented one-bedroom house. Now the couple were living in the lap of luxury. Soon the family was ensconced in their new crib.

At first, the Kardashian kids would spend alternating weekends with Bob but remained at Hidden Hills during the week, commuting to the various private schools that Bob had agreed to pay for as part of the divorce settlement. The girls attended the exclusive Catholic all-girls high school Marymount, even though they were still practicing Protestants. The school provided a solid education, but it also plunged the kids into a world of immense privilege, where their classmates hailed from the upper echelons of Southern California society, the children of celebrities and studio executives.

Inevitably, attending school with the rich and famous meant that it was important to stay on top of the latest trends and accumulate the best of everything. After they rose to reality-TV fame, the children's nanny, Pam Behan, reflected that she found the title of their famous show ironic, because from what she saw, the family was always try-ing to "keep up with the Joneses." Behan credited their mother with encouraging the obsession with material possessions that would one day be on full display for the world to see.

"I believe she was grooming her children for their current celeb-rity status their entire lives. They only wore the cutest clothes from the nicest stores, and were always perfectly well dressed. Even at a young age, they were fashion plates, and their image was being care-fully crafted. I do believe that the success they enjoy now is what she always hoped for and wanted for them and for herself."

Behan claims that the kids in her charge were sweet but unde-niably spoiled. In *Kardashian Konfidential*, the girls admit that they were indeed spoiled but stress that they weren't "spoiled brats." They explain that although most of the girls in their school had credit cards,

Bob wouldn't let them have their own. He would allow them to use his for basics, but not for luxuries such as Gucci bags. Each of the girls did get a car in high school, but in exchange for the automobile, Bob forced each child to sign a contract. They even include a photocopy of Kim's contract to illustrate the point. Among its provisions:

- Part of Kimberly's duties and responsibilities are to drive her sister, Khloé, and her brother, Robert, to their respective weekly activities. In addition, Kimberly shall run various errands for her father and help out whenever necessary. In the event Kimberly refuses or fails to drive her brother and sister to their respective activities or Kimberly refuses or fails to assist her wonderful father in any way, Kimberly's automobile shall be taken away for the upcoming weekend.

- Kimberly agrees that in the very unlikely event that she takes drugs of any kind, smokes cigarettes or marijuana and or drinks alcohol excessively, then her car will be taken away for a period of six (6) months. This provision is irrevocable and cannot be modified by either parent. It is absolute.

Contracts like this were one of the effects of having a lawyer for a father, and Bob frequently used similar documents to provide carrots and sticks to hold his kids accountable, at least when they were staying with him. Kim claims that shortly after she got her first car, a BMW, she rear-ended another car when she bent down to pick something up off the floor in bumper-to-bumper traffic. As a result, Bob made her pay for the repairs herself, which forced her to take her first job, at a clothing store in Encino.

The girls claim that as a result of their father's strict rules and determination to keep his children grounded, they were much less materialistic than their privileged friends. But just because they weren't handed everything on a silver platter doesn't mean they didn't want the same things that their friends took for granted. Bob's edict may indeed have had unintended consequences. In the spring of 1999, Bob had started to date a woman named Jan Ashley, whose late husband was the actor and producer John Ashley, who had appeared in a number of TV series, including a semiregular role on *The Beverly Hillbillies* as one of Ellie May Clampett's suitors. Bob was renting a house across the street from Jan when their relationship began. Seven months later, on Thanksgiving Day, they were married.

The honeymoon took place in Vail, Colorado, and Bob was anxious for his kids to bond with his new wife, so they came along for a ski vacation. Thirty days later, Jan mysteriously asked for an annulment and the marriage was over almost as soon as it had begun. Neither Bob nor Jan ever explained what went wrong, until in 2014 Ashley blamed the Kardashian kids for their marital troubles.

"Did the kids have anything to do with it? Of course they did!" she revealed. "All I know is he was upset all the time. Not with me, [but] with his kids and his ex-wife. They were after him for money, money, money. I don't think he could handle them. Money was an issue with them, as the Kardashians weren't well off at the time, although they like to portray themselves as rich. From their daddy, they wanted everything right then. He didn't have any money. He always pretended he had money. I'm the one who didn't care about money."

And although by this time Bob and Kris had apparently put their past troubles behind them and become friends, Ashley revealed that the pain of Kris's adultery still lingered. "He talked about [her cheating] day in and day out," Ashley said. "He talked about how she was guilty of everything. I asked him, 'How is she guilty of everything?' He said, 'She's guilty because she went out with all these guys and I didn't know about it.' "

Ashley reserves her harshest criticisms for Kourtney and Khloé, but there were two kids whom she seems to have absolved from blame. She described both Kim and Rob as "sweet."

Indeed, while her sisters constantly lamented the fact that they couldn't afford to buy the same expensive fashions and accessories as their friends, Kim became extremely resourceful and creative about bringing in extra income. "I'm a shopaholic," she later confessed. In order to finance her expensive shopping habits, she started her own business, using eBay to buy and sell used items, including some of the expensive clothing that her parents had bought for her.

"I discovered Ebay and I loved shopping," she later recalled. "I had to be on a budget. I didn't have credit cards. How do I figure out how to make this a business? I remember I bought these Manolo Blahnik shoes that were $700. [Bob] let me buy five pairs. I had to pay him back with interest. I sold every pair on Ebay for $2500. I became so obsessed with seeing that return, I would sell off the things I wouldn't be wearing."

The eye-popping profit, she explained, stemmed from her early knack for spotting trends. The Manolos had been featured in one of Jennifer Lopez's first videos, and women were clamoring for them. When she snapped up the last five pairs, she knew she could take advantage of the scarcity. From there, Kim conceived the idea of contacting the privileged friends she had grown up with in Beverly Hills and offering to clean out their closets, culling the clothes that they no longer wore, putting them up for sale on eBay, and sharing the profits. Her eBay account name was "kimsaprincess."

The idea for the business came to her when she was visiting the home of her godfather, boxer Sugar Ray Leonard, and his wife, Bernadette, she told *Player* magazine in 2006. "Bernadette's closet was massive and had so much stuff in it. I said to her, 'You really need to clean out your closet.' Well, we spent the whole night doing that." The unwanted items soon landed on eBay, and Bernadette was so impressed that she began recommending Kim to friends such as Rob

Lowe and Kenny G. She had soon earned the nickname Queen of the Closet Scene.

Meanwhile, Kim's high school classmates had another description for the future reality-TV star. In her yearbook, she was described as "Most Likely to Meet Her Husband at the Million Man March" (the 1995 gathering called by Louis Farrakhan to promote black pride). The reference alluded to Kim's known penchant, even then, for dating African Americans. When she was fourteen, in fact, Kim's first serious boyfriend was Tito Jo Jackson, son of Michael's brother Tito. Both Kim and Kourtney had attended preschool with a number of Michael's nephews. Kim's fourteenth birthday party was even held at Michael's Neverland Ranch, an occasion that she would remember as magical.

"That was the most magical place on earth," she told *People*. "When you drove up, there were baby elephants and chimpanzees in overalls, and there was all the rides. It was everything you can possibly imagine. The memories I have from that place will last for the rest of my life." She also still has pleasant memories of the Jacksons. "They were the nicest family I've ever met. Michael definitely was never this disreputable person."

T.J.—who Kim later revealed took her virginity—was the first in a long line of black boyfriends. Years later, she recalled that when she started going out with him, her dad "explained to me that he's had a lot of interracial friends, and it might not be the easiest relationship. He said I should prepare myself for people to say things to me. When I was growing up, when I was in high school, I'd get magazines and see interracial couples and think, 'They are so cute.' I've always been attracted to a certain kind of look."

Kris adored T.J. and claimed that she was heartbroken when the couple eventually broke up. While the other kids were still spending most of their time with Kris and Bruce as per the custody agreement, Kourtney, the oldest, had asked to live with her father. Although there were reports that she and Kris were constantly at each other's throats, she later explained that life with eight kids at her mom's was just too chaotic. Kim would also later choose to move in with Bob during her senior year of high school. "At my dad's," Kourtney recalled, "it was calm and he was easygoing."

In contrast, life in the Jenner household was anything but calm, especially after Kris gave birth to yet another child, Kylie Kristen Jenner, on August 10, 1997.

"Every day's a decathlon at our house," Kris told the *Los Angeles Times* in 1998. "We have 10 different activities going at once. With kids ranging from a 17-year-old teenager to a 7-month-old infant, life can be crazy. My friends ask what I'm doing and I say, 'I'm waxing one and diapering the other.'"

For the most part, Kourtney and Kim were self-described good girls, rarely getting into trouble. One notable exception occurred on an American Airlines flight to Atlanta in the summer of 1996, when the older girls were scheduled to meet up with Kris and Bruce, who was working as a commentator for the Games. On July 27, a bomb went off in Atlanta's Centennial Olympic Park, killing one person and injuring 111 others. Days later, Kris made the arrangements for the girls to join the rest of the family, but they were reportedly traumatized by TV coverage of the bombing and were convinced that they would be bomb victims if they attended. Kris would not take no for an answer and insisted the girls come anyway.

Traveling as unaccompanied minors, the girls took their seats on the plane, but before the flight could take off they became fixated on another passenger. "That guy has a bomb!" they shouted. "We want to get off the plane." Whether they were genuinely scared or whether it was simply a teenage prank has never been determined, but the plane was returned to the gate and the girls escorted off. They were suspended from flying for just one day. Only their stepfather's celebrity status likely prevented a far worse consequence for an act that is

considered a serious offense. Kris appeared to allude to her own skepticism about whether her daughters were genuinely frightened when
she wrote, "In hindsight I guess it should have been foreshadowing to
me about the kind of shenanigans Kourtney and Kimberly would get
into later."

Shortly after Kim turned nineteen in 1999, she announced to her
family that she wanted to move out into her own apartment. Kourtney had been the first sibling to break off from the tight-knit family
when she moved to Dallas to attend Southern Methodist University
following her graduation from Marymount. After her older sister left
for college, Kim claims she was devastated. The two had done everything together. Now she felt she was on her own. "I was nervous for
her, and we would talk every day," she later recalled. "It was a good
experience for her and I'm glad she went but it was just weird for
her to be away. She made me move in full time with my Dad so he
wouldn't be alone. When Kourtney and I were apart for that time, it
was probably my first push towards independence."

Now after living with her father for a year, Kim wanted to exert
her independence even more, or so she professed to Kris. She had
been dating a twenty-nine-year-old record producer named Damon
Thomas, whom she had met while freelancing as a wardrobe stylist
on a music-video shoot for one of Thomas's acts. When Kim reported
that she was planning to move to Northridge—even farther north
of central LA than Hidden Hills—Kris's suspicions were piqued. It
made no sense, especially given the distance to the high-end clothing
store where Kim was working in Encino. When she suddenly sported
a new car and flashy new clothes, with no explanation of where they
had come from, the entire family became curious.

On a whim, Kourtney decided to type her sister's name into a
search engine. Try that today and it would yield millions of hits. But
at the time, it yielded only one—the record of Kim's marriage to
Thomas three months earlier. The couple had secretly married in Las

Vegas after Kim told her family that they were going there only for a birthday celebration for Justin Timberlake, whom Thomas had been working with at the time. The family was flabbergasted. "I wanted to kill her," Kris later confessed, "but Kim was now old enough to make her own decisions."

"He was like, 'Let's go get married,'" Kim later recalled, "and I said, 'Ok.' I'm a people pleaser and I kind of wanted to please. I didn't really think it out. I definitely planned on telling my family and my sisters that I had gotten married. I was just young and I didn't know what I was doing." Kris gave Kim twenty-four hours to tell Bob what she had done.

Kourtney said that he wasn't at all pleased with the news and gave his daughter the cold shoulder for days. "My dad kind of had a rule," Kim recalled. "If you got too serious with a boyfriend or if you moved in or if you did anything he didn't approve of, you got cut off financially."

Meanwhile, Kris had plenty to worry about on the home front with her youngest Kardashian daughter. While Kourtney and Kim were self-described "teen queens," their sister Khloé recalls that they were "not an easy act to follow." While the older girls were cruising through high school as part of the "in" crowd, Khloé was having problems navigating her own teen years. "It was not easy being a Kardashian sister at that time," she would later admit. Part of the difficulty stemmed from the fact that she looked different from her sisters and was very self-conscious about her appearance.

After the divorce and the O.J. trial, Khloé revealed, people constantly gave the younger kids food. As a result, she recalls, she and Rob grew to be "fat little kids." It didn't help that she did not resemble her older sisters to begin with. While attending the same school as Kim and Kourtney, nobody believed she was a Kardashian. "You look nothing like them," she was constantly reminded. Eventually, she became so stressed out about her appearance that she lost a massive amount of weight. It wasn't an eating disorder, she insists. Rather, she started an extreme exercise regimen that included Tae Bo and horseback riding. She went from a size 10 or 12 to a size 0, she recalls. She describes all the symptoms of a classic eating disorder, though she claims she was determined not to let herself succumb to such a fate, especially after she saw an anorexic teenage girl at her grandparents' Palm Springs housing complex who looked "unattractive and sad, sickly even." Khloé's parents, she recalls, didn't think there was anything amiss about her rapid weight loss. They simply attributed her skeletal frame to the effects of puberty. But although the weight loss didn't set off warning bells, they soon grew alarmed at other aspects of their youngest daughter's behavior.

Although her sisters were known as the "good girls," Khloé was by her own admission anything but. Her mother had taught her to drive when she was thirteen years old so that she could take her baby siblings to the hospital in case of an emergency. And although she never had to use her driving skills for that purpose, she frequently snuck out at night to visit the boyfriend that had set her on the wayward path, an older man who had taken her virginity when she was fourteen—an act that would have been prosecuted as statutory rape if her parents had known his true age.

Once she stole her mother's car and it caught on fire. "I remember my friends and I saw this car and we were like, 'Whoah, that person is screwed! And then I was like, 'Shit that's my car,'" she later told *People*.

Her grades had started to slip, and she was acting up at home. She also started shoplifting and club hopping, though Khloé later insisted that alcohol and drugs were not among her teenage vices. It was in fact Paris Hilton, she recalls, who helped her slip into her first LA club, by putting a red wig on her, having her hold an unlit cigarette, and telling her to claim she was a *Playboy* centerfold.

She later revealed that she had spent a considerable portion of her teenage years hanging out at the house of a celebrity whose name she refused to mention.

They were involved in stuff that "I shouldn't have been around," she recalled, describing something "really horrible" that happened to her, during which she could have been seriously hurt and barely got out alive. A week after the incident, she remembers getting a call from a friend of the "sicko freak" who purportedly wanted to apologize for his actions.

On her way to meet him, she was involved in a serious car accident that sent her head first through the windshield of her Mercedes. Emergency crews had to saw through the car to extract her. Taken to the hospital with a concussion and lacerations, she was released soon afterward but forced to stay in bed recovering for a number of weeks. Khloé claims that she still suffers memory loss as the result of the accident.

When she finally called it quits with the older boyfriend and resolved to set her life back on course, she knew it wasn't going to happen by returning to the high school where she had been made miserable for years in the shadow of her popular older sisters. "She absolutely hated school," recalled her nanny, Pam Behan. "Every single morning, she had a new and different excuse for why she couldn't make it to class. 'Pam, I have a headache. I can't go to school,' she told me one morning. 'Okay, I'll get you some Tylenol and a glass of water,' I said. 'Please get dressed, Khloé, and come and eat breakfast.' The next day it was something different. 'I have a horrible stomachache,' she moaned, as if she were about to die. 'I'm so sick, I can't make it to school.' "

Finally her parents thought it best that Khloé drop out of Marymount—where she had fallen severely behind academically—and continue her high school studies in a homeschooling program run through Alexandria Academy. Kris, however, wasn't the type of mom to sit down at the dining-room table and teach her daughter math.

Nor did she have the time, what with her own hectic schedule. The program allowed students to work at their own pace instead of in a structured school environment. To help Khloé catch up, Robert hired tutors to work with her in an intensive course of study that enabled her to complete the equivalent of three years of high school in one year. She even graduated with honors, with a 3.8 GPA.

Although the kids at various times clashed with Kris to the point of enmity, they adored their father and rarely fought with him, despite his strict adherence to rules and strong moral code. So when he informed them in the summer of 2003 that he had been diagnosed with esophageal cancer, the news was devastating. At the time, Kris was dealing with her own stepfather's cancer diagnosis. She had put aside most of her business ventures to be with her mother in La Jolla and help her run the store while Mary Jo cared for Harry.

When Bob told her that he too had been diagnosed with cancer, the first thing she did was sit down and write him a long letter informing him of her regret at having hurt him all those years before. "I have so many wonderful memories," she wrote, "and I am grateful to you for being such an incredible man. . . . I very foolishly threw all that away and for that I will always be sorry. I was a very stupid and foolish girl. . . . I hope you will one day understand it really had NOTHING to do with you but obviously something went terribly wrong."

For the kids, the news was even more emotional, though Bob had hidden the severity of his diagnosis from them: The cancer was already at stage 4 and the chances of recovery virtually nil. "I think my dad was in denial or just trying to hide it from us," Kim would later recall. To break the news, he summoned the girls to his house for a family meeting, though he failed to tell them that the diagnosis was terminal. Rob was living with him at the time and had already heard the news.

About two weeks after his diagnosis, and before the worst of his symptoms started to manifest, Bob had married a real-estate agent he had been dating named Ellen Pierson. The timing may have appeared odd but, according to Ellen, the couple had been dating for five years and he had proposed all the way back in 2001. "We planned a wedding," she told *In Touch*. "We didn't just run out and get married. In fact I met with the girls just the week before to go over all our plans. We had a beautiful wedding with the girls and all his family at our home."

Bob went downhill fast. Only eight weeks after he was diagnosed, he passed away. Just before he died, Kourtney, Khloé, and Kim were called to Bob's house to say their final good-byes. They remembered that he asked if they could fetch the toy monkey, Jocko, that he had kept since his childhood, and which was in his bedroom closet.

His passing on September 30, 2003, at the age of fifty-nine hit the whole family hard. But by far the most devastated was nineteen-year-old Khloé, who recalled crying hysterically whenever anybody mentioned her father. "I disappeared from my family," she said. "I didn't understand why God would let it happen."

She remembers months of night terrors, an ulcer, and severe stress that caused all her hair to fall out. It would be a full two years before it grew back, during which she wore a wig to cover her matted scalp. "I was kind of in denial," she later told E!. "I had said my good-byes but not really like I should have."

Worse still, she engaged in what she would later describe as self-destructive behavior. "I got crazy with alcohol," she recalls, "and became very self-destructive and aggressive too. I was always in a club and the night would end with me angry and crying and screaming. I was mean and unhappy."

When she was packing up her belongings from her old room after the funeral, she remembers asking Ellen whether she could have Jocko. When her father's widow refused the request, she confesses to running to the closet and stealing the monkey, along with a pair of her father's old boots. Kim revealed that during her last conversation with her father, he told her he knew she would be okay, but he asked her to take care of the little ones. "He was really concerned about my brother, what he would do," she said.

For a decade after Bob's death, there was no record of animosity between his kids and Ellen Kardashian. That changed in 2013, when she sold her ex-husband's handwritten journals to *In Touch*—including entries that contained some extremely unflattering comments about Kris Jenner. The worst included numerous allegations that she had abused and neglected her children—most written during the period of the couple's bitter divorce. In one particularly unflattering entry, for example, Bob describes Kris's locking herself away in her bedroom for days at a time to sleep because of all the partying she was doing. Another entry accuses her of repeatedly forgetting to pick up her kids at school because she was too busy cavorting with her lover Todd Waterman.

In various sections of the diaries, Bob predicts what would become of each of his children. He claims that Kourtney would end up resenting Kris, whereas Kim would "become her mother," drawn to successful men who reflect glamor. Khloé would "do whatever she wants, when she wants." He was the most worried about Rob, who, he fretted, was "very confused."

Upon the release of the diaries at the height of the Kardashians' reality-show fame, the girls immediately hit back at Ellen. "How can such a piece of trash even mention my father's name?" Tweeted Khloé. "You married him on his death bed while he was not even aware of his surroundings. You should be hiding in shame for all the lies you sell to tabloids."

In April 2013, the family filed a federal lawsuit against Ellen for copyright infringement—changing their story from the original claim that the diaries were forged to the charge that they are copyrighted material that belonged to the children. "The defendant," states the claim, "is engaged in a despicable and unlawful scheme to hold in secret and convert and now exploit the material."

Ellen defended her right to release the journals and vouched for their authenticity. "These are authentic handwritten journals I have shared, that my late husband Robert Kardashian so carefully wrote during 1989 and 1990 at a most trying and touching time in his life. They are my personal possession and he left them to me on his passing."

The feud exploded into full public view after members of the family took a shot at Ellen on their reality show, describing her as a "slippery snake" who was telling lies and spreading rumors about the family. The family claimed that they had hired a private investigator, who determined that Ellen had filed for bankruptcy twice. On air, they decide to pursue legal action against Ellen.

"I'm not really surprised when I hear this woman has filed bankruptcy a couple times. I mean it's obvious motivation for her to want to sell stories. We're definitely going to do something to stop it and that's that," Kim says on the show. The family is seen meeting with an attorney to plan how to deal with Ellen's "lies."

When Khloé says that Ellen "married my father on his deathbed," Kris responds, "She propped [Robert] up on a pillow, basically in his own bed and married him in his pajamas." Kourtney corrects her: "Mom, he wasn't on the bed, he was on the couch," to which Kris says, "Well, propped him up on the couch and married him."

"These statements are false and imply that Robert was an invalid and physically and mentally incapacitated at the time of his marriage," Ellen's court filing reads. "The truth is the couple was married at their home in Encino on a hot summer day, July 27, 2003, where Robert wore a 'Tommy Bahama' style shirt (not his pajamas) and Ellen wore a sundress."

Ellen charged that the episode had been crafted to contain the damage caused by the release of the diaries and the toll that they were starting to take on Kris Jenner's image.

"The Kardashians developed and deployed a 'spin' designed to neutralize the exceptionally negative opinion that Robert had of Kris

Jenner," Ellen charged in a defamation suit that she brought against the family and the two production companies that produce the show. "The Kardashians' strategy was to neutralize the unrefuted details in Robert's diaries and notes by suggesting that they were in fact fabricated by Ellen. The Kardashians' strategy was to create a fake scenario where Robert's story and words would become the narrative of this surviving widow which the Kardashians would then claim was motivated not by truth but by greed."

The suit goes on to allege that the "shameful rewriting of history" was taken at the behest of Kris and "motivated by profit." Ellen describes it as an insult to the legacy of Robert Kardashian.

In *Kardashian Konfidential*, the three daughters detail the agony of their father's final weeks and the time they spent comforting him after his cancer diagnosis. They describe Kourtney's spending many evenings watching old black-and-white movies with him, including *The Postman Always Rings Twice*, during his final days. They describe how he threw up profusely and how he wanted to eat only Cream of Wheat, which Kim frequently made for him. But in her counterclaim, Ellen provides her own version of his final days and the presence of his family.

"When he passed away his children were not there," she states.

> *My daughter was there and three friends of ours. [Bob's children] were there early in the morning. I don't know why they didn't come back. They knew that it would be soon, and they knew it would be that evening. I think it was very difficult for them as it was for everyone. They came at different times. From time to time they would come together. . . . The girls would stop in when they wanted to. I really think that it was very important for him to have his family. He was very family oriented. That was his life, with his children. So yes, I know that he was very sad about that. . . . Robert would have been very sad had he known*

that his children were not there by his bedside. At the moment Robert took his last breath, none of his children could be bothered to be by his side, opting instead to attend a party at Kourtney's home.

In her deposition for the case, however, Kim had her own version.

She changed the locks on the doors when my dad was sick and told us to not come visit our dad, not come see him. We let that go for a few days then finally we're like, "That's our dad, he is dying, we will come over there." And we called him and we said, "Dad, open the door. We know she's gone." She was at, like, a salon appointment. We came back to the house and we got in there and we took a key. And we had to, like, force our way in the house. So decisions to keep family out, even his friends all came with us and we're like we're all going to go there and barge in and make this woman let us see our father.

Kim also described the marriage ceremony itself, claiming that her father was barely coherent that day and was so ill that he couldn't stand. "Based on my observations and interactions with my father," she stated, "I believe that he was suffering from extreme mental and physical fatigue and that he was not fully aware of his surroundings that day [the wedding]. Based on my knowledge of my father over my lifetime, it was apparent to me that his mental state was compromised and I believed it was due to his illness and medications. My father had to be sat on his couch until the ceremony, which took place at the couch. For the Wedding Ceremony, my father had to be propped up, to a standing position in front of the couch, for the few minutes of the ceremony."

Ellen takes issue with that charge as well. "At no time during the one-and-a-half year engagement, planning of the wedding or marriage did the Kardashian children object to their father's decision to marry Ellen, even with the knowledge that Robert's medical diagnosis was fatal," her counterclaim stated.

In another episode of their reality show, Kim is seen telling Kourtney and Khloé, "Dad's ex says that Mom used to beat me and hit me and kick me and, like, she claims Dad told her." But Ellen was quick to respond: "This statement is false because Ellen did not ever make these claims. These claims were published from a diary and letters written by Robert Kardashian and the Kardashians purposely and falsely attributed the statements to Ellen."

In April 2014, the family and Ellen reached an out-of-court settlement in the case. Four months later, the Los Angeles Superior Court dismissed the majority of Ellen's defamation claims against the Kardashians and the two production houses also named in the suit. The court awarded $84,000 to the defendants as compensation for attorneys' fees and other legal expenses.

The legal drama over the diaries, however, wasn't the only time Ellen had clashed with the family. In 2012, Ellen revealed that Kourtney had attempted to challenge the provisions in Robert's will that left most of his possessions to his widow.

"According to the calls I received from the attorney," she told a reporter, "Kourtney felt like she wanted to have her father's handwriting analyzed to make sure that he actually had written those things down that he left me. And she did. Kourtney actually had his handwriting analyzed. But every time she called the attorney about something, he would call me to let me know. It was never-ending. There were many things, many things about the will."

At the center of their 2003 dispute, Ellen said, was a Mercedes-Benz vehicle.

"The biggest thing she contested was the car," she recalled. "I finally put an end to the problem after six months with the Mercedes and I sold it. I bought myself another car so that I wouldn't have to hear her call and scream and yell at me every single day about that, about wanting her father's car. It was never-ending."

Kourtney had also demanded an item that Robert kept at his Palm Springs vacation home. "Kourtney wanted the desk that was in the desert that was her father's," Ellen said.

> *There was always a reason why she wanted something, and that was because she said she put her initials in it when she was a little girl. I felt badly, and I had the movers come ship it to her. There were some pieces that her father had brought out of art work she wanted and had reasons why she wanted them. I packaged up as much as I could, and I sent it back. But every time I gave her something, she wanted something else. She also accused me of taking something that I had no clue of and had never seen. When I would give her something, she would call me back the next day and want something more. Then I would get lists in the mail. I would get a call from the attorney saying she's back here (at the house). She contested everything that was given to me personally.*

It is likely futile to attempt to figure out the truth behind the she-said/she-said claims of the Kardashian family feud. We'll likely never know what really went down during Robert's final weeks. But the rare peek at the human drama behind the legal wrangling illustrates two things. The face the Kardashian clan shows the public is rarely what it seems. Anyone who crosses the family and its powerful matriarch quickly discovers that they have a powerful vehicle for damage control at their disposal, and they aren't afraid to use it.

These would be recurring themes in the saga of the Kardashians.

*   *   *

During the final months of her stepfather's life, Kris virtually ran every facet of her mother's La Jolla children's boutique, Shannon & Co., while Mary Jo tended to her dying husband. The experience was so exhilarating, Kris later recalled, that she decided to start a children's clothing store of her own.

After two years at Southern Methodist University, Kourtney had switched to the University of Arizona, where she studied fashion. Kim was already married and doing her own thing, while Khloé was still a basket case, recovering from her father's death. So Kris asked her oldest daughter if she would like to partner in a store similar to the one in La Jolla, where Kourtney often helped out on weekends.

Soon Kris was scouting locations and Kourtney was putting her fashion expertise to good use, selecting the merchandise lines that they would introduce in a fashionable little Calabasas storefront, not far from the Jenner home. They called it Smooch, and it soon became apparent that mother and daughter had a flair for business. Their friends and neighbors flocked to the new store to deck out their children in the tasteful high-end outfits that would soon become de rigueur in Hidden Hills. "This was our way of plugging through that horrible time [after Bob died] and just plugging ahead," Kris explained.

"I threw myself into the store," Kourtney later wrote. "I came early and left two hours after closing every day. It became my baby and my obsession and I really put my emotion and my time into it." For Kris, its success would be one more stepping stone to a future business empire. For Kourtney, it would lay the path for a retail empire of her own. Meanwhile, Kim's closet/eBay venture was thriving. The same couldn't be said for her marriage.

When Damon Thomas filed for divorce from her in 2003, it soon became clear that the marriage had been a disaster from the start—

hardly a surprise, considering that Kim had run off as a nineteen-year-old and married a high-flying music mogul ten years her senior. Again, however, the picture of what happened in the marriage and what went wrong depended on who you believed. According to Kim's statement as the respondent in the divorce papers, she was subjected to repeated domestic abuse. Thomas, she claimed, hit her for the first time just a few months after they were married.

"One incident," she wrote, "occurred on the day that Damon and I were going skydiving with Justin Timberlake. Before we left home, Damon hit me in the face and cut my lip open. I fell into the bed frame and banged my knee hard." On another occasion, she claims, Thomas learned she had paged someone, which led to yet another violent incident: "He became enraged and punched me in the face. My face was bruised and swollen as a result. I thought about calling the police but was afraid and decided not to do so." In a third example of domestic violence, she writes, "[Thomas] came at me and slammed me against the closet wall. . . . He held me up against the wall with his hands around my neck and threatened to choke me. He then took one hand and punched the wall right next to my head."

Besides physical violence, Kim also details a number of incidents of psychological abuse. Although she had a job at a high-end boutique when they first met, Thomas insisted that she quit, because he didn't want her coming into contact with any of her old boyfriends, who would know to find her at the store if they wanted to see her. Thomas "wanted to know where I was at all times," she stated. "He often arrived home at 4:30AM and expected me to prepare a meal for him at that hour." Kim was also forced to "ask permission" to go out to dinner with friends or even to go shopping.

"He didn't want me to go to the mall or with friends," she stated. "He told me he didn't want men to have the opportunity to 'hit on' me. Damon decided what we would do and when we would do it. He was very much the 'King of the castle.'"

She also claimed that her husband gave her thousands of dollars and demanded she get liposuction and that Thomas assaulted
her when she returned home during the divorce to retrieve personal
items from the bathroom.

In addition, Kim said, Thomas would start arguments at family gatherings and tried to convince her that her mother and sisters
were "evil." To brand her siblings as "whores," Kim alleged, Thomas
once showed nude photos of one of her sisters to Robert Kardashian.
Thomas told a different story about the demise of the couple's three-
year marriage.

"She can't write or sing or dance, so she does harmful things in
order to validate herself in the media," he told *In Touch* magazine.
"That's a fame-whore to me. It's just not cool at all." He also claimed
that Kim is not the supportive sister she portrays in public, who
would do anything for her family.

"Kim is obsessed with fame," he told the magazine, and would
step on anybody, including her sisters Kourtney and Khloé, to get
ahead. "She's jealous and competitive with her sisters. Jealousy is a
big thing with her." He believed that Kim leaked excerpts from their
divorce documents, especially the claim that he beat her, which he
vociferously denied. "It's just absolutely not true," he said, pointing
out that Kim never filed for a restraining order or a protective order;
she accused him of these acts only to get "a lot of money" out of him.
Indeed, Thomas added, he was the one who filed for divorce first,
because Kim was cheating on him with "multiple guys." He claimed
that when they briefly reconciled, she convinced him to finance
"extravagant shopping sprees" and a number of plastic-surgery proce-
dures, including a boob job and liposuction. "She wanted to have that
lifestyle," he said. "She wanted to be what she ultimately became."
Damon said he had no problem financing this lifestyle, but the final
straw came when he saw Kim with Jennifer Lopez's ex, Cris Judd,
on a magazine cover. "I saw my wife with another man, wearing the

clothes that we had just bought after her lipo," he said. "It was not something as a husband you ever wanted to see."

The marriage was eventually dissolved in 2004, and Thomas was ordered to pay Kim $56,000.

By the time Kim separated from her husband, Smooch was starting to get off the ground, and Kim was feeling a little left out watching her older sister carve out a place for herself in the fashion world. But the little boutique was too small to add another sister to the operation. The girls started to talk about maybe opening up another store one day, run by all the Kardashian sisters. For now, however, Kim plunged right back into her closet-organizing and eBay service. When word got out that she was back in business, she once again had a full list of clients who wanted to declutter their wardrobes, including a number of celebrities.

One of those clients just happened to be an heiress with whom Kim had attended the prestigious Buckley preschool when she was four years old. When Paris Hilton contacted her old friend and told Kim that she needed to "restock" her closet, it was a fateful call.

CHAPTER SEVEN

Before the Kardashians, the world spent a lot of time keeping up with Paris Hilton. As with the now-ubiquitous reality-show family, the name Hilton was already quite familiar to the American public by the time Paris burst to fame in 2003. It was Paris's great-grandfather Conrad Hilton who gave birth to an empire when he arrived in Texas just after the First World War, as the oil boom was reaching its peak. He had intended to buy a bank, but the purchase fell through when he couldn't come up with enough funds. Instead he ended up buying a lively forty-room hotel called the Mobley in Cisco, Texas, when he noticed that the rooms were changing hands three times a day to accommodate the eight-hour shifts of oilfield workers. The purchase ended up being more profitable than a bank would have been when Conrad parlayed his new expertise in the hospitality business into a chain of hotels throughout Texas, including a fourteen-story structure that was the first to bear his name—the Dallas Hilton—in 1925.

By the end of the Second World War, Hilton hotels were everywhere, and Conrad Hilton was a very rich man, describing himself as "the innkeeper to the world." In 1925, he married Mary Adelaide Barron, with whom he had three children, including Paris's grandfather Barron, before divorcing in 1934. Eight years later, Hilton married Zsa Zsa Gabor, a flamboyant socialite who would become known as "the original Paris Hilton." The two had one daughter, Constance Francesca, who Zsa Zsa later claimed was conceived when Conrad raped her while they were married.

Barron had eight children, including Richard, who would carve out a lucrative Southern California real-estate business of his own. In 1979, Richard married Kathy Avanzino—an actress who had attended high school with Michael Jackson and was one of his closest friends—and together they had four children. The oldest they cheekily named Paris, even though there is no hotel bearing the name Paris Hilton in the French capital.

As one of the heirs to her great-grandfather's multibillion-dollar fortune and the recipient of a trust fund created by her father, Paris never needed to work. Growing up in New York—where her father worked as an investment banker before moving west—she enjoyed a life of indulgence and luxury, living for a time in one of the world's most luxurious hotels, the Waldorf Astoria, which was owned by her family. Yet from an early age, she harbored professional ambitions, and she was willing to work hard to achieve her goals. At fifteen, she was signed as a model by Donald Trump's Trump Model Management agency, having honed her craft appearing in a number of charity fashion shows as a child. "I wanted to model and Donald was like: 'I want you at my agency,'" she explained. "I called Donald and told him, 'Don't tell my folks but I am signing with your agency.'"

Trump remembers the precocious teenager well. "Paris is someone who really understood from an early age the meaning of the word 'celebrity.' She understood what it meant and that it had great value," he recalled. As a teenager, she walked the runway during New York Fashion Week, appearing in campaigns for a number of major lines. At sixteen, she and her younger sister, Nicky, were even featured in the Best Dressed section of the *New York Post*.

Although well underage, Paris soon became a fixture of the New York club scene, where she honed her soon-to-be-legendary party skills as the It Girl of the era. During the day, she attended the Dwight School, a prestigious Upper West Side prep school that had turned out such notable alumni as Truman Capote, Roy Lichtenstein, and Fiorello LaGuardia.

Although she possessed an undeniable flair from a young age, the early media coverage of her presuperstardom modeling career and club hopping always noted her status as an heiress. When the UK newspaper *The Guardian* asked what she thought of the media pre-occupation with her family name, Paris replied, "I think it's retarded. . . . They call me 'Paris the Heiress.' I was going to go to school to study hotel management, but I don't want to be behind a hotel desk. My sister, she's really into all that. I'm more of an artsy person. I'm getting ready to record my album, I have my modeling and acting."

The first time the world outside of a tiny segment of the New York social scene got a glimpse of the Paris Hilton that we all know today was in a 2000 *Vanity Fair* photo spread, produced by the iconic photographer David LaChapelle, entitled "Hip Hop Debs." In it, Paris is photographed in, among other locations, the living room of her grandmother's Beverly Hills mansion, giving the finger to the camera and dressed in a see-through top. The photos would become known as the "nipple shots" and would catapult Paris to instant notoriety. They would also cause great consternation among her storied family, with one of her cousins sniffing that she was "ashamed" to be related to Paris. Tellingly, other relatives accused Paris's mother, Kathy, of encouraging such behavior, not the first time that her mother was linked to Paris's outrageous antics. In the accompanying *Vanity Fair* text, the writer, Mary Jo Sales, quotes one of Paris's friends: "All Paris wants to do is to become famous . . . to wipe out the past, to become somebody else."

If it was fame she was after, she got her wish in the summer of 2003, when a tape featuring Paris and her ex-boyfriend Rick Salomon—who at the time of the release was married to Hollywood actress Shannen Doherty—first surfaced on the Internet. Recorded with a night vision camera, the tape featured Paris and Salomon having sex and had reportedly been shot two years earlier, when Paris was twenty and Salomon thirty-one. When rumors of the tape surfaced, Paris at first denied its existence. Then when it began to circulate, her parents issued a statement declaring that they were "saddened at how low human beings will stoop to exploit our daughter."

There were claims and counterclaims, and suddenly Paris Hilton had gone from someone known mostly to readers of Page Six and *Vanity Fair* to someone that all of America was talking about. It was auspicious timing. The controversy just happened to coincide with a new Fox TV show called *The Simple Life*, which was scheduled to debut on December 2, 2003, only three weeks after the tape surfaced. The show would feature Paris and her childhood friend Nicole Richie—daughter of singer Lionel Richie—as fish-out-of-water Hollywood socialites thrust into rural living and forced to leave behind all the luxuries of their spoiled rich-kid lives, inspired by the '60s sitcom *Green Acres*.

The notoriety of the sex tape guaranteed an audience. The premiere, in fact, garnered monster ratings, with thirteen million people tuning in to watch Paris and Nicole move in with an Arkansas family, the Ledings, for a month. *People* magazine credited the sex-tape scandal with the show's strong debut. "Critics retched, but viewers watched," the magazine noted that week.

"I think a lot of that stemmed from the curiosity that was built in the media about who Paris Hilton was," recalled her manager, Jason Moore. "She lived the ultimate image and was the ultimate brand based on the right name, the right look, the right height, the right hair color, the right eye color, the right everything for a formula that far exceeded anybody else at that time. She was the ultimate package that corporate

America would want to make for itself as a marketing tool, but it was already made for them. They say to be a famous person, people want to be you or fuck you, and she encompassed both of those."

Paris had denied any knowledge of the sex tape and claimed to have had nothing to do with its release. "I didn't want to be known as that," she later told Piers Morgan. "And now when people look at me they think that I'm something I'm not just because of one incident one night with someone who I was in love with." She described it as "the most embarrassing, humiliating thing that has ever happened to me in my life. . . . This was not just some random person, it was my boyfriend who I was with for a few years and who I really loved and trusted. It was such a violation of everything. I was so hurt and so in shock and it's been hard for me to ever really trust anyone again, especially guys, because it's the most horrible thing you could do to a person."

Yet only a week after *The Simple Life* aired, she appeared on *Saturday Night Live*, with her parents and younger brother in the audience, and participated in a send-up of the controversy—with sexual innuendo that left no doubt as to its meaning—that had many wondering whether the release of the tape had been a publicity stunt to guarantee her show's success. In the skit, Jimmy Fallon interviews her:

FALLON: Is it hard to get into the Paris Hilton?

PARIS: Actually, it's a very exclusive hotel, no matter what you've heard.

FALLON: Do they allow double occupancy at the Paris Hilton?

PARIS: No.

FALLON: Is the Paris Hilton roomy?

PARIS: It might be for you, but most people find it very comfortable.

FALLON: I'm a VIP. I may need to go in the back entrance.

PARIS: It doesn't matter who you are. It's not going to happen.

Within weeks of the reality show's debut, Paris had ascended to megastardom, seemingly out of nowhere and without any discernible talent. Unbeknownst to most observers, her rise to fame was being orchestrated by her manager, Jason Moore, who had big plans for what he called "the branding" of Paris. He had first recognized her potential a year earlier after seeing a seven-page parody of her and Nicky in GQ magazine featuring two fictional sisters, Frenchie and Dallas Marriot—described as "spoiled party girls" who are raised by their parents, Denver and Piper, and hang out with the DAT Pack (Daughters of the Affluent and Tony).

"I read a piece in PAGE SIX that said Frenchie was traipsing around Tribeca in a flasher's jacket, a fishnet bra and a black Dolce & Gabbana thong," Piper says in the story. "Well, Dolce & Gabbana doesn't make a black thong. Honestly! It's so outrageous, the stories you hear."

In another passage, Dallas says the two of them have more offers than they can deal with and are always "exploring their options" but that eventually she would like to move to the Paris Marriott. "Ah, Paris," she sighs, looking out the window wistfully. "I totally love that property."

Controversy broke out following publication, when the Marriott hotel chain took issue with its portrayal, even though the fictional sisters' last name was spelled differently. "After that article, I recognized she was a brand," Moore told CNN. "It wasn't a Smith or Franklin that they parodied. It was a brand name and that's when I recognized that she is going to be bigger than anyone thought about, which was before anyone was thinking about anything at all." He explained that he had formulated a plan for Paris's rollout long before the TV show aired and had studied the way major rock stars such as the Rolling Stones and Grateful Dead had developed their branding. "Those guys aren't releasing new material, but they're making money hand over fist every year from what? Touring. Selling merch. Building more fan base. Exploiting more territories. Planting more seeds. The key was planting seeds with regard to everything we did. Even if it didn't feel big and it didn't feel necessary, if there was a seed to be planted, we planted it. She understood that a ripple will, after a while, create a wave."

Together they created plenty of waves as Paris became a full-fledged paparazzi phenomenon, landing on magazine covers, in tabloid gossip columns, at charity functions, and on fashion runways. "I said to Paris, we're on tour," Moore recalled.

Every venue is a stage. Always be in front of the fans, always perpetuating your brand, your merch, building new relationships. Encore, goodnight and we'll be back. It was important that we celebrate [native] culture too so you don't come in and step on them. Paris was amazing, she would immediately get a local designer and wear their clothes. The media and paparazzi loved it because she was wearing their hometown. Then you do something charitable. Then you party. And then do it over and over and over again. It was a machine. It was a Mike Tyson knockout.

In 2004, Paris published a memoir, *Confessions of an Heiress,* in which she took issue with what she called society's preconception of how to be an heiress. "It involves wearing white gloves, big hats, and pearls, having some dowdy debut or a coming-out party, and going to fancy, snobby all-girl colleges—boring, old-fashioned stuff like that," she wrote. "I totally disagree. There is no sin worse in life than being boring—and nothing worse than letting other people tell you what to do."

The continuing controversy over the sex tape was anything but boring. In 2004, the infamous tape was released commercially by Salomon under the title *One Night in Paris,* after a series of legal maneuvers that left people more confused than ever about what had happened and whether one or both parties on the tape had been involved in its distribution. An Internet porn company, Marvad, claimed in court documents that it had struck a deal with a friend of Salomon in August 2013, months before *The Simple Life* first aired, to distribute the tape. Marvad alleged that they had Salomon's permission and that Paris Hilton had "consented to the public exploitation of the video."

In July 2004, Salomon came to an out-of-court settlement with Paris, agreeing to pay her $400,000 and a percentage of profits from the tape's sales. She would later claim that she never saw any money from the tape. But she hardly needed it, because its notoriety helped build her an empire in excess of $100 million.

By the time the second season of *The Simple Life* aired in 2004, Paris was getting $25,000 to $100,000 just to appear at a club, and even more to DJ. Before long, with Moore's help, she had developed an assortment of fashion accessories, including a purse collection for a Japanese label and a jewelry line marketed on Amazon, which she described as "beautiful and very high quality, yet affordable and available to everyone."

Next came the first of many perfumes for her own company, Parlux, which proved to be an almost instant success, with sales increasing by 47 percent in just one year. Paris Hilton fragrances would gross more than one billion dollars over the next decade. Soon came the first of forty-four Paris Hilton stores, a racing team, a lingerie line, and even a Paris Hilton Beach Club chain. "I'm not just putting my name to any old product," she explained. "I'm hands-on. I sleep with a notepad next to my bed and design everything from the bags and sunglasses right down to choosing the smell of my perfumes."

Paris was riding high, and then she suddenly started crashing down. In September 2006, she was arrested on a DUI while driving erratically in Hollywood just after midnight. She registered a blood alcohol level of .08 percent, above the California legal limit. She was released shortly after arriving at the police station, and a trial date was set for the following January. The next morning, she called in to Ryan Seacrest's radio show to say that the incident had been blown out of proportion; that she had just been "really hungry" and was racing to In and Out Burger after having one margarita with friends. "It was nothing," she insisted.

She said she was surprised the press had made a big deal out of it. "Everything I do is blown out of proportion," she said. "It really hurts my feelings."

When the case came to court, she pleaded no contest to alcohol-related reckless driving, was placed on thirty-six months' probation, and was fined $1,500. Her license was also suspended and she was ordered to enroll in an alcohol-education program.

Days later, police pulled her over and informed her that she was driving on a suspended license. They forced her to sign a document acknowledging that she was not allowed to drive. But six weeks later, on February 27, she was stopped once again after being clocked driving seventy miles an hour in a thirty-five-mile-per-hour zone with no headlights on, and she was charged with violating her probation. Her publicist insisted that she was unaware that her license had been suspended, but a copy of the statement she had signed in January was in fact found in her glove compartment.

In May, the scene outside her court hearing was a circus, as the media gathered to find out whether she would pay any consequences for her repeated violations. It emerged at the hearing that Paris had never reported for the alcohol-education program she had been ordered to enroll in as part of her probation. Nor did the judge, Michael Sauer, find credible her claim that she did not know her license had been suspended, noting that police had found the "smoking gun"—the document that she had signed acknowledging this fact. "I'm very sorry and from now on I'm going to pay complete attention to everything," Paris said before the judge ruled. "I'm sorry and I did not do it on purpose at all."

Delivering his ruling, the judge issued a withering rebuke to her legal team, saying, "I can't believe that [her] attorneys did not tell her that the suspension had been upheld. She wanted to disregard everything that was said and continue to drive no matter what." Sauer proceeded to sentence her to forty-five days at the Century Regional Detention Facility in Lynwood. Well aware that celebrities are often accorded special privileges in jail, the judge made it clear that Paris was to get no special treatment. To ensure that this was taken seriously, he decreed that she would not be allowed work release, furloughs, alternative jail, or electronic monitoring.

Visibly upset by the ruling, Paris's mother jumped up and sarcastically asked the judge, "Can I have your autograph?" Afterward, she told a reporter outside the courtroom who asked what she thought of the decision, "What do you think? This is pathetic and disgusting, a waste of taxpayer money with all this nonsense. This is a joke."

Her lawyer, Michael Weitzman, was quick to react. "I'm shocked and disappointed at the sentence by the judge," he told reporters. "To sentence Paris Hilton to jail is uncalled for, inappropriate, and ludicrous. She was singled out for who she is. She's been selectively targeted. Paris was honest in her testimony. We plan to appeal. Shame on the system."

After attending the MTV Movie Awards on June 3, 2007, Paris reported to jail to serve her forty-five-day sentence. But only four days later, Los Angeles County sheriff Lee Baca signed an order releasing her to serve the remainder of her time at home under electronic monitoring, due to an unspecified "medical condition." It later emerged that the condition was a supposed psychological disorder, and it seemed to many observers that Paris had been given special treatment, especially since Judge Sauer had been very specific in his original sentence: "No electronic monitoring." When Sauer heard about the sheriff's actions, he immediately summoned Paris for a hearing the next morning. There, he reimposed the original sentence and sent her back to jail. When she heard his ruling, Paris shouted out "It's not right!" and broke down in tears, asking to hug her mother.

At the request of her lawyers, she was held for psychiatric examination for five days, before being sent back to Lynwood to serve the remainder of her sentence. In true Paris fashion, when she was finally released two weeks later, she had a special outfit delivered to the facility and changed in a bathroom before exiting past hordes of paparazzi in a chic jacket, jeans, and heels, and in full makeup. She would later use the outfit to launch a new clothing line.

At first, the notoriety of the arrest and subsequent legal proceedings appeared to solidify her brand. "Paris Hilton being arrested just makes her more famous," said veteran Hollywood publicist Michael Levine. "She has devoted her entire adult life to appearing to be the princess of parties." Her handlers wasted no time attempting to cash in on the new attention. Moore even trademarked her signature phrase from *The Simple Life*, "That's hot." But a phrase already existed that came to be even more closely associated with the heiress. Those who chose to disparage her usually dismissed her as "famous for being famous." The phrase had its roots in a 1961 book by the social theorist Daniel J. Borstin, who defined a celebrity as "a person who is known for his well-knownness." Until 2007, there was only one celebrity whose name would instantly come to mind when the phrase was used. Soon there would be another.

CHAPTER EIGHT

By 2006, Paris Hilton's friendship with her longtime BFF, Nicole Richie, had visibly soured. They were still under contract to produce *The Simple Life*, but now the episodes featured separate adventures and frequently alluded to their feud as part of the story line. Off-screen, Paris appeared to have a new best friend, a still-unknown Kim Kardashian, who was often photographed with her at LA hot spots. The two had known each other since preschool and their mothers were close friends, but Kim had never really hung out with Paris until after her divorce from Damon Thomas.

"While my friends were away in college and drinking and partying," she later recalled, "I was at home being a wife, cooking and cleaning. . . . I started hanging out with my friends that I had grown up with since I was two years old. I started to see a new life. I never partied before. I never went out."

She originally reconnected with Paris when the now-famous heiress asked her to organize her massive wardrobe, which was jammed on racks all over her house and garage. Kim had recently returned to her closet-organizing business, and she soon came up with a plan. She convinced Paris to convert an entire bedroom in her Beverly Hills mansion into a huge walk-in closet. Kim later recalled that it was no small task.

"I had to organize and color-coordinate it, and help her with my styling advice, what she needs to get rid of, what she needs to fill back in, you know, do personal shopping," she said. "With her, it was mostly getting rid of stuff because she's a compulsive shopper. Now her garage is filled with clothes again. It's overwhelming."

Paris was so impressed with Kim's design skills that she asked her to work with her as a personal stylist when she went on the road. In 2006, Kim would appear briefly in three episodes of *The Simple Life*. In one scene, she helps Paris organize her wardrobe, and in another, she helps her administer a pregnancy test to her Chihuahua, Tinker-bell. In later years, a myth would emerge that Kim had once worked as Paris's personal assistant. An Internet meme compiled screen grabs from Kim's episodes, featuring made-up dialogue implying that Paris ordered Kim around like a lackey. Kim was not in fact Paris's assistant, nor was she her actual best friend. But they were a regular fixture on the LA club scene for about two years in the mid-'00s.

"We'd go anywhere and everywhere just to be seen," Kim later told *Rolling Stone*. "We knew exactly where to go, where to be seen, how to have something written about you. All you had to do is go to this restaurant, or this party, talk about whatever you want to talk about, and it would be in the paper the next day."

Later, Paris would also fondly recall those days. "Yeah, we had so much fun. She's a great wing woman, someone to hang out with, fun to be around, beautiful," she said. Little did Paris know at the time that her fun-loving sidekick was watching and learning. Until May 2006, most of the paparazzi were unaware of the identity of the brunette who often arrived with Paris at hot spots around LA. That changed on May 24, when paparazzi photographed Kim emerging with Nick Lachey—lead singer of the boy band 98 Degrees—from an afternoon showing of *The Da Vinci Code* at a Brentwood cinema.

Lachey had famously broken up with Jessica Simpson, his costar on the popular reality show *Newlyweds*, a few months earlier, and the tabloids were curious to know whom he had replaced her with.

"The next night," Kim recalled in *Kardashian Konfidential*, "I was out with Paris Hilton and we were going to a club on Sunset. We were in her car and paparazzi started taking pictures. Usually they would shout, 'Paris! Paris! Paris!' But the night before they'd gotten these pictures of a mystery girl with Nick and by then they'd figured out who I was. So they started yelling out, 'Kim! Kim!' I wanted to hide, and Paris and I looked at each other and just laughed. She said, 'Whatever you do, just smile. And don't say anything under your breath because they now have video camera too.' I thought, 'This is so weird. I don't know what's going on.' It was surreal."

In its May 31 edition, *People* magazine reported that, according to sources, Lachey had been "dating stylist Kim Kardashian" for about a month. "They're sweet on each other," a source close to the couple told the magazine, revealing that the two had met at a party for Arizona Cardinals quarterback Matt Leinart.

The relationship turned out to be short-lived, lasting a little over a week. But the story of how Kim burst into the public eye is one that has been repeated ad nauseam over the years. It reminds me of the myth that Lana Turner was discovered at Schwab's drugstore. But just as the Schwab's tale was carefully crafted by Turner herself as a Cinderella story, it appears that there's more to Kim and Lachey's movie date than meets the eye.

Years later, Lachey would speculate that Kim's emergence into the public eye was no accident and imply that she or her people had deliberately engineered it. In 2013, *Details* magazine asked him whether he felt responsible for catapulting Kim to her "ubiquity."

"That's one way to interpret it," he replied. "Let's just say this: We went to a movie. No one followed us there. Somehow, mysteriously, when we left, there were 30 photographers waiting outside. [*Laughs*]

There are certain ways to play this game, and some people play it well."

Thanks to her newfound paparazzi attention, people now knew who Kim Kardashian was. So when word of a sex tape featuring Kim leaked out early in the new year, the buzz was deafening. After Kim separated from Thomas in 2003, she had ambitions to branch out from her closet-organizing service and work as a stylist in Hollywood. It would take awhile to break into the business, but one of her first clients happened to be Brandy Norwood, the actress and R & B singer. Years later, in fact, Brandy's manager mother, Sonja Norwood, would accuse Kim of passing the singer's American Express credit-card number to her siblings and running up unauthorized charges of more than $120,000. Kim steadfastly denied it and the case was settled out of court. But at the time, Brandy apparently thought enough of Kim to fix her up with her younger brother, Ray J, who was also an R & B singer, though not nearly as successful as his sister.

Their romance was short-lived, but at some point in 2003 they found the time to record a raunchy sex tape, in which they take turns going down on each other. As the rumors of the tape's existence heated up in early 2007, the name Kim Kardashian was suddenly hot.

In February, the tabloid TV show *Extra* hired Kim to appear as a celebrity correspondent in an episode during New York Fashion week. The same episode features Kim confirming the existence of the rumored sex tape: "She's the daughter of O.J.'s famed attorney, Robert Kardashian, and from O.J. to Jessica Simpson to Britney and Whitney, all Hollywood roads lead to Kim Kardashian," the episode teased. "But Kim is becoming famous for more than being close pals with Paris Hilton—she's currently starring in a new celebrity sex tape that has tongues wagging. Now, in an exclusive interview, Kim is coming clean to *Extra* about the sex tape she made with Brandy's brother, Ray J, who is now rumored to be dating Whitney Houston."

"A tape does exist. . . . Ray J and I are friends," Kim confirms for the camera. "Whatever we did was our personal business. . . . I hope that it remains private." The same week, Los Angeles–based Vivid Films—a porn outfit that specializes in the distribution of celebrity sex tapes—announced that it had purchased Kim's tape from a "third party" for a million dollars and would release it in stores and over the Internet on February 28 under the title *Kim Kardashian: Superstar.*

Kim immediately issued a statement announcing plans to sue Vivid. "This tape, which was made three years ago, and was meant to be something private between myself and my then-boyfriend is extremely hurtful not only to me, but to my family as well," she said. "I am filing legal charges against the company who is distributing this tape since it is being sold completely without my permission or consent."

Vivid chairman Steven Hirsch immediately responded to the legal threat.

"We are comfortable that we have the legal right to distribute this video, despite what others may say," he said. "We have been around for 20 years and if we didn't feel comfortable putting it out, we wouldn't. We would like Kim and Ray J to be a part of it and hopefully we can work that out."

Kim's invasion-of-privacy lawsuit called Vivid's actions "despicable, offensive, outrageous, oppressive, and malicious." But less than two months later, the lawsuit was over almost before it began, when Vivid announced that it had reached a settlement with Kim.

"We met with her several times and finally reached a financial arrangement that we both feel is fair," Hirsch announced. "We've always known we had the legal right to distribute this video which became an instant best-seller and we've always wanted to work something out with Kim so she could share in the profits." The settlement was said to have included a $5 million payment to Kim but, curiously, the settlement allowed the distribution of the tape to proceed as planned. Although initial reports indicated that the settlement contained an agreement that the company would stop distributing the tape as of May 31, 2007, it is still featured prominently for sale on the Vivid website eight years later.

Suddenly, Kim Kardashian was hot and, just as suddenly, the E! network announced that it was planning a reality series built around the lives of the Kardashians and Jenners. It seemed that right around the time the sex tape started circulating, Kris Jenner had barged into the office of Ryan Seacrest and pitched the idea for a show about her family that just happened to feature the woman whom everybody now was talking about. Kris would serve as the show's executive producer.

The announcement came a week after E! revealed that *The Simple Life* had been canceled after four seasons. Americans, it seemed, had grown tired of Paris Hilton and her antics, which had long since reached their best-by date. And yet the news that Paris's reality series was about to be replaced with the adventures of another Beverly Hills socialite who had achieved notoriety through a sex tape struck many observers as just a little too coincidental. Speculation was already mounting that Kim had engineered the release of the tape to jumpstart her stardom and to follow the career trajectory of her old friend Paris.

Indeed, Ray J himself added ammunition to the charge when he explained how the tape apparently made its way to Vivid. "I shot the tape and she kept the tape, so she said the tape got lost I guess when she was moving," he told an interviewer, in a tone that implied he was skeptical.

Not long after the tape's release, the popular entertainment site Hollywoodlife.com quoted a purported friend of Ray J's, revealing that the singer was in on it with Kim. "Both Ray J and Kim leaked the tape. They made that tape on purpose and that purpose was fame! Kim was all for it and then, when the tape became public, she acted like she was really upset. Everyone on the inside knew that it was all an act. She wanted to be famous like Paris and it worked."

Another source, who works in the adult-film industry, alleged that a mutual friend of Kim and Paris had advised her that if she wanted to achieve fame, a sex tape would be the way to go, and helped her put the video together. The source claimed that Kim had discussed the idea of producing a tape with her family beforehand.

Hollywoodlife interviewed a Los Angeles attorney, Mychal Wilson, who believed the tape could not have been distributed without the consent of both Ray J and Kim.

"It appears that both Kim Kardashian and Ray J consented to make the sex tape," said Wilson. "Clearly, they both are aware of the taping as they are mugging for the camera. Kim and Ray J's sex tape appears to be high quality and well shot. Additionally, both parties would have consented to signing on the distribution deal with Vivid Entertainment."

Another LA attorney concurred. "The most likely scenario is that they both decided to leak the tape," explained Anthony Salerno. "Let's just say, if Ray J had gone behind Kim's back and tried to sell the tape, Kim could have easily called on her lawyers to stop that tape from being shown to the public."

The former supermodel Janice Dickinson took these sentiments a step further, claiming not only that the stars willingly participated but also that Kim's own mother struck the eventual distribution deal. "Kris Jenner signed a contract with Vivid," she told Radar Online. "Kris approved the video, she signed it along with Kim and Ray J." This corresponded with what Kim's former friend Sheba—whom I was dating at the time—told me in 2010: that it was Kris Jenner who engineered the deal behind the scenes and was responsible for the tape seeing the light of day, though it's unclear if Sheba was passing on firsthand knowledge or just repeating rumors.

I knew Janice Dickinson well from the days when I went undercover as a male model for my exposé of the fashion industry, *Shut Up and Smile*. She had always struck me as somebody of great integrity, as evidenced by the way she handled herself as one of the women who accused Bill Cosby of drugging and raping her. She is also very familiar with the behind-the-scenes machinations of the reality-show industry, having served for four seasons as one of the celebrity judges on the popular reality show *America's Next Top Model*, and hosted her own reality show, *The Janice Dickinson Modeling Agency*, from 2006 to 2008.

Still, I thought, the only way I could make sense of the whole sex-tape controversy and find out how these things work would be to go to the source. Aside from posing as a male model, I had also gone undercover as a drug dealer, a private detective, an escort, and a hairdresser's assistant for various projects. Now I would pose as a porn peddler to infiltrate the distributor of *Kim Kardashian: Superstar*—the adult-film giant Vivid Films.

First, I needed an angle, one that would get me through the doors of Vivid to discover what's involved in distributing a celebrity sex tape. I briefly toyed with the idea of making my own sex tape, but there's only so far I'm willing to go for my craft. Moreover, having viewed Ray J's assets on *Kim Kardashian: Superstar*, I could accurately say that I didn't measure up. And although I am the only Canadian to top the *New York Times* bestseller list in more than seventy years, I wasn't sure that I qualified as a celebrity.

However, I happen to live in a Miami complex that is chock-full of famous people. One whom I am acquainted with is my fellow author Elizabeth Gilbert, but I was pretty sure that when she wrote *Eat, Pray, Love*, public fellatio wasn't what she had in mind for the latter category. In fact, I would be hard-pressed to convince any of the personalities I bump into at the pool each week to bare their assets for the sake of my journalistic career. An actual sex tape was clearly out of the question. But I immediately thought of somebody who was a good enough sport that she might go along with pretending that she had a tape of her bedroom antics up for sale.

A friend of mine was a fairly well-known model who had appeared on *Dancing with the Stars*—a higher level of celebrity than either Kim Kardashian or Paris Hilton had achieved at the time of their cinematic debuts. Still, both women had something else going for them before their tapes started to circulate—their famous names. I needed something else to sweeten the deal. I came up with the perfect bait. With an idea in mind, I made a call to Vivid headquarters.

I informed them that I was calling as a middleman in possession of a sex tape featuring a well-known model—one who had appeared on *DWTS*—having sex with "one of the world's top basketball players." They were definitely interested but noncommittal. They needed to see the tape, of course. I asked my model friend if she would be willing to come with me to the offices of Vivid to make our pitch. She informed me that she had an upcoming shoot scheduled in LA and could work in a pitch meeting if I could be available on those dates.

When I flew to LA and got in touch about our jaunt to Vivid, however, she immediately crushed my hopes. She had told her manager about the plan and he had unequivocally forbidden her to participate in the scheme. It could be career poison, he warned. Feeling guilty about bringing me across the country for nothing, she suggested a friend, Laurie, who she thought would be game. She wasn't at the same level of fame, but she was a model and she definitely looked the part for a taped sex romp that the public would be willing to pay for. Moreover, she happened to know both Kim and her husband, Kanye West.

I was to meet Laurie at the Churchill Pub on Third Street for breakfast. My assistant, Grace, was supposed to join us. The tall, mulatto brunette—whose look immediately identified her as a model—showed up twenty minutes late. She was dressed in sweatpants, pink Asics kicks, and a T-shirt, looking like she had just come from a yoga or gym class. I spotted her and waved her to my table in the back. She introduced herself. "I'm starving," she told me. "I hope the food is good here because I have a big appetite. Just worked out for two hours." She told me she only agreed to meet with me under three conditions: (1) I couldn't use her full name; (2) I bought her breakfast; (3) I paid her taxi fare back to her apartment in West Hollywood.

Laurie started telling me stories about Kanye West back in the day, how he used to have multiple women on the go and how his ego was always "bigger than life."

"He was always good with the ladies, a modern-day Don Juan," she said. "But after his mother died he seemed to change. He became more serious. He wanted to meet the right woman."

She said she had known Kim for almost a decade, though not well. She used to occasionally hang out with her during her partying days at various clubs in LA, including Skybar and the rooftop at the Standard.

"Kim was always a big scenester," she said,

a woman possessed with achieving fame and fortune without having real raw talent. Ever since I knew her she had a master plan and didn't try to hide it. She knew what she wanted. If there was a big celebrity in the house, Kim would go over to them and schmooze her way to sitting at their table and drinking with them. One night a group of Lakers had a table in VIP and they had several lovely young girls sitting with them drinking. In a matter of seconds, I saw Kim have the security guard open the rope for her and let her in. She sat with Kobe Bryant and his buddies the rest of the night while the three friends she was with had to stay in the regular area. It was incredible because Kim was unknown then. She was always good at getting what she wanted, and quickly.

While we talked, she ate an acai bowl with a smoothie and then ordered a round of scrambled eggs and bacon with toast. For such a thin woman, she had a huge appetite. "I for one was not surprised Kim married Kanye," she said. "Kim was always very open about wanting to meet a man more rich, famous, and powerful than her. She definitely found that guy in Kanye. It's funny because they really don't seem compatible. I've bumped into Kim a few times since they got married and she's never with him. I think they got married with some sort of agreement to have kids together but to lead separate lives."

Finally Grace showed up. Laurie really didn't give me any good info on Kanye and Kim, except for one tidbit about how she had heard from Kanye's friends that the main reason Kanye married Kim was to be part of a big family.

"Losing his mother was devastating," she said. "He never got over it until he met Kim and loved how big a family she had. He was smitten with Kris Jenner. In fact, I don't think he would have married Kim if Kris Jenner wasn't on the scene. In Kris he found a new mother figure. She treated him like her own. He was enamored with how smart, loving, and business-savvy Kris was. He had found the perfect family to marry into."

Grace called an Uber car to pick us up because we had a jam-packed day ahead and needed to get over to Vivid. In the car, a Jeep Cherokee, we rehearsed what we'd tell the people at Vivid about our sex tape involving a model and a famous basketball player, the most famous player in the world. Once we arrived at the white building on Cahuenga Boulevard that houses Vivid, we got out and stood outside for a few minutes before going in.

Grace said she was a bit nervous and wanted to have a cigarette. When we went inside, we were greeted by a burly security guard, who said we needed authorization to enter. I told him I had something very exclusive for Vivid. Still he wouldn't let us in. Instead he agreed to phone upstairs to see if they would meet with us.

He got Tessa Allmon on the phone. He passed it to me and I explained to Tessa what I had. I asked her if I could speak to the head of Vivid, Steve Hirsch. I had interviewed Hirsch at length a few years ago in the same building for a documentary I'd directed about Charlie Sheen during the height of his wild antics with goddesses and erratic behavior. Hirsch was extremely cooperative on the Sheen film, even bringing in a couple of his porn stars who knew Sheen to give me interviews, including Capri Anderson. (She had claimed she was roughed up by Sheen at the Plaza Hotel in 2010 during one of his coke binges. He denied it and the case was settled out of court.) But on this day Hirsch was too busy. Tessa told me I'd have to call Vivid's head of PR, Jackie Markham, in New York to discuss the matter. What a colossal waste of time. Fortunately, it had cost me nothing more than a breakfast. But there was also the small matter of my airline ticket and hotel accommodations. I hadn't traveled 3,500 miles only to find out I could have accomplished the same thing with a long-distance phone call.

The minute we got outside, I called another publicist, Norah Lawlor, to see if she'd represent the model and help promote and sell the sex tape. Lawlor Media Group's main office is on Park Avenue, but many of Norah's clients live and work in Los Angeles. In fact, she used to represent Janice Dickinson, and she first came to my attention while Janice was appearing in my film *His Highness Hollywood*.

"Who is it?" Norah demanded when I told her about the basketball star who played a starring role in the tape. I told her I would tell her in time, but I first wanted to know if this was up her alley. "This is perfect for the tabloids, sweetie. My best friend is the editor of *The Enquirer* and also *Radar*."

"Who, Dylan [Howard]? You're friends with Dylan?" I asked.

"Dylan, Lachlan [Cartwright], Barry Levine; I know them all. First of all, can you tell me who?"

"No, but it's huge," I replied cagily. "A-list." That got her attention.

"First we need to talk to the *Radar* people, then I have to speak to TMZ, *Daily Mail*. Those three first," Norah said. "I have to go to first people first. It's a triple-down and then they do deals with this one and that one, release the video, and write about it. It's a whole thing that happens."

I asked Norah if it was in the best interests of the model to release the sex tape to further her career. She kept pressing me about who the athlete was. I told her, the world's most famous basketball star. She said, "Oh, shit, Lebron. Will Lebron release it anyway or is it all in her hands?" Norah asked.

"In her hands," I replied.

"She would be in deep shit," Norah said. "I mean, can she try to do a deal with him to get paid off?" I told her she wanted to become famous to further her career. "Is she a well-known model?" Norah asked. "She's up and coming, not famous," I replied. "Could it boost her notoriety?" I asked.

"Look what it did with Kim Kardashian," Norah replied. "That's how she sort of got famous."

How much would you charge for this? I asked her.

"Probably just a fee," Norah said. "You know, five K." Then, if the model wanted "full service," including an ongoing campaign to keep her name in the media, the rate would be another five thousand dollars per month or more, depending on the services.

"Best is to release it to print first and then TV would come after. This is good, though. I'd love to be involved. That's what I do. I was trained by the tabloids. There's not many PR people who know the tabloids. I mean, who can call the editor in chief of *The Enquirer*? Not many."

I asked her if the tape was worth something to a media outlet and how much it could fetch.

"I can call and check for you. The only people who really pay are the *Daily Mail* and *The Enquirer*. I'd have to feel it out.

"I mean, listen—as a woman, do I think she should do this? No!" she continued. "But if she wants to be a celebrity, that's another question. It depends where she wants to go. She should show you the tape on a computer just to make sure the tape is real."

My next call was the Vivid publicist to whom Tess Allmon had referred me. When I reached Jackie Markham at her New York office, I told her that I knew a woman in Miami who had a sex tape featuring a well-known athlete. Would she be interested in taking a look at it?

"Is she on the tape?" she asked.

"Yes. She's a model," I told her. "And the basketball player is the most famous basketball player in the world."

"Lebron?"

"I can't say," I replied, laughing.

"Well, if you're going to let us see it, we'll know in a minute," she pointed out.

"Right. Would you be interested in seeing it?"

"Yeah, but the problem is this: When it comes to actually marketing and selling a sex tape, both parties need to sign off."

"There's no way around that?" I asked.

"Not that I know of, unless the law's changed. It would be considered an invasion of privacy."

"So, there's no way she can get that tape out, then?" I asked.

"Nope."

"I mean, how did Kim Kardashian get hers out, and all those other people?"

"A third party brought it to Vivid," she explained. "Vivid got in touch with the Kardashian family and explained the truth, which is if [their representative] doesn't buy it and pay for it, there's a good chance that other sites will put it up, portions of the sex tape, and not charge for it, and they'll never get anything."

"I better get back to her. Can I put her in touch with you? I'm just the middleman here and I don't want to be involved in this directly."

"She should talk to Steven [Hirsch]. He can explain how this works. If Steven winds up talking to Lebron, he'd tell him, 'If you just want to let this go and try to keep it a secret, that's fine. But chances are—and this has happened over and over and over again, so we know it to be true—it's going to get out one way or another. If not all, parts of it will get out, in which case he won't get a penny. So why not work for us, and we'll make sure that it will not only get out but that it will be distributed the way you want. You'll get a nice payment for it. You'll probably get a royalty, et cetera, et cetera."

"What could something like that fetch?" I asked. "Any idea? If it's authentic?"

"If it is who you say it is, my guess is an enormous amount of money."

"What's an enormous amount?" I pressed. "Without committing to anything."

"I can tell you right now. Kim Kardashian's movie came out in '07, and she's made millions."

"So this could turn into millions? Is that correct?"

"It could absolutely."

"Can I have this woman call you if she's interested?" I asked.

Markham then spent a significant amount of time trying to get the model's name and my contact info. It was clear she was definitely very interested. She wanted to get her hands on that tape. I could picture the dollar signs in her eyes.

I told her that the model had dreams of making "gazillions," but that it sounded from our conversation like unless she got the basketball player to sign on, she could forget it. "Correct me if I'm wrong. Is that the gist?"

She was convinced we were talking about Lebron. "Yeah, and, you know, he's come so far in such a short time, he doesn't really have to worry that it will hurt him in any way," she explained.

She asked again how she could reach me. I told her my friend would be in touch and I quickly hung up, a little wiser about how these things work and fairly convinced that Janice Dickinson's information was accurate. It is clear that Vivid would not have announced plans to distribute Kim's tape without a clear indication from the family that they would give the go-ahead once they had come to terms on a price.

The so-called lawsuit and press release about Kim's dismay appeared to be nothing more than an attempt to portray herself as the victim of an unscrupulous thief or Ray J himself. Whether she planned it from the beginning is still an open question, even though the remarkable parallel to her friend Paris Hilton's own rise to fame seems to leave the answer to that question fairly obvious. However, I asked myself a question I would ask time and again in various forms while chronicling the rise of the Kardashian dynasty:

If indeed Kim or Kris engineered the release of the sex tape to further their careers, so what? Marilyn Monroe once said, "Hollywood is a place where they'll pay you a thousand dollars for a kiss and fifty cents for your soul. I know, because I turned down the first offer often enough and held out for the fifty cents."

If the Kardashians were willing to sell their souls for five million dollars, at least they weren't selling themselves cheap like poor Marilyn.

The Kardashian girls early on in their careers.

Photo by Chris Polk/FilmMagic

Bruce Jenner won the Olympic gold in Montreal in 1976.

Photo by James Drake/Sports Illustrated/Getty Images

Kris and Bruce Jenner
with their two young
daughters, Kylie (left) and
Kendall (right), in 2000 at
a Disney Premiere.
Scott Nelson/AFP/Getty Images

Robert Kardashian (center), with his good friend and client, O.J. Simpson.
Vince Bucci/AFP/Getty Images

Kim Kardashian used to be inseparable from Paris Hilton. Kim's ex-boyfriend Ray J and close friend Serena Williams are pictured with them. *Photo by Chris Polk/FilmMagic for Bragman Nyman Cafarelli*

Kim with ex-husband Kris Humphries, Khloé Kardashian with estranged husband Lamar Odom, and Kris Jenner. *Photo by Denise Truscello/WireImage*

THE KARDASHIAN

Kim: 2006
Photo by Michael Tran/FilmMagic

Kim: 2014
Photo by Larry Busacca/Getty Images

Kourtney: 2006
Photo by Chris Weeks/WireImage

Kourtney: 2015
MARK RALSTON/AFP/Getty Images

TRANSFORMATIONS

Khloé: 2006
Photo by Enos Solomon/FilmMagic

Khloé: 2014
Photo by Jason LaVeris/FilmMagic

Kris: 2006
Photo by Mark Mainz/Getty Images

Kris: 2015
Photo by Jon Kopaloff/FilmMagic

Caitlyn Jenner receives the Arthur Ashe Courage Award at the ESPYS in 2015. *Photo by Kevin Winter/Getty Images*

Estranged couple and parents of three young children, Scott Disick and Kourtney Kardashian have had a turbulent relationship.
Photo by Bauer-Griffin/GC Images

Rob Kardashian has battled many demons the past few years.
Photo by JB Lacroix/WireImage

Kim's butt: real or fake?

Photo by Raymond Hall/GC Images

Photo by Larry Busacca/Getty Images for DuJour

Kim and Kanye with daughter North at Charles de Gaulle airport in Paris.

Photo by Marc Piasecki/GC Images

Kendall and Kylie Jenner are the future of the Kardashian Dynasty.

Photo by Jason LaVeris/FilmMagic

There are as many different versions about how *Keeping Up with the Kardashians* came to happen as there are Kardashians. According to Kris Jenner, the idea germinated with Deena Katz, the casting director of the reality show *I'm a Celebrity . . . Get Me Out of Here*, on which Bruce Jenner had appeared as a contestant in 2003. The story Kris tells is that Deena was over at the house one day and observed the everyday chaos. Kris was booking speeches for Bruce while simultaneously answering the phones and talking to the intercom to inform the various kids that they had calls. When Katz saw Kris intercom ten-year-old Kylie, she was flabbergasted. "This is the craziest house I have ever been in," she purportedly said. "You really need a reality show." It was Katz who suggested that Kris contact Ryan Seacrest's people.

Seacrest had exploded to fame as the host of the immensely popular *American Idol* show and had recently formed a production company, looking for projects. Katz set up the meeting and Kris raced right over to pitch the concept.

In *Kardashian Konfidential*, the girls credit another family friend with the idea:

One of our mom's best friends is Kathie Lee Gifford. She's on the Today *show and she's also the godmother of our little sisters. . . . She's very religious, and unlike most of our mom's friends, she likes to talk about religion. We usually only see her a couple of times a year, but we see her now more often because we go on her show. Whenever Kathie Lee would visit us, she'd say, "You are such a crazy family! Where are the cameras? We need cameras in here!" She thought our family would make a really funny show. . . . And literally a week later we had all these people with cameras in our house filming, and it was on the air really soon after that.*

Whoever came up with the idea first, Seacrest was open to the idea. *The Osbournes*, which aired from 2002 to 2005 on MTV, had followed the antics of a famously dysfunctional family, Ozzy and Sharon Osbourne and their kids, and had proved ratings gold for the music network, garnering its highest ratings. It happened to be one of Seacrest's favorite shows. A year before Kris pitched the show about her family, A&E had debuted a show about rocker Gene Simmons's family, and it too had proved an immediate success. Seacrest, like most of America, had been observing the meteoric rise of Kim Kardashian following her sex tape and wondered if her family was as colorful as she was.

He dispatched one of his employees to film a Kardashian family barbecue and get a sense of the dynamic. "I remember perfectly," he told *Haute Living* magazine. "[The cameraman] called me from their house and said, 'It's absolutely golden; you're going to die when you see this tape. They're so funny, they're so fun, there is so much love in this family, and they're so chaotic—they throw each other in the pool!' We watched it and rushed the tape to E! immediately, and that was the beginning."

But according to E!'s vice president of original programming, Lisa Berger, she was not immediately sold on the idea. "The family had been around town with the sister idea [for a series]," she told the *Hollywood Reporter*. "When we got a call from Ryan Seacrest Productions asking if we had met with the Kardashian sisters, I said, 'Honest to God, I'm not sure if there's a show there.'" But Seacrest wasn't about to take no for an answer. If Berger saw what he had seen on the tape, he was sure she would change her mind. He also heavily played up Bruce Jenner's participation to convince her that they weren't complete unknowns. Finally she sat down to meet the whole family, and Berger was sold.

"The addition of Kris and Bruce made the show what it is," she recalled. "What was most noticeable was Kris's sense of business. She wasn't a typical overbearing showbiz mom, but she knows how far she can push her kids and how far she can push the show."

Seacrest enlisted Bunim/Murray Productions, which had produced *The Simple Life*, and now all that was missing was a title. That fell into place when the Bunim/Murray showrunner, Farnaz Farjam, arrived out of breath for a meeting a few days into production and announced, "I'm sorry I'm late. I'm just having a really hard time keeping up with the Kardashians."

As filming began, the producers sensed that they had struck gold. "This family is sort of a ready-made sitcom," Kris's fellow executive producer Jonathan Murray later observed. "You've got Bruce as the conservative dad, you've got Kris as the crazy mom and you've got Kim the beautiful daughter and Khloé the crazy wisecracking sister. It's like a producer's dream."

When the first episode finally aired on October 14, 2007—only months after getting the green light—Americans didn't really know what to expect. It's hard to believe today, but nobody knew anything about the family other than the fact that one of the daughters had starred in a notorious sex tape.

"At the heart of the series—despite the catfights and endless sarcasm—is a family that truly loves and supports one another," announced Seacrest before the first episode aired. "The familiar dynamics of this family make them one Hollywood bunch that is sure to entertain."

Bruce Jenner was a name familiar to older Americans, but those who remembered him weren't really the target demographic. That may be one of the reasons why his name was not featured in the advance hype, nor indeed in the show's title, even though, as the *New York Times* would observe, "he is the only person in his household to have actually accomplished anything."

It is instructive to hear Kris Jenner discuss the family meeting she called before shooting began. Gathering Bruce and the clan together, she reports that she informed them that there was only one formula for the show's success. "I think the only way to make this show successful is to really be real about it," she allegedly told them. It's entirely possible that she meant it at the time.

In the very first scene, before the opening credits roll, the viewer is introduced for the first time to Kim's ass, as Kris observes her bending to retrieve something from the fridge and disparagingly refers to her "junk in the trunk." It was an inauspicious start, but also entirely appropriate. Because, before too long, it seemed that Kim's ass would have an empire all its own. And like virtually everything in the ensuing ten seasons, this was not an accident. Minutes later, viewers meet Kris Jenner for the first time and learn that she is not only the mother but also the manager of her clan.

The significance of Kris's central role would become apparent early in the episode, when we see Kim on her way to an interview with Tyra Banks, in which the topic of her sex tape would inevitably come up. "When I first heard about the tape, as her mother I wanted to kill her but as her manager I knew that I had a job to do," Kris confesses. In her review the next day, Ginia Bellafante of the *New York Times* cynically translates this scene for her readers.

"As a parent, Ms. Kardashian's mother, Kris Jenner, was concerned for her daughter, she explains. But as her manager, she thought, well, hot-diggity," writes Bellafante.

Indeed, Kris would eventually concede as much when she admitted to the *Hollywood Reporter* that she had essentially decided to capitalize on the tape. "I would never think I knew enough to care for a situation like that. What's that Kenny Rogers line? 'You got to know when to hold 'em and know when to fold 'em.' All I knew was that I had to make some lemonade out of these lemons fast. Real fast. . . . My job was trying to take my kids' 15 minutes and turn it into 30."

Although the term *momager*—which she would trademark in 2012—would not come until later, it became apparent to both writers as early as that first episode that Kris was the heart and soul of the family. They might have tuned in to watch Kim, but it was Kris and her antics that would keep viewers riveted, even if the media could not at first see the appeal. Indeed, the critics savaged the show right off the bat. The *Times* compared it unfavorably to what they called the "gold standard" of the genre, Gene Simmons's *Family Jewels*.

Unlike that show, writes Ginia Bellafante, "The Kardashian show is not about an eccentric family living conventionally; it is purely about some desperate women climbing to the margins of fame, and that feels a lot creepier." Amaya Rivera of *Popmatters* agreed, laying out the basic premise of the show at the same time.

"As far as plot goes, it's hard to imagine anything more boring," she writes.

> *Kim, Khloé, and Kourtney, all in their late 20s, pal around, argue and fight with one another, and occasionally with their brother Rob—and that's about it. They take care of and probably negatively influence their 12-year-old half sisters Kylie and Kendall, while their mother Kris (notice all the K'S!) plays best*

friend to all of them, living it up with the three older girls in Vegas for example, while Bruce Jenner plays the straight man, continually befuddled by the wackiness around him. . . . There is something disturbing about the Kardashians' intense hunger for fame. But even worse—it is downright boring to watch this family live out their tedious lives.

When the ratings rolled in, however, it was quickly apparent that viewers disagreed. The first episode garnered just under one million viewers, and within a month the show was the highest-rated Sunday-night cable show in the all-important eighteen-to-thirty-four female demographic, garnering a total viewership of 1.3 million.

The viewers had apparently spotted something that the critics had not. It was not so much the dysfunctional family that kept eyeballs glued to the screen. On that score, the Kardashians and Jenners hardly measured up to the wacky Osbourne clan. But they had clearly never seen a mother like Kris, and that hit home during episode 4, when the show appeared to really hit its stride.

It's not that the first three episodes had any shortage of risqué scenes. In the very first episode, for example, Kim is showing her friend Robin Antin, creator of the Pussycat Dolls, her sixteenth-anniversary gift for Kris and Bruce—a stripper pole installed in their bedroom. Kylie, nine years old and wearing three-inch heels, marches in and announces, "Look what I can do," before gyrating and performing a suggestive routine on the pole, to the delight of her older sister. In the middle of the routine, Bruce happens to walk in with a stern expression and admonishes his daughter, saying, "I just don't think that's appropriate. It's not funny," before slinging her over his shoulder and carrying her out of the room. In the same episode, Khloé conducts a mock interview with Kim to prepare for her upcoming Tyra Banks appearance.

"Why did you make a sex tape?" she asks her older sister.

"Because I was horny and felt like it," Kim replies.

In the second episode, Kris hires a nanny named Bree to look after Kylie and Kendall while she is working at the store. Sure enough, while she is gone, the nanny ends up sunbathing topless by the pool and parading through the house in front of Bruce wearing a bra top.

But that pales in comparison to the premise of episode 3, which has Joe Francis—the sleazy producer behind the Girls Gone Wild topless spring-break videos—calling Kris from jail, where he has been serving time for racketeering and subsequently keeping contraband in his cell. He wants the Kardashian girls to fly to Mexico to be spokesmodels for his new Girls Gone Wild bikini line. While they are off cavorting south of the border, Kris hires Bruce's son Brody Jenner to babysit for Kylie and Kendall. Brody invites his friend and manager Frankie over, and we see the girls cavorting around the stripper pole, lifting their shirts and mimicking Girls Gone Wild while Frankie videos their antics, offers to be their manager, and says he plans to post the videos on "YouTube or something."

In its episode review the next day, the Buddy TV blog called the whole episode "rather sad" and asked a pointed question: "The fact that the parents would allow these incidents into the show . . . makes me wonder just exactly what Kris Kardashian is willing to do to get 'exposure' for her family."

It only took one more episode to find out.

Episode 4 starts off with Kris receiving a call from *Playboy* asking if Kim will pose for their celebrity issue in December. Surely anybody who released a sex tape would have no problem posing for the tamer-in-comparison men's magazine. Kim's mother—who had claimed to be mortified by her daughter's raunchy tape—heads down to the store to share the news. "They really, really, really, really want you to do it," she tells Kim. "Wouldn't it be fun?"

Kim is less than enamored of the idea. She shares her thoughts with the viewers. "Ever since the sex-tape scandal, I have to be very careful about how I'm perceived," she confides. Cut to Kris in the store saying, "I think it would be an awesome experience for you, if nothing else. On top of all of that, it's a ton of money."

Kim protests, wondering if she will be seen only as the girl who takes her clothes off. "Can she do anything else?" she wonders if her public will be asking. Soon enough, the family gets in on the act, and we see Kim sitting down and debating the merits. "It's the December cover, it's a really big deal," she says, revealing that she's been assured *Playboy* will keep it classy. They worry that Bruce will not approve. "We know what Bruce will think. He's very conservative," Kris says. The girls point out that he was once on the cover of *Playgirl*, so he's one to judge.

Asked what she thinks Kim should do, Kris is unequivocal. "I think she should do it; it will be really great."

For the first time, we get a glimpse of the business side of the burgeoning empire. "Of course you want her to do it, with your ten percent commission," says Kourtney. When Bruce enters the room and finds out what's going on, he tells Kim that she would be taking a big risk, at which point the girls tease her and suggest she pose instead for *Penthouse*. "Do it with class and undress that ass."

Later, we hear Bruce telling Kris that he's the only one who voted no. "I mean, she's got a sex tape out and now she's doing *Playboy*. Please, this is your daughter," he says in disgust. Kris assures him that Kim doesn't have to pose completely undressed. "Okay, she doesn't have to show nipple," he retorts. "She's showing everything else."

Cut to the *Playboy* photo shoot, where we see Kim posing in lingerie. The creative director approaches her to suggest she take her top off, as Kris looks on. "I just don't want to be so exposed for any of the shots," she says, looking genuinely uncomfortable. In the dressing room, she tells her mother that she is not comfortable posing topless. Kris reassures her that they simply want her to take her clothes off so that they can cover her with something else. We then see a *Playboy* employee telling them that he has been talking to Hef, who wants to see the shoot "pumped up." Kim continues to resist being shot topless, even though she already had been in her first ad campaign months earlier, for the Christopher Brian apparel collection, where she posed topless wearing just jeans. Anybody who had seen that campaign— shot before Kim was well known—would suspect that her reluctance was feigned for the cameras, but for those who knew her only as a sex-tape star, it was likely mission accomplished.

Days later, we see the family looking over the finished results, with Kim telling her sisters how Kris had tried to get her to show more skin. "All you have to do is lay there and look gorgeous," her mother replies.

To this, Kim challenges Kris, "Mom, why don't you do it?" Kris feigns astonishment. "A naked photo shoot? I would let somebody see me naked, like a photographer?" Next thing you know, Kris has agreed to the idea. Kim tells the viewers that she has decided to play manager for a day and give Kris "a taste of her own medicine." We then see Kris in a photo studio, naked except for an American flag wrapped around her, and wearing Bruce's gold medal around her neck. "Can we just do one with her boobs exposed?" Kim asks.

It ends with Kim telling the camera that she can't believe how comfortable her mom is being naked. Eventually Kris presents the photos to Bruce as a present. If one had to pinpoint the moment that the Kardashians became a cultural phenomenon, it is this epi- sode. It launched them into the zeitgeist, in which they would soon become lodged in a love-them-or-loathe-them place in the American psyche.

Suddenly, people were buzzing about the crazy mom who tried to convince her reluctant daughter to pose nude for *Playboy* and "Oh, by the way, you may have heard that Kim Kardashian is a slut but she is actually very shy and didn't want to pose nude until her mother forced her." Suddenly, people wanted to see more.

CHAPTER TEN

Only a month after the first episode of *Keeping Up with the Kardashians* aired, E! announced that it had ordered a second season. "The buzz surrounding the series is huge, and viewers have clearly fallen for the Kardashians," the network's VP for series development announced.

For many, the instant success of their TV show and its accompanying fame and fortune would have been enough. For Kris Jenner, it was only a beginning. Today it is common to hear the media referring to the Kardashians as a "brand." From the moment the first episode of *Keeping Up with the Kardashians* aired, that is exactly the word that was going through Kris's head. As a manager with a financial stake in her daughters' careers, the most logical step would have been to focus on the highly bankable Kim, who was already in great demand before she became a reality-TV personality. She had done a high-profile campaign for Christopher Brian apparel, and the calls had already been pouring in with offers of personal appearances, modeling assignments, and other ventures. Kris had already quietly incorporated a company, Jenner Communications, to handle it all, along with Bruce's career and the new TV show.

On top of Kim's burgeoning popularity, she was also the low-est maintenance of the kids by far. Khloé had recently been busted for a DUI and failure to enroll in an alcohol-treatment program and sentenced to a jail stint at the same facility where Paris had served her time. Although she appeared happy-go-lucky on air, she was still deeply troubled behind the scenes and was known for her hard-partying ways. Rob was focused on school, and Kourtney was busy running the D-A-S-H boutique in Calabasas that she and her sisters had started in 2006 but was really her baby. Kris would later compare each of her daughters to a dance. Kourtney, she described as a tango— "spicy and difficult at times"; Khloé, a salsa—"sassy and all over the place"; and Kim, a waltz—"easy, smooth and beautiful."

Besides Kim, none of them seemed like a logical candidate for a career in the public eye—at least not outside the tight confines of their reality show. Kris thought otherwise. She saw the show as what she called a "vehicle" to create a family empire, and she was tireless in her mission. "There was no way to do this half-assed," she recalled in her memoir. "I knew I could not do this as a hobby, or part-time, or just a couple of hours a day. This job required that I live, breathe, eat, sleep it 24/7, and once I decided to do that . . . there was no turning back."

She was now more than just a wife and mother, she reflected; she was a "producer, manager, negotiator, a publicist, a business manager, a stylist, and at times a caterer and set decorator." And although Kris is known to engage in hyperbole and often to downplay the contribu-tions of her extensive staff, in the beginning she undeniably performed all those functions and more. In Kim, she also had a partner whose business savvy was arguably as sharp as her own, having watched and observed the phenomenal success of Paris Hilton close up.

However, Kim would tell journalist Jo Piazza that when she ini-tially sat down with her mother to talk about a business model as early as 2007, they agreed that they would not necessarily follow the Paris Hilton example, although it was a "good start." Instead, she explained, "We make our own model. My mom and I talk about it all the time." In the first year or two, however, it was hard not to draw obvious parallels between the two socialites, who had both shot to fame on the notoriety of their sex tapes.

In her 2011 book *Celebrity Inc.*, about the way celebrities cash in on their fame, Piazza analyzed the similarities and differences between Kim and Paris. She found that Kim had the advantage of learning from Paris's mistakes and, unlike Paris, had few friends beside her sisters. The tight-knit family had its built-in advantages, and Kim trusted nobody outside the clan.

Piazza believed the success of each reflected their respective eras. "Hilton represented all the excesses of Bush-era wealth and conspicuous consumption," she wrote, "whereas Kardashian, despite her upper-class income, displayed a work ethic worthy of the middle class. Ask any of the Kardashians about their success and they will pepper their answers with work, work, work."

Indeed, when *Redbook* editor in chief Jill Herzig spent time with the Kardashians for a profile, she was struck by two things.

"The Kardashians are nothing if not joyful," she wrote, "and they are the hardest workers you will ever meet. They wake up at 5AM, and they work until they fall down at night. Kim was tweeting from a Golden Globes party at 3AM, and then there she was at 6AM, chipper, professional and ready to do her thing."

Paris too worked hard to create her brand, but that was not the image she cultivated for her fans, who were happy to see her as a ditzy party girl spending her inherited millions. But as Piazza noted, Kim also gained an early reputation for being a "nice girl." Throughout her peak years, Paris was notorious for her bad behavior—drug busts, pantiless paparazzi photos, even controversial racist and homophobic tirades, such as the time she called a male friend a "faggot" or told the camera "we're like two niggers" while dancing at a club. Paris was also known to have no time for the little people and would often refuse to look her fans in the eye. At the time, it was an important part of her appeal.

"The part that I don't understand," observed Eric Hirschberg, president of the marketing giant Deutsch Inc., in 2006. "Paris has this meanness that's in her persona. And it's embraced. Girls from the kind of places she makes fun of on *The Simple Life* want to wear her perfume. Her job is to party. She seems to answer to no one. . . . And there's a bit of anarchy there—she's like the princess running around the palace knocking over vases."

Meanwhile, Kim from the outset would often linger for hours signing photographs or posing for selfies with fans, while always smiling and interacting with them. By most accounts, she doesn't do drugs and rarely drinks. She only shows up at clubs when she is paid to do so and always leaves before midnight. In fact, she rarely swears, and never in public.

"I remember this one time when I used the F-word—and everyone was like, I can't believe you said that!" she told *The Guardian*. "You never say that! I am really cautious about what I say and do. If I look at the message I'm portraying, I think it definitely is be who you are, but be your best you."

She was also very candid about her body-image issues, which struck a chord with many of her young fans and set her up as a role model of sorts, at least in the early years. The constant mention on the show of her "booty" became a recurring theme in the tabloids and Kris was quick to credit her Armenian appetite for her most famous asset.

"I don't ever really diet because I don't want to be miserable," she once told a reporter. "I love food." Kris quickly struck an endorsement deal with Kim to model Bongo Jeans, which promised to show off the famous butt to good advantage.

"I'm not your typical stick-skinny model," she said, promoting the jeans. "There are super-skinny girls doing ad campaigns and I don't think it's realistic. I don't like that [skinny] body image. I'm very proud of my body image."

And yet when GNC came calling about having the family promote "weight loss supplements," Kris was thrilled, sending just one more of the mixed messages that the public would receive from the Kardashians over the years, as the entire family is seen on the show ingesting the diet cleanse QuickTrim and shilling for it in interviews and on social media.

Jeans and supplements were only the beginning. Before long, the Kardashian name was tied to a long line of merchandise, fashion, and product endorsements in rapid succession. But who was buying?

Kim told a British reporter that she considers her typical fan "a younger girl, like 15 or 16, who loves fashion, loves to be a girly girl, loves beauty, glam."

That wasn't much different from Hilton's target demographic. Was there room enough for two socialite reality-TV stars to compete for the pocket money of young girls leading mundane lives and desperate to bathe themselves in the glamor and fabulous lifestyles of these celebrities?

By the time the Kardashians came along to do battle for the hearts and pocketbooks of this demographic, Paris—shrewd businesswoman in her own right and surrounded by handlers who had been crunching the data—sensed that she needed to tweak her ebbing brand.

"With Paris, there's so much debauchery and valuelessness to her brand, she'll have to figure out a way to get past that," Hirschberg told the *Baltimore Sun* in August 2006. "There needs to be some humanity."

Given what we saw when Kim Kardashian reached a similar point in her career a few years later, it's instructive to look at how Paris was trying to reposition herself in the months before her protégée burst onto the scene. In late 2006, she released an album, *Paris*, on the Warner label, clearly targeted at the urban market. It appeared to be working. Its reggae-inspired single, "Stars Are Blind," became the most requested song in both the New York and LA markets, and Paris immediately launched an aggressive media campaign to announce her rebranding.

"I haven't accepted money from my parents since I was 18," she told the *Baltimore Sun*. "I have things no heiress has. I've done it all on my own, like a hustler."

Words like *hustler* started to feature in her interviews, which began to take on a decidedly "street" tone. Watching the noticeable shift in her branding, one paper observed that she was self-consciously trying to align herself with "hip-hop's boot-strap ethos." Indeed, she began hanging out with hip-hop artists and was frequently photographed in urban music clubs instead of the vapid, party-till-you-drop LA hot spots with which she had always been associated.

"I love hip-hop," she declared in an interview promoting *Paris*. "I grew up listening to Dr. Dre. With the hip-hop world, they came from nothing, from the streets. I respect their turning into these huge stars with huge mansions, all on their own." And while she had for years played up her image as a wealthy heiress, which was a central theme of *The Simple Life*, she now disingenuously made a conscious effort to distance herself from that image, almost to the point of absurdity.

"When I moved to L.A., I swear on my life I didn't have anything," she said, failing to note that her previous address had been New York's swanky Waldorf Astoria. "I told my mom I didn't want any money. And I've done it all on my own. All this, I bought for myself: my cars, my house. Who can say that at my age who's an heiress?"

She proceeded to sign on to star in a futuristic musical-comedy/horror film called *Repo! The Genetic Opera*, in which she played a character named Amber Sweet, who is addicted to surgery and Zydrate, a potent illegal opiate extracted from dead bodies, which Amber obtains from a grave robber in exchange for sex. The movie wasn't particularly well received but it succeeded in giving her a grittier image. It's entirely possible that if Paris had successfully continued on this course, there would have been no opening for Kim and her family to usurp her place in the immensely lucrative teen-girl and young-female market that would be their bread and butter for the next decade. The turning point, from a brand-marketing perspective, appears to be Hilton's appearance on David Letterman's show only a week before *Keeping Up with the Kardashians* debuted on E!.

Paris was in full-tilt rebranding mode when she appeared on Letterman to promote a new fragrance line in September 2007. The talk show king's hip, sophisticated, urban audience was just the demographic that Paris was looking toward to expand her retail empire. Her recent stint in prison was a mixed blessing, because it had the potential to bolster her urban credibility but had somewhat undermined it when her connections had at first appeared to keep her out of jail and then helped keep her isolated in the infirmary for her entire stay.

Letterman had apparently agreed to her handlers' demands that he refrain from asking her about jail. It worked with Larry King who had, in his typical fashion, lobbed nothing but softballs at her. Similarly, Letterman was not known as a hard-hitting journalist but, after asking her if she liked New York, he wasted no time cutting to the chase. "So how did you find your time in jail?" he asked. Left uncharacteristically speechless, Paris answered, "Not so much," before squirming through a rapid series of uncomfortable additional questions about the food and whether she had made any friends. When an audience member yelled out, "I love you, Paris!" the host immediately asked if it was someone she had met in jail. "Now you're making me sad," she pouted.

Finally, she lost it. "I'm not answering any more questions about it," she retorted. "I'm here for my clothing line, my movie, and my perfume." When that still didn't stop the questions, she snapped,

"I've moved on with my life so I don't really want to talk about it anymore."

Seemingly willing to acquiesce and help her shill for her new perfume, Letterman proceeded to spray it on himself and then down the entire bottle as Paris looked on, mortified.

By the following morning, her rebranding had appeared to suffer a spectacular setback, as clips of her appearance and the resulting buzz reduced her to a punch line that she never really appeared to transcend. More important, it left a giant void for a new reality star to fill.

While promoting her new album a year earlier, Paris had declared, "The book, the perfume, the show, the album. I wanted to do the album last because I wanted to do it like no one else has ever done it before. I don't think there's ever been anyone like me that's lasted. And I'm going to keep on lasting."

Indeed, Paris never went away. But, as Jo Piazza noted, she appeared to cede the domestic market to the new upstarts as she refocused her fragrance and clothing lines overseas, especially on Japan, where Paris is still a marketing force.

When Kim emerged as a phenomenon soon after, there was one thing she definitely had in common with Paris Hilton. Both could command hefty fees just to show up at a club or event. By 2011, Kim was getting anywhere from $100,000 to $250,000 to fly to an ordinary club appearance, and as much as $1 million for New Year's Eve. "The appearances are good moneymakers," she told *Cosmopolitan*. "And they're also a great way for me to connect with people in places like Oklahoma, where I never would go otherwise."

At one such paid appearance at a Las Vegas pool party, somebody asked Khloé whether she thought Kim was the new Paris Hilton. "No. I think she is way better than Paris Hilton," Khloé replied. "I think she's the new Kim Kardashian. Kim has her own title. She doesn't need anybody else's."

Paris signaled that she was resentful of Kim's success when she told a radio interviewer that Kim's butt "looks like cottage cheese inside a big trash bag." For her part, Kim graciously pretended that there was no bad blood between the two former friends, even though she acknowledged that the two didn't speak anymore.

"I definitely respect everything she's done," she told a reporter, when asked whether there was a feud. "She's very cool and has done so much in her life, and she's taught me so much, just being a friend for so long. But I don't look at it like that. I mean, I guess you would see the comparisons—the reality shows and stuff like that—but I don't know. I'm kind of like the sisterhood, with my sisters and my family. I've never thought of myself like that."

By 2011, according to Piazza, more Americans had heard of Hilton than Kim Kardashian (97 percent to 90 percent). But in every other way, Kim had surpassed Paris, according to the Davie Brown Index, which determines a celebrity's marketing value to a corporate brand.

"Kardashian had a stronger appeal score (59 vs. 45 out of a possible 100)," Brown wrote, "was more likely to be a trendsetter (66 vs. 55), had more endorsement potential (63 vs. 48), and was more aspirational (56 vs. 42). More brands wanted to sign Kardashian for endorsement deals, more consumers wanted to buy products that would allow them to be like her, and the public simply liked her more than they liked Hilton."

It was quickly becoming clear that there was a new girl in town, and Paris had been deposed from her throne. And although there were many marketing strategies that the two former friends had in common while building their brands, there was one in which Kim was in a league by herself, social media, which didn't really exist when Paris was at her peak. By 2012, Kim had fourteen million followers on Twitter, surpassing even Barack Obama. Eventually she would storm the new social media platform Instagram, where she would amass more "likes" than even Katy Perry, the queen of Twitter.

Kris didn't really understand the ins and outs of social media. But it didn't take her long to figure out how to profit from Kim's massive following. She let it be known that Kim's Tweets were for sale, and soon her daughter was shilling for a wide range of products. Although her fees vary depending on the product and the circumstances, Joan Barnes, president of Atlanta-based Marketing Specifics, revealed to the *New York Post* that a social-blogging company told her it had arranged for Kim to be paid $25,000 by Armani for just one Tweet. It soon became apparent why she commands such exorbitant fees. The Tweet drove forty thousand users to the Armani website in less than twenty-four hours. "Somebody who paid a million dollars would be tickled to get that level of response for a campaign," Barnes told the *Post*.

Witnessing Kim's Twitter success, Kris urged all the kids to devote a certain amount of time to social media, including blogs, Facebook posts, Twitter, and Instagram.

Kim described for the *Hollywood Reporter* how she uses social media to incorporate her massive fan base into the family's marketing strategies.

"I have a blog that has 40 million hits a month," she explained. "People leave comments: 'What shoes do you wear, and what lip gloss do you use?' My mom told us, 'So why not be a brand for our fans and give them what they want?' Many of our ideas [about what to endorse] come from our fans and then our mother makes it happen."

Meanwhile, Kris was busy, adding new ventures for her family every day. In 2008, the entire family competed on the celebrity edition of the TV game show *Family Feud*, hosted by Al Roker, against the family of football player Deion Sanders.

Not long afterward, Kim agreed to appear on season 7 of the popular ABC show *Dancing with the Stars*. It seemed like a good opportunity to introduce her to a mainstream audience, and Kim jumped at the chance. She probably later wished that she hadn't, because she was paired with professional dancer Mark Ballas and became the third contestant voted off the show. The judges described her performance as "cold," and Ballas later said that Kim "wasn't the best dancing partner."

A year later, she tried her hand at drama, signing on to appear in four episodes of the Nickelodeon surfer-themed show, *Beyond the Break*, playing a girl named Elle who is very possessive of her artist boyfriend and is willing to crush anybody who gets in her way.

"The most challenging part of playing the role of Elle was just trying to be the mean girl," she told *People*. "I've never really been that outspoken girl. It's the confrontation that I'm not used to, so I think doing that was really kind of refreshing in a weird, sick way." A year later, she would get behind the camera to produce a reality show called *The Spin Crowd*, following the employees of a Hollywood PR firm. The show was not well received and was cancelled after only eight episodes, but not for lack of effort on Kim's part. According to the show's central character, Jonathan Cheban, Kim went above and beyond the call of duty to promote the show. "She is the busiest woman I have ever met," he observed, "and yet once the show started, she was out promoting it on the *Today* show and on Twitter. She never flakes on you. That's what sets her apart. Her business model is about morals and standards, never screwing anybody and never flaking out."

And if the failure of *The Spin Crowd* proved that not everything the Kardashians touched turned to gold, their decision to lend their name to a prepaid debit card reconfirmed it. At the splashy launch party at New York's Pacha nightclub, the family gushed at how excited they were about the Kardashian Kard. They even alleged that the card had a higher social purpose.

"When we were growing up, we didn't have credit; we didn't know what it was like to try and get your first credit card," Kim told *Entertainment Tonight*. "But with this one you don't need credit; you don't even need a bank account.

"We wanted to provide people with something where they could learn their budgets; there is a spending limit on it. We are so excited that so many people are into this idea."

But it soon became apparent that the Kard was riddled with a slew of outrageous fees, leaving the parents of teenagers, who were the target market, fuming. Although a typical prepaid debit card is free, a twelve-month Kardashian Kard cost $99.95 just to own, including a monthly fee of $7.95. On top of that, users had to shell out $1 every time they added money to the card and $2 per transaction to pay bills automatically with the card. Soon after the Kard was launched, the Connecticut attorney general issued a strong rebuke to its manufacturer, questioning whether the Kard's "pernicious and predatory" fees were legal.

"Among the prepaid debit cards now on the market, the Kardashian Kard is particularly troubling because of its high fees combined with its appeal to financially unsophisticated young adult Kardashian fans," wrote Richard Blumenthal. "Keeping up with the Kardashians is impossible using these cards. This card—or kard— appears to specifically target young adults in evoking the name and image of the Kardashian family who showcase lives of luxury and extravagance. Known for their reality show—*Keeping Up with the Kardashians*—the family is marketing a dangerous financial fantasy."

Only a month after the launch and a barrage of negative publicity, the Kardashian family attorney announced that they were pulling out of the venture, claiming that the "negative spotlight . . . threatens everything for which they have worked."

Their association with QuickTrim also came under fire, after a group of customers filed a class-action suit against the Kardashians for "unsubstantiated, false and misleading claims" in ads, interviews, and Tweets about the efficacy of the supplement. The sisters had been hawking the pills and cleanses for years in various forums, including the reality show, Twitter, and interviews where they talked about the wonders of the supposed miraculous weight-loss supplement, which, according to the lawsuit, implied that QuickTrim "curbs cravings," "promotes weight loss," and "burns calories."

"Just did an amazing pilates class with @KimKardashian," Khloé Tweeted in 2010. "That and a little QuickTrim and my bikini bod will be ready in no time."

Their association with the product had reportedly netted the family millions since 2009, but it soon emerged that the primary ingredient was in fact a massive dose of caffeine, which the Food and Drug Administration had ruled was not a safe or effective weight-loss tool.

Eventually, the lawsuit was dismissed by a New York court, which ruled that a similar lawsuit had already been settled in California. But it was yet another reminder that the family needed to be more vigilant in their choice of endorsements if they were to safeguard their brand.

To that end, the family and especially Kim were playing a hands-on role in the creation of their own products. As Kim knew well, Paris Hilton's most successful venture was her line of perfumes—Paris Hilton for Women—which had mushroomed into a $2 billion fragrance empire, especially overseas.

Kris wasted no time in securing the infrastructure to start a family-branded perfume business of their own. In 2009, Kim launched a perfume line heralded by what would become her signature fragrance, Kim Kardashian by Kim Kardashian. It soon became the number-one-selling fragrance of the year for the beauty chain Sephora. By November 2010, Kim had reached number one on top of the celebrity loyalty list—which gauges consumer engagement with entertainment personalities—compiled by the consumer research company Brand Keys.

"There was a time when Paris Hilton topped that list, when she was the most famous person for being nothing we had ever seen," noted branding expert Robert Passikoff at the time. He also noted that many consumers associated Kim with entrepreneurship, much more so than other celebrities, including Paris Hilton.

And although the family was widely mocked and their show regularly dismissed as vapid fluff, the stuff of tabloid trash, the respectable media was beginning to take notice of the Kardashians' remarkable marketing clout and multimillion-dollar product empire. Curious about who was buying these products, the New York Times sent a reporter to the launch of a new Kim Kardashian line at the fashionable Bebe boutique. Discovering a line one hundred deep, they asked the fans what Kim represented for them.

"The average girl," replied a twenty-two-year-old Pennsylvania woman who worked for a D.C.-based political-media-buying company. "She represents fashion," said a twenty-two-year-old Bronx waitress. "I like the way she dresses." "She has an ethnic sex appeal," said a twenty-six-year-old Queens paralegal. "I like how she created a franchise with her sisters. That opens a lot of opportunities for women who have a spark of beauty and want to shine. She reminds me of Sophia Loren." A twenty-one-year-old Australian tourist took note of Kim's famous figure. "She stands out from every other celebrity in the world. She is natural and curvaceous. There are too many thin celebrities out there who make women feel they are overweight."

Whether it was the twentysomething working women who attended the jewelry launch or the tween girls who snapped up the Kardashian Silly Bandz Glam Pack during the twistable-rubber-band craze a year earlier, the Kardashians had brilliantly tapped into a profitable niche and had become what celebrity talent broker Ryan Schinman had described as "Kardashian Inc."

The importance of Kim to the family brand was obvious and hard to escape. But the show had created at least two other celebrities, and Kris was not going to miss the chance to milk her 10 percent commission from her other offspring.

As early as the first season, in fact, it is now clear, Keeping Up *with the Kardashians* was deliberately molding the image of each Kardashian with an eye to potential marketing opportunities. While the debut episode famously attempted to rehabilitate Kim's slutty sex-tape image and position her as the good girl by turning the tables on a *Playboy* shoot, it is instructive to look back on episode 5 of that same season.

In it, the family gathers at Robert's favorite Armenian restaurant to observe the fourth anniversary of his death. Later, Khloé—still devastated by remembering her beloved father—is seen having a meltdown at the D-A-S-H boutique. She ends up going to a club and getting drunk. On her way home, she is pulled over by the police and given a field sobriety test, which she fails.

The next day, Kris goes out to lunch with Kim, who eventually tells her that Khloé is in jail. Kris freaks out and calls Robert Shapiro, who got O.J. acquitted. Eventually, Kris picks up Khloé and they argue about whether to tell Bruce. When they do, he gives her a lecture and says he wonders what her dad would have thought.

It is entertaining and dramatic TV, except that Khloé was actually busted for DUI in March, before *Keeping Up with the Kardashians* even got the green light. The whole thing had been staged. But a brief onscreen disclaimer had in fact warned that "This episode features re-creations of actual events," so the producers had covered themselves with viewers who were aware of the chronology. Still, it was a harbinger of things to come, and would add fuel for critics who assert that just about everything about the show is scripted.

More significantly at the time, however, it set up Khloé as the bad-girl foil to her good sister Kim. Although Paris Hilton's star was already waning, she had proved that there was a significant demand for the bad-girl image that she represented.

CHAPTER ELEVEN

Having cultivated separate images for each of the girls, it was time to find a way to carve out their own sub-brands independent of Kim. The way Kris tells it, Kourtney announced out of the blue one day that the girls wanted to open up a new D-A-S-H store in Miami. If they were going to open a store there, "why not add a television component?" asked Kris. And so the first television spinoff was born—*Kourtney and Khloé Take Miami*. The show would follow the girls as they moved to Miami for the summer, designed and stocked the store, and hired the employees, who would become known as "D-A-S-H Dolls."

By now, anybody familiar with Kris's business acumen knew that Kris and the producers were likely brainstorming ways for the two sisters to move out from under Kim's shadow to help expand the family brand. Eventually, I presume, somebody proposed a spinoff about opening a second store, and voilà.

Of course, nothing could possibly be less dramatic than two sisters ordering merchandise and overseeing the renovations of a store. In order to spice things up and create the kind of situations that Kardashian followers had come to expect, the producers arranged to get Khloé her own Miami radio show. And in keeping with the edgy image that was being built for her, the show was hardly run-of-the-mill, standard fare. Instead she was given a five-week "trial run" of a late-night Miami talk show, airing from midnight to 3:00 a.m., titled *Khloé After Dark*.

The radio show itself, for anybody who bothered to tune in, was something of a dud. Reviewing the first show, the *Sun Sentinel* called it a "badly edited late-night infomercial for the South Beach shop owner and reality TV star." But that was hardly the point. Clearly the show was simply a vehicle to generate some seemingly impromptu situations for the TV show. And sure enough, by the second episode, there was enough drama to generate the kind of buzz guaranteed to keep viewers tuning in.

In the very first episode, Kim visits to help promote the new store but ends up getting into a fight with Khloé, who comes close to pulling the plug on the new operation. Nothing particularly groundbreaking, but Kim's presence guaranteed a strong premiere. By the second episode, however, the girls didn't need their famous sister's star power. It created enough buzz on its own to virtually guarantee the show a successful run. In a scene shot during the first installment of Khloé's radio show, Khloé did a segment on the prevalence of drugs in Miami, noting that people thought she was a "coke whore." During the segment in which she interviewed a "drug expert," she revealed that one of her employees had found coke in the changing room of the new store. She had stuck the drugs in her purse and she just happened to still have them on her. Taking the purported container out of her purse, she declared, "I have never done coke; I'm just not into that stuff. Look what I found at my store! It's, like, coke; I don't know, but what do you do? Do you, like, snort it through here?"

She then mimed snorting the coke, saying, "I'm so high! It's not mine, it's just cocaine, it's not mine!" This prompted a producer to lecture her about the propriety of her actions, telling her it was "dumb" and "stupid" while reminding her that just possessing cocaine is a felony. The radio show was suspended while Khloé was forced to undergo drug testing to prove she wasn't under the influence while on the air.

As if that wasn't enough drama for one show, Kourtney happened to take an art class where she made a friend, Jackie. They went to a lesbian club with the cameras in tow, and suddenly Kourtney was a bisexual.

Of course, the show's publicity machine went into high gear, reminding people that Khloé was still on probation for her 2007 DUI and that the coke in her purse could have sent her to jail, even though nobody ever actually saw the coke and it is hard to believe that Khloé would be stupid enough to carry coke around that wasn't hers and then pull it out live on air. Just to raise the tension, Kourtney gave media interviews in which she insisted the coke was indeed real.

Khloé told *Life and Style* the story of how she happened to come by the drugs.

> My employee was picking up a pile of clothes that customers had tried on, and it fell out. She called me into the dressing room, and it was in a little glass vial. I was leaving the dressing room, and a lot of customers walked in. I didn't know what to do, so I threw it in my purse. I was like, "I'll dispose of this in a second," and I went to help them. Then I forgot about it. Nothing registered until after the fact. Now, talking about it, I'm like, "OK, that would be really bad if I got (charged) with drug possession." But I don't do drugs. I don't have drugs in my purse. I'm not someone who needs to do drugs. . . . I'm too energetic and crazy as it is. I wouldn't want to see me on drugs.

Of course, no police came calling and nothing happened to Khloé as a consequence of her actions. But the show's ratings went through the roof, E! renewed it for a second season, and the Kardashians had chalked up another conquest in their never-ending drive for success.

For those who came into contact with the sisters during their Miami run, their sojourn in the city only reinforced growing rumors of divalike behavior. My friend Tim Johnson worked at the Clevelander, the popular South Beach hotel and restaurant where the sisters launched their Miami boutique and filmed segments of their show.

"It was mayhem," Johnson told me.

> They drove the hotel and staff crazy with a lot of outrageous demands. In the end it really wasn't worth all the publicity because we needed to accommodate them with so many demands, including a security team that I had never seen at any other event in Miami. The entire staff was not allowed to approach them and we were told to look away from them anytime there was eye contact. We basically had to work like robots. It was extremely hot when filming went on and they kept delaying and delaying the shoot because Kourtney kept complaining about heat exhaustion. There was so much complaining going on we really didn't know what to do.

Because the Miami D-A-S-H boutique is practically located in my backyard, I decided to pay a visit to see what all the fuss was about. Just to make it interesting, I brought along a friend named Trey on an undercover mission. When we arrived at the Collins Avenue store in the heart of South Beach, we found just a few customers milling about, mostly tourists who were visiting the store because they were fans of the shows. One customer, Tina, described herself as a "worshipper" of the family. Not many people seemed to be buying stuff.

Trey, who works as a fitness-club manager in Miami Beach, sometimes moonlights as a plus-size model when the opportunity arises.

Most recently, she was featured in a plus-size bikini shoot in Miami for a Hungarian magazine.

As we browsed through the merchandise, Trey complained that the clothes and accessories were overpriced and that the quality of the merchandise was "nothing special." She observed that much of it was manufactured in China. "Usually that means sweatshop," she complained. "I know people in the fashion business who manufacture in China. They tell me that almost every manufacturer in China is associated with sweatshop conditions. That concerns me a lot because the Kardashians are supposed to be a progressive family, with their interracial relationships and their concern about their origins in Armenia. I hope and pray that they are not exploiting workers in China."

I talked to a couple of the "D-A-S-H Dolls," who admitted that the Kardashians rarely visit D-A-S-H Miami. "I've never seen them," one salesgirl told me. "I guess they're too busy with the TV show."

Rhonda, a twenty-two-year-old tourist from Raleigh, North Carolina, told me she was appalled by how expensive the clothes were. "Ridiculous," she said. "I can shop at Forever 21 and buy a top or pants that are more stylish at a fraction of the price. I came here because I watch the show, but it's obvious they are trying to gouge consumers with their fame. That's not right. I will never set foot in this store again."

Meanwhile, Trey, twenty-nine, asked to speak to the store manager about applying for a job. The manager immediately told her there was a long queue of girls wanting to work there and that "at the moment there are no positions."

She sensed that it was her size that was the real factor. "They didn't even let me fill out an application," she said when we met up afterward. "Most of the sales staff were thin and beautiful. I felt insulted. Kim and Khloé are not exactly Kate Moss themselves. They have curves. It incenses me that I can't get a job there because I think they look at me as being too old and too heavy."

Although the Miami store might not be anything special, the show about its creation drew millions of viewers. The successful spin-off would not just add to the family's immensely profitable empire. It would also help create more Kardashians.

When I was dating Kim's former friend Sheba, she made an interesting observation. "The sisters don't look for boyfriends the way most girls do. Instead they look for new cast members for the show." Under normal circumstances, Scott Disick would have been exempt from that cynical assessment. He was dating Kourtney, six years his senior, for months before the show even aired and was even featured on the first episode of *Keeping Up with the Kardashians*. And considering the circumstances in which they met, she might have done well to be wary. It was Joe Francis, the family friend who runs the Girls Gone Wild soft-porn empire, who claims he introduced the two in 2006, though it would appear by his time line that the two actually met in 2007. "I introduced Kourtney and Scott at my house in Mexico," he later recalled. "Scott came as the guest of a friend of mine, and they met in my master bedroom."

Scott's tumultuous relationship with Kourtney would make for an important subplot during the first season of *Keeping Up with the Kardashians*. It soon became apparent that a love interest was good for both ratings and tabloid buzz, especially because he was often spotted with other women, which was dutifully reported in the gossip columns, along with his hard-partying lifestyle. In season 2, Kourtney confronts Scott about his cheating, creating both relationship drama and the show's first villain. The couple breaks up but the magazine covers and tabloids delight in chronicling the couple's liaisons. Sure enough, Kourtney finds out she's pregnant, complete with an on-air pregnancy test, but it's no happy ending as the tension only escalates. Khloé ends up slapping Scott and accusing him of getting her sister pregnant just so he can get back together with her, which of course means that he gets to return to the cast.

Conveniently, the birth of the first new Kardashian, Mason Dash Disick, provided a stirring finale for season 4, which aired two months after the baby's December 2009 arrival. It even included graphic footage of the birth, shot by Scott in the delivery room. The critics if not the fans noted that Kourtney came off looking more glamorous than the typical first-time mom, because she just happened to be in full makeup with perfectly coiffed hair as she gave birth. That might have had something to do with the fact that Kris—never one to allow a family milestone to go unexploited—negotiated a staggering $300,000 package deal with *Life & Style* that included the pregnancy announcement, an exclusive reveal of the sex of the baby, the birth announcement, the first baby photos, and the first photos of Kourtney's postbaby body. With the hefty sum in hand, the couple stayed together just long enough to provide the tabloids with more drama when they broke up soon after, along with a riveting subplot with which to hook viewers for *Kourtney and Khloé Take Miami*.

Sure enough, the new series featured Scott making a "surprise" appearance, wanting to get back together, and much rumination by Kourtney about whether they should do so. Coincidentally, Kourtney found out she was pregnant again just in time to deliver monster ratings for the first season of the new series and a perfect story arc for the second, when a massive audience tuned in for the birth of baby number two, Penelope.

Only the most cynical observer would conclude that Scott and Kourtney's relationship drama—and the accompanying increased ratings that go with it—would convince the family that it might be profitable to add yet another cast member. So when Khloé met NBA player Lamar Odom—fresh off two championships with the Los Angeles Lakers—those who believe in love at first sight were thrilled when the two announced their engagement three weeks later and tied the knot five days after Lamar presented his new fiancée with a nine-carat diamond ring. Bruce Jenner walked his stepdaughter down the aisle, while guests were banned from bringing cell phones to the wedding. It soon became apparent why the restriction was put in place when OK magazine published the exclusive wedding photos. The magazine, it turns out, paid $300,000 for the privilege, with Kris pocketing her $30,000. But that was chump change compared to the lucrative endorsement deals the new couple landed soon after.

Kim wasn't the only Kardashian who could peddle family-branded fragrances. Lamar's love for Khloé, fans were told, was "unbreakable," and that became the name of the unisex perfume they launched together. Of course, in order to market the perfume and secure the staggering appearance fees once commanded only by Kim, the new couple needed a vehicle. In a remarkably candid moment in 2011, Khloé would confess to a reporter that the family's various enterprises—reported to have made them $65 million in that year alone—were the real goal. The TV shows were merely the vehicles to push the merchandise and ancillary revenue sources.

"These shows are a 30-minute commercial," she revealed to the *Hollywood Reporter*. It wasn't altogether different from what the sisters had written in *Kardashian Konfidential*: "We have a lot of fun doing *Keeping Up with the Kardashians*," they wrote, "and it's a perfect commercial for our products. We're trying to make the most of our current success and we don't apologize for it. . . . That's what smart businesswomen do."

To that end, it seemed appropriate that E! announced yet another spinoff. In the spring of 2011, *Khloé and Lamar* made its debut, following the couple's tumultuous marriage and featuring Lamar's two children from a previous relationship. The show kicks off with a surprise revelation, as Lamar reveals that his estranged father, Joe, is a heroin addict. "I'm not asking him to be a father," Lamar muses. "I'm asking him to act like a father."

Sure enough, in one of the serendipitous, completely unplanned dramatic events that Kardashian shows are noted for, Joe happens to surprise Khloé while she is at a book signing. Khloé the loving wife then attempts a reconciliation between father and son, but Joe ruins the potential reunion when he later calls Lamar asking for money. "Give me a couple dollars, man, I'm wiped out," he says over the phone. Seeing the true nature of her father-in-law, Khloé decides that a reconciliation is not in the cards after all.

Meanwhile, before the spinoff even went on the air, E! announced that a new series would follow Kourtney and Kim as they opened another D-A-S-H boutique, this time in New York's trendy SoHo district. In fact, Kim had had little to do with D-A-S-H since the first one opened in Calabasas, and fans knew that she had little interest in the day-to-day running of the stores, which was the domain of her less-busy sisters. It seemed a stretch to focus a whole new series on Kim's involvement in the franchise. It could run the risk of overexposure, which marketing experts had long cautioned could devalue the brand.

When the store eventually opened in 2010, the launch garnered some rare negative publicity. At the time, the director of the SoHo Alliance community group blasted the sisters for what was generally deemed a disorganized and rowdy launch party. "I think it is reprehensible that they would Tweet their fans to purposely create this zoo on our streets," said Sean Sweeney. "The Kardashians are attempting to bring all that is wrong with Los Angeles to Soho, as well as to their fans—a generation of classless, tasteless and clueless sheep."

Nor were the media kind about the new venture at the time. "The store doesn't feel much like a store. It feels like a set for a show," fashion critic Lisa Marsh wrote on Style List. "The inventory is sparse and the mood less than service-oriented. There wasn't anything I wanted to buy, and I had a hard time picturing others making a bee-line for the goods, too."

The first signs of trouble had already started to emerge. It's hard to imagine today, but during the first three years of the family's invasion, there wasn't yet a thundering herd of media voices heralding the Kardashians' role in the decline of Western civilization. Still, the first hints of that coming wave were visible at the time the new spinoff hit the airwaves.

Spencer Pratt knew a thing or two about reality-star overexposure. He happened to have created the ill-fated Fox reality series *The Princes of Malibu*, which featured both Brody and Brandon Jenner, Bruce's adult sons, before they became known as part of the Kardashian clan. The series lasted only two episodes before being canceled. Later, Brody was cast in the hit reality series *The Hills* after allegedly dating one of its stars, Lauren Conrad. His appearance on the scene subsequently sparked a dramatic feud between Conrad and another prominent cast member, Heidi Montag, which became the primary focus of the series and garnered years of tabloid coverage. In 2009, just when the Kardashians were hitting their peak, Pratt and Montag married, earning them the moniker "Speidi," and for a time they were receiving more magazine covers and tabloid coverage than even Kim Kardashian. They milked the relationship for all it was worth, appearing together on *I'm a Celebrity . . . Get Me Out of Here* and the UK edition of *Big Brother.*

In February 2011, Kim had starred in a racy Super Bowl ad for Skechers Shape-Ups, which was banned for its suggestive dialogue. In the ad, Kim tells her shirtless trainer, "You're amazing, the best I've ever had," before leaving him for a pair of Skechers, which she implies get her in shape without having to go to the gym. Three months earlier, she had graced the cover of *W* magazine completely naked, her naughty bits covered by the headline "It's all about me . . . I mean you . . . I mean me." Inside, she is seen fully naked, covered in silver paint, with most of her body exposed, including a completely topless shot and a bottomless shot from behind.

Kim would later be seen in previews for her new spinoff crying about the *W* cover and what had allegedly been promised by the magazine's creative director. "I'm so fucking mad right now," she tells her publicist. "She promised me I would be covered with artwork on top of me. It was so uncomfortable. I'm really honestly freaking out. It really pisses me off; this is serious porn. They weren't going to show my ass crack or my nipples. This is full fucking porn. I'm never getting naked again. I feel so taken advantage of. I don't want people to be, like, 'All she's good for is being naked.'"

Responding to the controversy, Pratt gave an interview in which he warned that such tactics could end up tarnishing her brand. "Kim has totally lost the plot," he told a Fox affiliate. "She should have kept up her good-girl act and image. Now we are seeing her whine about all those naked magazine covers and then doing a raunchy Skechers ad. That makes her a hypocrite. She had better be careful. The people who buy her products aren't guys, they are girls, and girls don't want to see Kim naked during the Super Bowl."

Indeed, others were beginning to sense that her appeal was already starting to diminish. "The whole world according to Kim Kardashian is starting to come crashing down," warned Jay Grdina, CEO of the popular celebrity website Kikster.com. "Her allure and appeal has become a dull luster at best. I think that the civilians have finally caught on her game and realized that everything about her is fake. Kim's traffic on our site isn't 30 percent of what it was a year ago, and I really think it's a direct result of her massive over exposure and the fact that her constant crying about her own actions is getting old."

Would her appearance in yet another family spinoff help matters? many wondered. It soon became clear that the new series was not about launching a store at all but rather about introducing a new cast member. Kim had been dating New Orleans Saints running back Reggie Bush since around the beginning of the original series, and the two were often photographed together on the red carpet or at openings. Their relationship was occasionally featured on *Keeping Up with the Kardashians* before they broke up in 2009, but Bush was never really comfortable with the cameras nor with what he called the "Kardashian lifestyle." His conservative family was also said to disapprove of his relationship with Kim because of her sex tape. They did briefly reconcile in the spring of 2010, but the relationship once again fizzled.

Since her breakup with Bush, there were reports of other men—including singer John Mayer—but Kim had not been involved in a serious relationship. Suddenly she was dating the New Jersey Nets' power forward Kris Humphries. Their relationship had reportedly begun in the fall of 2011 when the NBA season was well under way, so it is hardly conceivable that the two could have spent much time together, especially since Kim was based in Los Angeles and Kris was in New Jersey when he wasn't on the road.

The premise of the new series—besides the artifice of opening the new SoHo store—was that Kim was single and looking for love when she arrived in New York. Indeed, she gave an interview to *MTV News* shortly before the series launched, in which she declared that she was not dating anybody. She had most recently been seeing model Gabriel Aubry, but he had never appeared to be a serious boyfriend and she had let it be known that she believed he was merely trying to attach himself to her fame.

"It is the first time that I'm single," she told the music network. "I never have been single in my life. So [after] getting married as a teenager and then getting into a relationship, each lasting, like, four years—after that, something inside of me, I just felt like I wanted to be single. I only was, like, really dating one guy on the show, but I learned the hard way that maybe a few guys that I would go out to eat with probably wanted to be with me for other reasons than getting to know me. It was more about being on a show. I decided to be super open about that."

On November 29 the previous year, however, she had been photographed courtside at a Nets game in which Humphries was playing. Days later, she and the star athlete appeared out and about together in

New York. By early January, as rumors of a romance with Humphries began circulating, Kim Tweeted a photo of Kris as a child, writing, "I want my son to look like this."

Meanwhile, in episode 3 of the new spinoff, Kim tells her sisters that she received an email from her former bodyguard Shengo Deane, whom she once dated. This prompts a discussion with Kourtney, Khloé, and Scott about whether she should get together with him. "What else have you got going on?" Scott asks. It soon became apparent that the New York spinoff was going to be the vehicle to watch Kim end her singlehood in full view of her rabid fan base and, judging by social media, millions of teen girls and twentysomethings were desperately hoping that Kim would finally find her Prince Charming and live happily ever after.

"Kim is promising that while she's in New York, she's going to be single and not get into a relationship," Kourtney tells the camera. "But Kim is in love with being in love. The second she starts dating someone, she has a boyfriend."

Kim reinforces her reluctance to start dating. "I like being single," she tells the family. "If anything went down, it would be just, like, a hookup."

Her sister asks her when she's ever had just a "hookup."

"Anybody you kiss becomes your boyfriend," protests Kourtney. Later in the episode, Kim ends up dating Shengo and winds up in bed with him. The episode doesn't reveal that Shengo still happened to be married to an Australian woman named Zuzana at the time.

"Knowing Kim," Kourtney declares, "she's probably already planned her whole Australian wedding, eucalyptus trees and all." Later, the sisters go for tea and Kim confesses, "I don't want to be single forever."

Zuzana would later reveal that she had no hard feelings toward Kim, saying, "Shengo saw her as the golden ticket to fame." Eventually we see Kim end the relationship with Shengo on air, even though it's unclear from the time line and the show's shooting schedule how she could have been still dating the Australian when, in real life, Kris Humphries was already in the picture. Certainly, as her and Shengo's relationship unfolded on air, she was already publicly dating Humphries, with whom she had been photographed leaving a Prince concert in February. Only a few weeks after the first season ended, fans were stunned to pick up the May 25 edition of *People* and learn the news.

"It was a dream come true for Kim Kardashian as she walked into her Beverly Hills home May 18," gushed the magazine in an exclusive. "Her boyfriend of six months, New Jersey Nets forward Kris Humphries, was waiting in her bedroom on bended knee."

"I didn't expect this at all," Kim told the magazine. "I was in such shock. I never thought it would happen at home, and I never thought now."

Kris Jenner purported to be in the dark about her daughter's plans. "Kim dropped this bombshell and went to Europe for a couple of days," she told a Fox affiliate. "I mean, hello? So I have no idea what she's going to do but I'll find out in a couple of days. But Kris and I have the same name, same spelling—kinda creepy, right? He automatically fits, so that's the good thing."

When season 6 of *Keeping Up with the Kardashians* kicked off less than three weeks later, millions tuned in to find out how it had all gone down. In the first show, however, the engagement had not yet happened. "Kris and I are now boyfriend and girlfriend," Kim says in her confessional. It would guarantee that viewers would keep their eyeballs glued to the screen in the coming months. They would have to wait until episode 12, when the family traveled together to Bora Bora so that Kris and Bruce could renew their vows, and Humphries tagged along. Kourtney confesses that she has not yet made up her mind about Kim's boyfriend. "None of us have spent any serious time with Kris," she says. "He's very sarcastic, and I just don't know what to make of him yet." After Rob and Humphries have an altercation, they make up by playing a cruel prank on Kim, and he ends up bonding with the family. He even wins Kris Jenner's seal of approval.

In her confessional, she says, "I'm definitely more comfortable with Kris than before we went on this trip, because I didn't know him at all. I get now how Kim is head over heels for this guy. Who knows, he might be the one."

Later, she told *People*, "He is so amazing and sweet and after spending time with him I came to realize he was such an important part of the family. He gets along with every single one of us, and that is not easy to do. When you date one of us, you date all of us. We're all going out with Kris."

Humphries plays a round of golf with Bruce and tells him, "So, Bruce, the real question is, you're wondering why we came out here. 'Cause, man, I wanted to come to you first and ask you if I could marry Kim."

After Bruce grants his permission, telling his future son-in-law that asking for it was a smart move, Humphries confides that he plans to pop the question that same week. Later, he tells Kris that he has asked Bruce if he may marry Kim. "That's such good news!" she gushes, throwing her arms around him. "When I look at Kim," he says in his confessional, "I see the mother of my children, and I see someone that I want to spend my life with."

We then see Kris and Kris head to the SLS Hotel to arrange to pick up the engagement ring from Kim's friend Jonathan Cheban, who arranged the purchase. Kris Jenner dubs it "Operation Pumpkin" because the whole thing is a "Cinderella story." The plan hits a snag when Jonathan informs them he doesn't yet have the ring. It is so valuable, he explains, that it has to be shipped in a Brinks truck to a place of business, so he arranges to have it shipped to the D-A-S-H boutique, where Khloé signs for it, unaware of what's in the package.

Eventually, we learn that it's a 20.5-carat diamond ring worth $2 million, but there's trouble in paradise when Kim and Humphries have an on-camera fight about where they're going to live after they marry. Finally, we see Humphries in Kim's bedroom, laying out rose petals to spell out WILL YOU MARRY ME?

"This is the biggest moment of my life," he tells the camera. He chose the bedroom because "to me, our love is simple and I don't want all the distractions. I just want it to be in her home, quiet and perfect."

When Kim enters, Kris is waiting on bended knee, hiding the ring behind his back. "Oh my God. This is, like, the moment that every girl has dreamed of their entire life," she says in her confessional.

"You're crazy," she giggles, approaching him.

"Will you marry me?" he asks.

Kim pauses and then spots the massive diamond ring. Mouth agape, she says, "Oh my God. Yes."

The episode ends with Kim gushing, "I am honestly so excited. I feel that my life has changed so much in a year. I'm really looking forward to this amazing journey that I'm going to bring Kris on and I really think we've changed each other's lives."

That set the stage for a hyped event the likes of which America had rarely seen. Not long after the engagement, a reporter asked Khloé and Kourtney whether the couple planned to broadcast their wedding on the show.

"Well duh!" "It comes with the territory," Kourtney replied. Khloé immediately added, "I mean, I would assume it would be . . . we sell our souls to E!, but that's obviously up to Kim and Kris."

Speculating about the same question, the *Today* show asked, "If a Kardashian does something, and it isn't aired on television or splashed through magazines, did it really happen?"

They wouldn't have to wonder long, just long enough for Kris Jenner to finalize the contracts. A whopping 3.2 million people had tuned in to watch the televised wedding of Khloé to Lamar Odom two years earlier, making it E!'s highest-rated broadcast ever at that time. This was arguably a much bigger occasion and had the potential to attract a massive audience. And it appeared that Kris had been busy making sure that her 10 percent would be maximized in every conceivable way.

The *People* exclusive, it soon emerged, had not gone cheap. The magazine had paid $300,000 for the privilege of breaking the news and an additional $1.5 million to run the first wedding photos. In addition, *OK* magazine had agreed to pay $100,000 for photos of the bridal shower. *US Weekly* was shelling out a similar amount for photos of the honeymoon. But that was peanuts compared to the amount Kris landed for the couple to broadcast the nuptials on E! in a two-part special, reported to be worth as much as $15 million.

The wedding was scheduled to take place on August 20, but the hype reached deafening tones within days of the announcement. "It's going to be royal wedding number two," Khloé told E! and, judging from the subsequent media fanfare, this wasn't hyperbole. "I could only imagine Kim having the hugest wedding," she added. "Kim has always been a hopeless romantic. She thinks she is a Disney character; like, everything is a great love story. It's so sweet and cute. It's just Kim. I feel like she is very much in love with love."

In keeping with the Disney analogy, E! announced that their wedding special would be entitled "Kim's Fairytale Wedding: A Kardashian Event."

In order to keep people interested long enough to watch the special, scheduled two months hence, details about the affair were kept to a minimum. On the afternoon of the wedding, a number of celebrity guests used social media to announce they had been invited.

The wife of NBA player Carmelo Anthony Tweeted, "Butterflies in my stomach for @KimKardashian & @Krishumphries . . . beyond excited for today! The Anthonys are on our way! Love is in the

Air!" Ryan Seacrest attended with his girlfriend at the time, Julianne Hough. That day, he Tweeted, "On the way to @kimkardashian's wedding . . . Traffic so bad on the [Highway] 101 I had to stop at cold stone creamery."

Afterward, he added few details about the ceremony, simply describing the occasion as "beautiful . . . Kim looked regal, a perfect night. I just danced with the whole family."

The lavish ceremony was reported to cost anywhere from $500,000 to $10 million, depending on the source, but it would emerge that most of that had been donated in exchange for the publicity. Kim was said to be wearing a diamond headpiece that was worth $2.5 million. Vera Wang gifted the bride with a $20,000 custom-made wedding gown, while hundreds of thousands of dollars in floral arrangements were donated by luxury florist Mark's Garden. Leaving no opportunity unmonetized, Kris Jenner had even negotiated a $50,000 fee for Kim to host her bachelorette party at the Tao nightclub in Las Vegas.

Asked why so many businesses were clamoring to be associated with the nuptials, marketing consultant Linda Ong told the *Hollywood Reporter*, "The Kardashians represent a new type of exotic subculture. Today, when most people are just trying to survive, seeing them thrive gives us all hope."

The first sign that all was not right appeared days later, when *People* ran the wedding issue, "Kim's Wedding Album," for which they had paid a whopping $1.5 million. Many were surprised to discover that Kris Humphries was not on the cover, only Kim in her wedding gown. Was this the deal that Kris Jenner had brokered, and if so, why did she exclude her new son-in-law?

People's assistant editor Jennifer Garcia appeared on *Access Hollywood* to address the controversy. When the cohost, Arsenio Hall, appeared to mock Kris's absence from the cover, Garcia explained that the magazine had sorted through thousands of wedding photos, at which Hall piped in, "Looking for ones that didn't have Kris?"

"That's not true," Garcia replied defensively. "It's all about the bride. We wanted her. It's her day, we wanted her on the cover."

When the special finally aired two months later, we learn that much drama had ensued before the big day. First, Kris Humphries and Khloé take digs at each other. Later, Kris walks in on Khloé talking about him with a friend and confronts her about bad-mouthing him behind his back. She tells him that she's not trashing him but rather that she questions his intentions. Kris is furious. "How dare you question someone else's marriage? Are you sure you're not just using Lamar? He's a Laker, he's got championships. How often are you going to find a tall, successful guy to have kids with?"

"Wow, I'm going to kill this girl!" he mutters to himself.

After Kris tells Kim what went down, she confronts her younger sister.

"I don't want this bad energy at my wedding, and if all of you are talking shit behind my back there's no reason why any of you should be at my wedding!" she yells.

Khloé fires back, "So, wait, you don't want me at your wedding?"

"No," Kim replies, storming off and slamming the door.

Khloé fumes in her confessional: "I don't know what it is about Kris, but I feel like every time he's around me, he just wants to start digging in at me." We later witness a conversation between Khloé and Kourtney in which they diss Kris behind his back, and suddenly the viewer is left to wonder whether Kris is really the knight in shining armor that everybody had hoped for.

We see Kim annoyed with her fiancé because she feels that he is not doing enough to help with the arrangements and is leaving her to do everything herself.

KRIS: This is getting out of control. Why don't we refocus on the purpose of all this and make it more about us than what people expect?

KIM: What do you mean, we have to lower our standards? I have a lot of pressure and a reputation to keep. People are comparing us to William and Kate. We can't mess this up. We'll figure us out later.

KRIS: I think we should slow down and talk about this.

KIM: I can't slow down, it's on. I don't want to talk about this right now. I have too much on my plate. The last thing I need is more problems to solve. Sorry. You have to toughen up.

At the rehearsal, we hear Kris telling Kim, "I'm still gonna scream at you when I get a chance," to which Kim retorts, "Go for it. I'll fuckin' slice you."

As the rehearsal dinner gets under way, the couple are still fighting. Kim is unhappy that Kris is sporting a mustache, whereas he claims that "this is all I feel that I have left, my mustache. It's the only way to send a message to Kim."

"He hates me," Kim tells a friend, who tells her it's normal before a wedding.

"We hate each other," Kim replies. "Is that normal?"

Kim and Kris end up sitting at separate tables during the dinner, their backs to each other. The next day, they squabble again about whether Kim plans to change her last name to Humphries after the wedding.

Normally, such scenes are merely used to build dramatic tension and keep the viewers' interest. Little did anybody know that it was actually foreshadowing.

It didn't take long for the first rumors to emerge that the new prince and princess were not destined to live happily ever after. The first reports followed the couple's honeymoon on Italy's Amalfi Coast. While Kim had gushed to *US Weekly* that "our honeymoon was so perfect! We caught up on alone time," Perez Hilton reported a different version after they returned to New York. He quoted a source who allegedly knew the couple well.

"Kim felt the marriage was over almost as soon as it began. . . . Kim was distant from Kris [during the honeymoon] and when the duo weren't posing for pictures, she was cold as ice. Kris couldn't figure out what he was dealing with. . . . All Kim could talk about was all of the great press she was getting after the wedding. Kris felt like he was just an accessory in her life."

The honeymoon was cut short so that Kim could begin filming season 2 of *Kourtney and Kim Take New York*, which was scheduled to focus heavily on the new couple's married life. Cameras followed them as they moved in with Kourtney, Scott, and Mason to a New York hotel suite while Kris found himself temporarily unemployed because of the NBA lockout that delayed the start of the season until December. Soon there were reports that Kris was frequently seen partying in New York clubs, with no sign of his new wife.

In October, the senior editor of *In Touch Weekly*, Dorothy Cascerceri, reported,

> *Kim and Kris have rarely spent time together since they got married two months ago. She's constantly working, jetting off to exotic locations like Dubai and filming her reality show, "Kourtney & Kim Take New York"—all without Kris. Sources say Kris feels like she's way too busy for him, so he's been putting all of his free time to other use. In recent weeks, he hit several New York clubs—The Ainsworth and Beauty & Essex—and was spotted flirting with girls and basking in the attention of other women. When the two actually do spend time together, a source says they are "icy" and "cold" to each other. Kim has said time and time again she's eager to become a mom especially in light of how close she is to her nephew, Mason. I'd be surprised if these two split before Kim has a bun in the oven, but by the looks of the way*

they interact on their show, it doesn't seem they have a marriage
built to last.

Meanwhile, *Life & Style* reported, "Rumors are swirling that Kim
Kardashian and Kris Humphries are on the brink of splitting, just two
months into their marriage." The magazine claimed to have spoken
to a producer of *Kourtney and Kim Take New York*, who told them,
"Kim's mapping out 2012, including holidays, and Kris isn't a part of
it. Any itineraries for the future don't include Kris very much."

Kris Jenner denied that the marriage was in trouble but hinted at
problems when she revealed that the couple appeared to be "going in
two separate directions."

"She's working, he's working—he's trying to stay in shape for basketball," she told *People*. "I think they'll figure it out as soon as they
get back to Los Angeles."

Kim suggested that the living situation was an issue. "We have to find
our home base," she said. "He lives in Miami and Minnesota. I'm in L.A.,
so we had to find where that home base is going to be. We're waiting for
the lockout to end to see where he's going to play. . . . I'm a very tough
crowd. [My relationship with Kris] is a work in progress. It's not something either one of us is going to fake. I just need to know him more."

And then the bombshell hit. On October 31, 2011—only seventy-
two days after their lavish, televised wedding—Kim filed for divorce,
citing "irreconcilable differences."

"After careful consideration, I have decided to end my marriage.
I hope everyone understands this was not an easy decision," Kim said
in a statement issued to media outlets. "I had hoped this marriage was
forever but sometimes things don't work out as planned. We remain
friends and wish each other the best."

Kris was said to be blindsided by the announcement. "I love my
wife and am devastated to learn she filed for divorce," he Tweeted.
"I'm willing to do whatever it takes to make it work."

By the next day, multiple media outlets were speculating that the marriage had merely been a publicity stunt, noting that the announcement just happened to come a day before the release of Kris Jenner's memoir, *Kris Jenner . . . And All Things Kardashian*. Radar Online quoted a source close to the show suggesting that the marriage was more of a business arrangement than a genuine love match. "Kim was looking for a husband and Kris was selected for her, amongst others," the source alleged. "She wasn't really into him but she hoped she would be able to develop some feelings, but it never happened. Kris turned out to not be as malleable as everyone hoped he would be, he was pictured out partying with other girls, Kim really couldn't care less for him, she decided to end it."

Even reputable newspapers joined the flurry of speculation. "Was Kardashian Marriage a Sham?" the *Chicago Tribune* asked in a headline the day after the divorce filing. Kim only poured fuel on the flames when she Tweeted about the opening of a new Kardashian-themed store in Las Vegas on the exact day that the divorce was announced. "Our store #KardashianKhaos is opening tomorrow at 9am at @The MirageLV We are so excited!! Kardashian Khaos has arrived!"

More than one newspaper calculated that the couple had made the equivalent of $250,000 a day for the brief period they were married and wondered if they now had plans to give back the nearly $18 million they had received from the photo and TV rights they had collected.

The couple's prenuptial agreement had barred Kris from publicly discussing Kim in a negative light or revealing disparaging details about the marriage but, as is common practice to get around these things, he appeared to use his family members as surrogates to get his side of the story out.

A month after the divorce filing, Kris filed an application in LA Superior Court for an annulment on the grounds of "fraud." These were the same grounds Renée Zellweger had cited when she filed to have her four-month marriage to country singer Kenny Chesney annulled. At the time, there was widespread unconfirmed speculation that Zellweger had discovered that her husband was gay. In a 2007 *60 Minutes* interview Chesney denied being gay. "It's not true. Period," the country star said. "Maybe I should have come out and said, 'No, I'm not [gay]' but I didn't want to draw any more attention to it."

Now, Humphries's application on the same grounds fueled speculation that he had been used by the Kardashians. Kris's aunt Dedria Humphries, who had attended the wedding, told the London *Sun* that she believed the marriage had been a ploy to boost ratings for the Kardashian TV shows.

"It was a sham," she said. "My understanding of marriage is people are going to give it more than seventy-two days unless there's serious abuse. If I felt somebody had duped me and used me in front of the whole world, I would be very angry. An annulment says it wasn't valid in the first place. She should admit that it was a sham at the very least."

Kris's uncle Mike Humphries was even more blunt, blaming Kris Jenner for engineering the marriage. "I would love for her to get thumped," he told the paper. "She's the mastermind. You can just see that's the brains making that thing go. The wicked part is she's using her family to make that thing. All of it's really due to her."

Having lived in Miami for years, I had met Kris Humphries—who owned a Miami Beach condo not far from my own apartment complex—on a number of occasions, including once during the period when he was dating Kim. He always seemed like a nice guy, and he definitely loved to party. About a week after his split—at a time when he still professed to be miserable—I encountered him in the lounge of Miami steakhouse STK. He was drinking heavily and surrounded by young women. I recall a leggy blonde approaching him and asking him to pose for a selfie. After a few photos, he invited her to drink champagne with him and his friends.

A few days later, Kris took a Bikram Yoga class in South Beach, where my friend April Young taught. April told me that Kris seemed nice but became enamored of one of the stunning Bikram instructors. After the class, he asked her out, but she told him she had a boyfriend. He persisted, not seeming to care whether or not she was single. "It was a bit odd," April told me. "He knew that she was taken, but it didn't seem to bother him." I asked her how he did in the class.

"Although he's an athlete, he was a bit awkward," she recalled. "He definitely needs to do more classes and to work on his format. He struggled quite a bit. He was definitely humbled doing hot yoga."

A few months later I encountered Kris again at South Beach's Story Club. Inside, I saw him in the VIP section, with at least half a dozen young, pretty girls at his table. In the media, he played the victim and made the world believe he was still in love with Kim. But he didn't show any sign of being a victim on the South Beach club circuit. He seemed to be having the time of his life.

Gradually, details of what had supposedly gone wrong in the marriage began to trickle out. Kim's people had let it be known that there was considerable tension between herself and Kris about where they would live after the wedding. During the wedding special, Kris had told her, "Maybe you should just move to Minnesota with me. We could move into my little house on the lake; we could just start popping out babies."

Now E! was promising to supply plenty of dramatic footage that had been shot during the couple's brief marriage, which would lead viewers to tune in to the upcoming second season of *Kourtney and Kim Take New York*. Already the previews were providing a hint of what might have gone wrong. Building on the theme of the couple's disagreement before the wedding on future living arrangements, Kim is seen complaining to Kris.

"How am I going to have my career and live in *Minnesota*?"

"Baby," Kris retorts, "by the time you have kids and they're in school, no one will care about you."

Given the family's control over the show, and clips such as these, it was a safe bet that the Kardashians were going to use their spin machine to make Kris look like the bad guy and Kim the aggrieved victim.

By the time the season finished airing in January 2012, however, viewers had a more nuanced take on what had gone wrong. The couple is seen squabbling about living arrangements but also more mundane issues. In one episode, Kim gets mad at her husband when he implies that her friend Jonathan is gay. In another, she wonders if she can trust him after he sneaks off to a party in Toronto with Scott without telling her. In a later episode, Kris gets annoyed when Kourtney and Khloé put a snake in his bed and then cover his room in toilet paper as a prank while Kim is away in Dubai.

A massive audience of 4.5 million viewers tuned in to the final episode, in which we finally see what happened, or at least the edited version. Ominously, Kim tells her husband, "We need to talk." Kris tells her that he wants things to be the way they were at the beginning, but Kim reveals that she feels "dead inside." He admits that he has been too hung up on his basketball career and hasn't been making her a priority, but he vows to try to make it work. "You are a priority to me," he tells her. They take a Pilates class together as an attempt at bonding, but when he complains that she is interfering with his workout, she storms out in a huff.

"It's not what I thought it would be; he fell in love with me and I fell in love with him—and now my feelings have changed," she says in her confessional.

It's obvious that she's made up her mind by the time that she expresses guilt about the lavish wedding ceremony. "I invited all these people to this huge wedding and flew everyone out, wasted everyone's time and everyone's money—everyone's everything—and I feel bad!"

Even Kourtney turns on Kim, when Kris wants to move his things into Kim's LA house and Kim discourages the idea, suggesting that maybe he should just bring a suitcase. "You're such a bitch, Kim!" Kourtney tells her when she overhears.

Kim's not the only one with doubts. We see Kris tell a friend that he may want a divorce. "I'm just over her," he says.

When the end finally comes, we see the two riding silently to the airport. Neither comes off as the obvious culprit. Instead, the series appears to show the strains of conflicting schedules and differing goals. And yet, almost as soon as the season finished airing, the backlash had turned into a tsunami, with what seemed to be the collective wrath of America concluding that the marriage had been a publicity stunt and that the Kardashians had duped their fans in the name of profit.

One of the first to pile on was Kim's former publicist Jonathan Jaxson, who was her press rep from the beginning of *Keeping Up with the Kardashians* until 2009. In an interview on the Elvis Duran TV show, Jaxson claimed that the marriage to Humphries was a sham and that she had reservations about it before the wedding took place.

"She knew weeks before getting married she didn't want to do it," he said. "She's never gotten over [ex Reggie Bush]." He then revealed that, as her publicist, he had seen her pull publicity stunts since the beginning of her career. He recalled an incident in 2007, when Kim tipped off the paparazzi as she was exiting a Beverly Hills jeweler, to make it appear that Bush had proposed.

"She was going to go shopping with her grandmother and her mom and we said, 'Let's do something to get more press for you,' " Jaxson recalled on the show. "She said, 'Perfect. Let me go to a ring store and walk out as if Reggie Bush were proposing to me.' " Jaxson also claimed that this was the exact same ring that Kris Humphries later gave Kim during his "surprise" proposal.

He also claimed that the couple made a lot of money off their wedding: "They had a lot of contracts, they had endorsements. To say they weren't paid is a lot of foolish garbage." He claims that Kim was forced to go through with the wedding because of the endorsement deals that her mother had negotiated.

When Jaxson took to the morning talk shows to discuss these and other incidents from his tenure with Kim, her camp was furious and went on an immediate offensive. First they attempted to undermine him, using TMZ to suggest that his relationship with her consisted of only two small projects, including a blog. When Jaxson produced a slew of evidence attesting to a close working relationship, they then filed a lawsuit against him, seeking $200,000 damages for violating the confidentiality agreement he had signed as part of his contract.

Nondisclosure agreements are the shield that protects celebrities from having their dirty laundry spilled by the assorted household staff, employees, and associates that they come in contact with. The Kardashians are especially fond of such agreements, as I discovered when I began to attempt to interview people who work on the show and other related projects. When I approached one Miami-based technician, who had been referred by a friend as someone who could spill much relevant information, the TV veteran merely hissed, "NDA. They'll sue my ass off if I tell you anything." I work off-the-record, I assured him. I never reveal names. That wasn't good enough. "Between Seacrest and Kris Jenner, they've got eyes and ears everywhere."

Indeed, on a marble table inside Kris's house lies a pile of non-disclosure agreements that everybody who enters must sign. Nearby a framed sign reads, WHAT WE SAY HERE, WHAT WE SEE HERE, LET IT STAY HERE, WHEN WE LEAVE HERE.

The consequences of violating a nondisclosure agreement are usually severe, what one producer described to me as "career suicide and very expensive." So it was a surprise when Jaxson went public with his claims. But he soon revealed what had given him such license.

"To the best of my knowledge, I have never signed an agreement dealing with confidentiality with Kim Kardashian. I have an agreement in my possession that does not have either party's signature on it."

It appeared that Kris had let Jaxson's NDA slip through the cracks. I had recently witnessed the consequences of a similar lapse while researching a book on the late Whitney Houston. I obtained an FBI file that revealed the Bureau had been called in to investigate a possible case of extortion involving the singer. It seems that a former employee had threatened to spill the beans on Houston's longtime lesbian affair with her assistant Robyn Crawford and was demanding $200,000. Within days, Whitney's father and business manager had sent over a check to the extortionist's Chicago attorney, along with a nondisclosure agreement.

On her blog, Kim dismissed Jaxson's accusations. "First and foremost, I married for love. I can't believe I even have to defend this," she wrote. "I got caught up with the hoopla and the filming of the TV show. I probably should have ended my relationship."

Still, although his revelations were embarrassing, Jaxson admitted that his speculation was based on the word of friends that he and Kim shared rather than any firsthand knowledge. Eventually, he ended up apologizing and retracting his claim that the marriage was a sham.

Soon after Jaxson came forward, the popular website Reality Tea—specializing in coverage of reality-show news—claimed to have discovered concrete evidence that the show was staged. They analyzed a scene that was purported to have been taped in Dubai in October and compared it to a paparazzi shot of Kim and Kris Jenner leaving a studio in December, in which mother and daughter are wearing the exact same clothes, makeup, and hairstyles as they were in the scene supposedly shot in Dubai. In the televised exchange, Kim confides to her mother that she is struggling with her marriage to Humphries. "I don't know, I'm just, like, learning a lot of things about him that I didn't really know before and, I don't know, married life just isn't what I thought it would be with him." The paparazzi photo shot in December appears to confirm that the scene was deliberately staged *after* the breakup, in order to make

Kim look more sympathetic. Still, it was just conjecture based on a photo and didn't prove anything.

Much more damaging, however, was a 165-page deposition given by Russell Jay, one of the executive producers of *Keeping Up with the Kardashians*, who was deposed by Humphries's attorneys as part of the ongoing divorce battle. *Life & Style* obtained the deposition and printed devastating excerpts in which Jay admitted that at least two scenes that portray Kris in a negative light were "scripted, reshot or edited." Jay reveals that although the dramatic proposal scene in Kim's bedroom was portrayed as a surprise, Kim knew beforehand that Kris was going to propose on camera, but she didn't know exactly when it would happen. Moreover, she demanded the scene be reshot because she wasn't happy with her reaction in the first take.

"I remember, like, Kim—she didn't know he was going to propose at that moment," Jay testified. "And she came in and she was completely surprised, and I think she had a bad reaction or something and she was embarrassed. So she said can we just, like, have me come back in one more time and be, like, really surprised."

In another episode, the cameras portray an outraged Kim, furious at discovering that Kris threw a party in their hotel room while she was out of town. Jay, however, admits that Kim was in the hotel when the party happened and was aware of everything, contrary to what is portrayed on the show.

He also revealed that Kim uses a "tear stick" to cry on camera.

Much more troubling, however, was Jay's revelation that she created scenes for the show entirely from scratch, which appeared to confirm the allegations first reported by Reality Tea. During one memorable moment, Kim shares with her mother that she is having a hard time being married to Kris and is struggling in the marriage. In his deposition, Jay admitted that this scene was actually shot *after* the breakup and made to appear as if it took place while the couple was still together. This is in fact the first incontrovertible evidence ever produced to confirm that *Keeping Up with the Kardashians* is staged.

It seemed like the hits just kept on coming, as a full-fledged backlash seemed to converge from all directions and from some surprising sources. Take, for example, an award issued by the National League of Junior Cotillions at the end of 2011, which named Kim the "Most Ill-Mannered Person of 2011." Her sin? "Making a private matter public and disrespecting the institution of marriage."

Then Salman Rushdie got in on the act, Tweeting a limerick that indicated that watching the Kardashians might once have been a guilty pleasure of the revered author of *The Satanic Verses*.

"1. The marriage of poor kim #kardashian was krushed like a kar in a krashian," he wrote. "2. her kris kried, not fair! why kan't I keep my share?" "3. But kardashian fell klean outa fashian."

Next, *Saturday Night Live* ran a merciless skit that portrayed the family as veritable idiots who are obsessed with anal bleaching. Kris Jenner is played by Kristen Wiig as a plastic-surgery addict, while Kris Humphries comes off as a moron who can barely string two syllables together. Afterward, Khloé and Kourtney Tweeted that they found the skit funny.

Even in the venerable paper of record, columnist Frank Bruni took aim, writing in the *New York Times*:

> *If you're just catching up on last week's news, I suggest you sit down. Fast. What you're about to learn is incredible. Unthinkable. If you drink, grab one. Certain shocks can't be borne without absorbers. Kim Kardashian is getting divorced. You read that right. It turns out that the nation's poster girl for old-fashioned virtues—our little Kimmykins of Sunnybrook Farm—brought something less than steadfast and humble commitment to her marriage, which unraveled only 72 days after a ceremony bathed in klieg lights, lousy with product placements and underwritten*

with a reported multimillion-dollar payment (which her family has vaguely denied) for television rights. Of course none of that casts doubt on her good intentions. So it's a real stunner, this rapid and bitter end. A nation reels.

Although his words were clearly satire, it is instructive that the *Times* and serious authors like Rushdie were paying any attention at all to the foibles of a reality-TV star. They weren't the only ones. In between the satirical digs and the vicious celebrity putdowns, media outlets were tripping all over themselves to analyze the impact the divorce would have on the Kardashian brand, trotting out PR experts and even divorce attorneys, such as Hollywood favorite Raoul Felder. He predicted that the Kardashians could find themselves in serious trouble "if the public comes to the conclusion that they were hoaxed." Similarly, if one of the media outlets that bought wedding rights came to that conclusion, Felder believed they'd have a case for demanding their money back.

"If one of the people who gave them money came to me, I'd say, 'You have a lawsuit,'" he said.

In November, an online petition was launched, under the banner "No More Kardashians," demanding that E! take them off the air. "We feel these shows are mostly staged and place an emphasis on vanity, greed, promiscuity, vulgarity and over-the-top conspicuous consumption," explained petition organizer Cyndy Snider at the time. "While some may have begun watching the spectacle as mindless entertainment or as a sort of 'reality satire,' it is a sad truth that many young people are looking up to this family and are modeling their appearance and behavior after them. I'll remind you here that the Kardashian family fame largely started with a 'leaked' sex tape." Within a week, the petition had gathered more than 100,000 signatures. But reality-TV blogger Mickey McKean predicted it would be months before the real fallout could be assessed.

"It is going to be interesting to see whether or not TV viewers are going to give a rip about the Kardashians after this divorce announcement," he wrote. "There is no question that a lot of viewers are becoming more savvy when it comes to reality TV; that they now know it is not reality and is in fact scripted. When viewers feel that they have been lied to—that their intelligence has been insulted—they know they have the option of turning the channel and watching something else on TV. Only time will tell after this big a$$ scam how many viewers will still be interested in *Keeping Up with the Kardashians*."

"There's a real danger that people will be angry because they feel that they have been taken for fools," crisis-management expert Glenn Selig told *TheWrap*. "It's one thing for reality stars to exaggerate something for an episode, it's another thing to go through with the marriage just to concoct a TV special. This could be the time when the line gets crossed."

Publicist Richard Laermer had some advice to help Kim weather the crisis.

"The only way people are going to stop hating her is if she goes away for a while," he said. "But I doubt this woman will ever do that. She'd go nuts to be away for even five minutes."

Judging by the reaction on social media, Kim's stock had fallen considerably by the end of 2011 because of the divorce. But nowhere was the backlash more evident than in Hollywood, where it seemed that celebrities were trying to outdo each other in expressing public disdain for Kim and her family.

Reese Witherspoon got the ball rolling at the 2011 MTV Music Awards. "It's also possible to make it in Hollywood without a reality show," she noted. And in case any viewers were unclear about whom her remark was targeting, she added that when she started in the business, "If you made a sex tape, you were embarrassed and you hid it under your bed, and if you took naked pictures of yourself on your cell phone, you hid your face."

The singer Michael Bublé took a less subtle shot while performing at the IHeart Radio Live concert in New York. "Ladies and gentlemen," he announced, "I have a very special guest. Please welcome Kim Kardashian." The audience was in shock until he quickly added, "Nah, just fucking with you! That bitch isn't coming on my stage."

His fellow singer Cher was no less impressed, judging by a Tweet she shared in 2011. "I don't watch reality!" she wrote to her fans. "Never saw a Kardashian but these Bitches should b Drop kicked down a freeway !Not kidding! No shit this Fkn nuts."

In an interview, the actor and comedian Jonah Hill actually admitted that he watched the Kardashian series for its amusement value but then reflected on the significance of the family's popularity. "The truth of it is, I have friends who work in TV and the Kardashians get higher ratings than their TV shows," he told the *Huffington Post*. "Shows that people actually work hard on—writing and creating and trying to tell stories. The fact that the Kardashians could be more popular than a show like *Mad Men* is disgusting. It's a super disgusting part of our culture. The Kardashians are as famous as our president. What does that tell you about how skewed our society is?"

And speaking of the president, it turned out that even Barack Obama wasn't immune to the pervasive reach of the Kardashian clan. Around the time of Kim's divorce from Kris Humphries, it was widely reported that the White House had "banned" the Kardashian shows. What actually happened was that Michelle Obama gave an interview to iVillage in which she brought up her husband's feelings about the phenomenon.

"Barack really thinks some of the Kardashians—when [the Obama daughters] watch that stuff—he doesn't like that as much," she revealed. But rather than confirming that her daughters were forbidden to watch the show, Michelle seemed to pour cold water on that idea.

"But I sort of feel like if we're talking about it, and I'm more concerned with how they take it in—what did you learn when you watched that?" she said. "And if they're learning the right lessons, like, that was crazy, then I'm like, okay."

Former Nirvana drummer Dave Grohl, leader of the group Foo Fighters, certainly appeared to have learned a lesson from the family. He revealed that they played a significant role in his decision to quit smoking pot. "I stopped doing drugs when I was about 20 years old," he told the British magazine *New Musical Express*. "But I recently thought, 'Oh, I'm going to start smoking pot again to cure insomnia.' I'd put the kids to bed, go upstairs and smoke a bit of pot. But then I'd get stuck in front of the Kardashians on TV for 45 minutes. And it freaked me out. I was like, 'I'm never doing this ever again. It's definitely not for me.'"

Kim was remarkably forbearing about much of the high-profile criticism, but she seemed to take it to heart when *Mad Men* star Jon Hamm took a shot at her and her former friend in an interview with *Elle UK*.

"Whether it's Paris Hilton or Kim Kardashian or whoever, stupidity is certainly celebrated," Hamm told the magazine. "Being a fucking idiot is a valuable commodity in this culture because you're rewarded significantly. . . . It's celebrated. It doesn't make sense to me."

Perhaps because she was a fan of *Mad Men*, Kim decided to respond. To her millions of followers, she wrote on her blog, "I just heard about the comment Jon Hamm made about me in an interview. I respect Jon and I am a firm believer that everyone is entitled to their own opinion and that not everyone takes the same path in life. We're all working hard and we all have to respect one another. Calling someone who runs their own businesses, is a part of a successful TV show, produces, writes, designs, and creates, 'stupid,' is in my opinion careless."

Hamm volleyed back. "I don't know Ms. Kardashian, I know her public persona. What I said was meant to be more on pervasiveness of something in our culture, not personal, but she took offense to it and that is her right."

Even James Bond got in on the Kardashian bashing, when Daniel Craig weighed in during an interview with the UK edition of GQ.

"I think there's a lot to be said for keeping your own counsel," he said. "It's not about being afraid to be public with your emotions or about who you are and what you stand for. But if you sell it off it's gone. You can't buy it back—you can't buy your privacy back. Ooh I want to be alone. Fuck you. We've been in your living room. We were at your birth. You filmed it for us and showed us the placenta and now you want some privacy? Look at the Kardashians, they're worth millions. I don't think they were that badly off to begin with but now look at them. You see that and you think, 'What, you mean all I have to do is behave like a fucking idiot on television and then you'll pay me millions.' I'm not judging it—well, I am obviously."

As the backlash intensified, it genuinely looked like it was going to derail the Kardashian phenomenon. It looked like their 15 million minutes of fame were over. Even ABC TV predicted the end might be nigh.

"Perhaps it's backlash over the hype from Kim Kardahian's seventy-two-day marriage to Kris Humphries, or just the normal trajectory of any unexplainable flash-in-the-pan phenomenon, but the country's long national nightmare regarding the Kardashians might be ending," the network reported in early 2012. It turns out the obituary was premature.

CHAPTER TWELVE

The *New York Post* reported in December 2011 that Kim was "keeping an uncharacteristically low profile" and had told her team to cancel all promotional obligations until her annual New Year's Eve gig at Tao Las Vegas. She also canceled a UK tour for her shoe line and an appearance at Z100's December 9 Jingle Ball, among other planned events. She had been scheduled to promote a novel, *Dollhouse*, which she had written with her sisters, but Khloé and Kourtney were forced to hawk the new book without her, which might account for its subsequent mediocre sales.

Kim later admitted a sense of deep foreboding when she witnessed the backlash against her. "At the time when I was going through the divorce I did say to everyone, 'You guys I think our careers are over,'" she told *The Drum*. "'I hope you've saved your money. And now we'll just continue to do our clothing stores and continue to do what we started off doing before the show.' I was being very paranoid. I just took some time off and the time was really good for me. I cancelled everything. I had a book tour, I had a fragrance launch, I had everything that you could possibly imagine and I just cancelled it all and I took time for me."

It's easy to see why Kim thought the brand was irreparably tar-

nished, judging by some media outlets' seeming delight in announcing that the Kardashian phenomenon was finished. In January 2012,
for example, the New York Post published a report that appeared to
confirm the downward trend.

"You may not have to keep up with the Kardashians much longer," the paper reported. "Everything the reality family touches turns
absolutely toxic—with party promoters, magazine editors and television execs all scrambling to blacklist them."

Noting that Kim was once paid $600,000 to appear at a New
Year's Eve party in Las Vegas, the paper interviewed Travis Bass,
owner of the popular Chinatown hot spot Red Egg.

"I'd pay her $600,000 personally not to go to Red Egg," Bass said.
"Kim Kardashian would be crushing to us."

Once, Kim's appearance on the cover of a magazine guaranteed
high circulation. Now, reported the Post, circulation at Us Weekly, In
Touch, Life & Style, and OK! dropped about 18 percent when a Kardashian was on the cover in December.

And even the TV show was starting to suffer ratings declines,
with E! reporting a 14 percent dip in viewership of the new season,
compared to the year before.

"I'm bored with them," revealed publicist R. Couri Hay, who had
paid Kardashian family members to visit New York clubs in 2008 and
2010. Now, he told the paper, he wouldn't dream of paying to bring
in "Kim Kardashian and her little clunky sisters."

Stories like this appeared to confirm that the divorce and subsequent high-profile backlash were having a devastating effect on the
brand. But the predicted demise wasn't going to happen if Kris Jenner had anything to say about it. Undoubtedly concerned about the
fallout from the divorce, Kris had counseled her daughter to stay out
of the limelight for a period until the dust settled. But behind the
scenes, Kris was as busy as ever and, contrary to reports such as the
Post obituary, the money continued to pour in.

When the first signs of a Paris Hilton backlash had appeared in 2006, her handlers had worked furiously to rebrand her by bathing her in what they called the "hip-hop ethos." If she was suffering over-exposure with one demographic, the reasoning went, it was time to build a new following. If small-town unsophisticated young women were beginning to tire of her, it was time to build up her appeal in a new urban market.

Whether or not it was a coincidence, Kim suddenly reemerged from her self-imposed exile in the spring of 2012 with reports that she was dating the hip-hop megastar Kanye West. The two had report-edly first met when she was still married to Damon Thomas in 2004. Kanye later recalled that he had felt drawn to her as far back as 2006, when he saw a photo of her in Australia with Paris Hilton. They next bumped into each other in 2007 at a Beverly Hills party, but Kanye was engaged at the time to designer Alex Phifer, and Kim was seeing Reggie Bush. In 2010, Kim had participated in an ill-fated recording, singing a heavily Auto-Tuned song, "Jam," produced by The Dream. At the time, Kanye was spotted in the recording studio, prompting rumors that the two were either an item or that they were collaborat-ing on the single.

"He's a musical genius, so I would be honored to work with Kanye," Kim said at the time. "It's all in fun. We're just trying to have a good time." At the time, Kris Jenner was reported to have scolded Kanye when she caught his eyes wandering. "Don't be looking at her ass," Kris allegedly said, to which Kanye replied, "I've never seen it, actually." When the single was eventually released, with half the pro-ceeds going to charity, the critics were not so charitable. The *Daily News* called the song a "dead-brained piece of generic dance music, without a single distinguishing feature," and opined that the single made Kardashian the "worst singer in the reality TV universe."

In March 2012, the first rumors of a romance between the two began to circulate, when they were photographed sitting together during Paris Fashion Week. A month later, they were dating openly. At first, it seemed like an unlikely pairing. The media were evidently not buying it, as judged by the heavy dose of skepticism served up about the new couple. In a *New York* magazine profile about the Kardashians' hold on popular culture, the respected publication too took aim at everything about the family while referencing the odd new coupling.

"The felony count in the indictment, though, seems to be the family's utter disregard for the boundaries that give the rest of us a sense of order in the cosmos," the writer observed.

> *It unsettles our ideas about how things work, or how they should work, to see the Kardashians thrive by blithely trampling over the customary lines between self and other, private and public, soul and body, work and play, real and fake. Is Kim's Twitter praise for those slingbacks purely heartfelt, or is she receiving $10,000 for it? Is she holding that green cocktail because she likes it, or because of an endorsement contract? Has she lately been dating men whose names start with K (Kris, and now Kanye West) out of mere koincidence, or because she's following the example of her mother, Kris Jenner, who seems to have chosen her daughters' names—Kourtney, Kim, Khloé, Kendall, Kylie— out of a branding manual rather than a baby book?*

Indeed, few were buying that the relationship with Kanye was anything but a publicity ploy aimed at shoring up the brand of both parties. But a closer look at Kanye's history would indicate that perhaps the pairing wasn't so far-fetched after all.

Kanye had burst upon the music scene in the late '90s as a producer for the Roc-A-Fella record label and by 2001 had achieved acclaim for his work on Jay Z's landmark release, *The Blueprint*, for which he produced four tracks and which announced his arrival as a major player on the hip-hop scene. Unlike many of his peers, Kanye was anything but street, having been born into a middle-class Chicago family. His father, a former Black Panther, left when Kanye was just a baby and would eventually become an award-winning photojournalist. This left the young boy to be raised by his mother, Donda, a respected academic who served as the chair of the English department at Chicago State University, where she spent thirty-one years before retiring to work full-time for her son.

The bond between mother and son was always very tight. In 2004, before Kanye's breakout release as a rapper, Professor West told the *Chicago Tribune* that Kanye's talent was obvious even as a young boy. "We were coming back from a short vacation in Michigan when he was 5, and he composed a poem in the back seat," she recalled. "The one line that sticks with me is 'the trees are melting black.' It was late fall, and the trees had no leaves. He saw how those limbs were etched against the sky, and he described them the way a poet would. People say Kanye and humility don't belong in the same sentence, but he's had that determination since he was 3."

For his part, Kanye was always devoted to his mother, and the two shared a strong bond. "My mother was my everything," he told *MTV News* in 2005, discussing his childhood. When he was only thirteen, Kanye cowrote a rap song, "Green Eggs and Ham," which his mother paid twenty-five dollars an hour for studio time to record. But Kanye was never a rapper, and few could have imagined him as a front man. Apart from his comfortable upbringing, he never really seemed at ease with the hip-hop look or style. When he started musing about recording his own rap album, few took him seriously, not even his collaborators at Roc-A-Fella.

When he approached the label, he was at first diplomatically rebuffed. "Kanye wore a pink shirt with the collar sticking up and Gucci loafers," recalled Damon Dash, the Roc-A-Fella CEO. "It was obvious we were not from the same place or cut from the same cloth."

Similarly, Jay Z couldn't picture the preppy, middle-class producer behind the mic.

"We all grew up street guys who had to do whatever we had to do to get by," he told *Time* years later. "Then there's Kanye, who to my knowledge has never hustled a day in his life. I didn't see how it could work."

Nor would any other label give him the time of day, notwithstanding his success as a producer. "It was a strike against me that I didn't wear baggy jeans and jerseys and that I never hustled, never sold drugs," he remembered. "But for me to have the opportunity to stand in front of a bunch of executives and present myself, I had to hustle in my own way. I can't tell you how frustrating it was that they didn't get that. No joke—I'd leave meetings crying all the time."

And yet his position at Roc-A-Fella had allowed him to commandeer studio time and lay down his own tracks as far back as 1999 in anticipation of eventually releasing an album of his own. In 2002, Kanye fell asleep at the wheel after a late-night recording session and was involved in a near-fatal car accident that left him with his jaw wired shut. Two weeks later, he went into the studio and recorded a song based on the experience, "Through the Wire," determined to complete the album, which he described as "my medicine." Finally in 2004, he released his breakthrough recording, *The College Dropout*, and achieved almost instant success. The album rocketed to number two on the *Billboard* charts and sold 441,000 copies during its first week, eventually selling more than 4 million copies worldwide. Straying from the gangsta style of most hip-hop at the time, Kanye forged his own distinct sound. The recording was widely acclaimed by critics, with the *New York Times* calling the record "2004's first great hip hop album." *MOJO* called it "manna for hip hop fans," while *URB* wrote that the album "manages to be both visceral and emotive, sprinkling the dance floors with tears and sweat." *Rolling Stone* praised Kanye's "signature cozy sound—dusty soul samples, gospel hymns, drums that pop as if hit for the very first time. He has also succeeded in showing some vulnerability behind a glossy mainstream hip-hop sheen." The magazine would later place *The College Dropout* on its list of the 500 greatest albums of all time. In fact, by the time he started dating Kim Kardashian in 2012, Kanye would have a remarkable three albums on that list. He would also garner twenty-one Grammy Awards and achieve preeminence as one of the most respected musicians of his era.

But in some circles, he was still known as much for his bombastic ego and his controversial antics as he was for his music. In 2005, only a year after he had burst into the limelight, Kanye—or 'Ye, as he was already being dubbed—was invited to participate in a nationally televised telethon to raise money for the victims of Hurricane Katrina, which had recently devastated New Orleans and left thousands of the most vulnerable and mostly black residents homeless. George W. Bush was already being widely criticized for lackluster federal efforts to help the victims during the initial period following the hurricane.

When Kanye appeared with Mike Myers on the telethon, they were given scripted patter for their segment, in which they would describe the devastation of the hurricane. Myers dutifully read his portion from the teleprompter: "The landscape of the city has changed dramatically, tragically, and perhaps irreversibly," he said. "There is now over twenty-five feet of water where there was once city streets and thriving neighborhoods."

When he turned it over to Kanye for his portion, the rapper departed from the script in what appeared to be an ad hoc tirade. "I hate the way they portray us in the media," he began.

> You see a black family, it says, "They're looting." You see a white family, it says, "They're looking for food." And, you know, it's been five days [waiting for federal help] because most of the people are black. And even for me to complain about it,

I would be a hypocrite, because I've tried to turn away from the TV because it's too hard to watch. I've even been shopping before even giving a donation, so now I'm calling my business manager right now to see what is the biggest amount I can give, and just to imagine if I was down there, and those are my people down there. So anybody out there that wants to do anything that we can help—with the way America is set up to help the poor, the black people, the less well off, as slow as possible. I mean, the Red Cross is doing everything they can. We already realize a lot of people that could help are at war right now, fighting another way—and they've given them permission to go down and shoot us!

Myers appeared to have no idea how to respond. "And subtle, but in many ways even more profoundly devastating, is the lasting damage to the survivors' will to rebuild and remain in the area," he read. "The destruction of the spirit of the people of southern Louisiana and Mississippi may end up being the most tragic loss of all."

When he again turned over the microphone, it appeared that Kanye was still not finished with his thoughts. "George Bush doesn't care about black people!" he announced.

NBC ended up cutting his comments from their West Coast feed, but the damage had been done. The network issued a hastily drawn-up statement addressing Kanye's rant. "Tonight's telecast was a live television event wrought with emotion. Kanye West departed from the scripted comments that were prepared for him, and his opinions in no way represent the views of the networks. It would be most unfortunate if the efforts of the artists who participated tonight and the generosity of millions of Americans who are helping those in need are overshadowed by one person's opinion."

The proclamation unleashed an immediate backlash among Bush supporters, who vented their wrath on this uppity black rapper, remi-

niscent of the backlash that greeted Muhammad Ali in 1967 when
he refused to be drafted into the army because "I ain't got no quarrel
with them Vietcong. No Vietcong ever called me nigger."

Bush would eventually describe Kanye's comments as "one of
the most disgusting moments of my presidency." He told the *Today*
show's Matt Lauer, "He called me a racist. And I didn't appreciate it
then. I don't appreciate it now. It's one thing to say, 'I don't appreciate the way he's handled his business.' It's another thing to say, 'This
man's a racist.' I resent it; it's not true."

Although he had looked shocked by his copresenter's remarks at
the time, Mike Myers would tell GQ that he was proud of Kanye's
comments. "I'm the guy next to the guy who spoke a truth. I assume
that George Bush does care about black people, I mean I don't know
him, I'm going to make that assumption, but I can definitively say
that it appeared to me watching television that had that been white
people, the government would have been there faster."

Kanye's mother, Donda, also supported her son. "We need more
people who aren't afraid to speak their minds," Donda West told the
Chicago Tribune. "I have always encouraged him to think and to speak
the truth as he sees it."

Unfortunately, Kanye's brave Katrina comments weren't the only
time he courted controversy with his outspokenness. In 2004, he
stormed out of the American Music Awards in a huff when he lost
out to country singer Gretchen Wilson for Best New Artist. Backstage,
he told reporters, "I was the best new artist this year." In 2006, Kanye
began a tradition of storming the stage, when his video for "Touch the
Sky" lost out in the Best Hip Hop Video category at the MTV Europe
Awards to Justice and Simian. Hurling obscenities, he said that he was
the rightful winner of the award because his video had "cost a million
dollars, Pamela Anderson was in it, and I was jumping off canyons. If
I don't win, the awards show loses credibility. I had the best video.
'Touch the Sky' was a great moment in TV."

Dubbed a poor loser, he later defended his actions, especially his use of profanity, to *MTV News*. "People were cursing throughout the whole night," he said. "It was encouraged. I know how to use proper English. I was more offended that the press had the audacity to think I wouldn't know when to curse. People were so surprised at what I did. I'm more surprised people thought I had changed."

Indeed, his ego was quickly gaining a reputation and overshadowing his musical brilliance. "I'm at no time arrogant or humble—I'm straightforward, like, 'This is how I feel,'" he said. "Matter of fact, I'm not going to any more awards shows. From now on, I got all the awards I need. I'm only making my music for the fans. . . . The streets know, and the fans know, that 'Touch the Sky' was killin' that video. . . . Don't even nominate my shit. Don't play with me. I don't need awards to validate me."

Alas, his vow to boycott awards ceremonies was short-lived, as Taylor Swift would learn when Kanye stormed onto the stage just as she was about to accept her award for Best Female Video at the 2009 MTV Video Music Awards. As she was about to start her acceptance speech, the rapper leaped on stage, grabbed the microphone out of her hands, and announced, "I'm sorry, but Beyoncé had one of the best videos of all time!"

Swift, only nineteen at the time, later described her feelings about the incident to *People* magazine. "I was standing onstage, and I was really excited because I'd just won the award, and then I was really excited because Kanye West was onstage. And then I wasn't excited anymore after that."

The stunt earned Kanye the enmity of countless celebrities, who immediately rose to Swift's defense. "Kanye west is the biggest piece of shit on earth," Pink Tweeted. "Quote me. Beyoncé is a classy lady. I feel for her, too. Its not her fault at all, and her and taylor did their thing. And douche bag got kicked out. HA." Katy Perry was no less enraged. "Fuck u Kanye. It's like you stepped on a kitten,"

she Tweeted after the incident. Even President Obama called him a
"jackass." Kanye later went on Jay Leno to apologize to Swift. "It was
rude, period, and I would like to apologize to her in person," he said.

In response to the criticism, he would later explain that he
engaged in these types of stunts because he was so passionate. "When
I did things like that or the 'George Bush doesn't care about black
people' moment, it wasn't a matter of being selfish," he wrote in *XXL*
magazine. "It's more like I was being selfless—that I would risk everything to express what I felt was the truth."

If these antics sparked controversy, they were nothing compared
to the fury unleashed when Kanye compared himself to Jesus on his
sixth album, *Yeezus*. "I know he the most High / but I am a close
high," he rapped on his single, "I am a God." With those words, Jesus
became just one of the many icons that 'Ye would compare himself
to, including Michael Jordan, Steve Jobs, and even one of the greatest artists of all time. "No matter how they try to control you, or the
motherfucker next to you tries to peer pressure you, you can do what
you motherfucking want. I am Picasso," he told his fans at a concert in
Paris. And if that wasn't a lofty enough comparison, he would one-up
it at the Big Chill Music Festival in 2011, when he compared himself
to another giant of the twentieth century. "I walk through the hotel
and I walk down the street like I'm Hitler. One day the light will shine
through and one day people will understand everything I did."

But if Kanye came off as an egotistical blowhard, given to outrageous hyperbole about his musical abilities, there was one area where
he was just as passionate but also uncharacteristically insecure. Kanye
West, it would appear, never dreamed of being a hip-hop star. His
true calling was fashion.

"I dreamed, since I was a little kid, of having my own store where
I could curate every shoe, sweatshirt and color," he told the *New York
Times*. "I have sketches of it. I cried over the idea of having my own
store."

For years, Kanye had been a fixture in the front row of the world's top fashion shows—Dior, St. Laurent, Givenchy. But all the while, he was plotting for the day when celebrities would be watching super-models parading down the runway in his own collections.

And if it was once hard convincing his music collaborators to let him record his own compositions, it was nothing compared to the obstacles he faced when he tried to conquer the world of high fash-ion. Kanye was so passionate about his dream that in 2009 he and his design collaborator, Virgil Abloh, did an internship at Fendi to learn the ins and outs of a fashion house. In 2011, he launched his first clothing line during Paris Fashion Week, DW Kanye West, a hastily put together collection of ready-to-wear women's clothing that he dedicated to Donda, who had died after a botched breast-reduction surgery in 2007. It was not a stellar debut.

"Good thing Kanye has a day job," wrote the *Wall Street Jour-nal* fashion blogger. "The only thing more painful than witnessing the dress was watching the model pitch down the runway in shoes so ill-fitting that her spike heels were bending at angles.

"One breastplate of a top—recalled the Flintstones. . . . There were lots and lots of tight leather pants. . . . Yet a vast quantity of lux-ury materials can't blind people to a lack of creative marksmanship."

The *New York Times* was equally disdainful. "His collection of sexpot low-bodice dresses and skintight pants, decked out with heaps of ginger fur, did not inspire the fashion crowd to tell him to give up his day job."

Not all reviewers hated it, though. "West proved nay-sayers wrong with his slick collection of sexy, hard-edged looks that were hands-down better—in terms of design and construction—than much of what's been shown during the first five days of Paris' spring-summer 2012 ready-to-wear collections," wrote the Associated Press critic.

But although he went into debt to finance his first collection, Kanye remained steadfastly committed to his goals. He believed it was his fame and notoriety, not his lack of talent, that were his biggest obstacles as a designer. "The biggest conversation I had was about the whole idea of a celebrity-designer or a rapper-designer," he told a reporter. "That was the biggest hurdle when you are trying to get people to work with you. . . . Fame is often looked down upon in the design world, so it's actually been something I had to overcome."

He returned to the drawing board, consulted with respected design mentors, and poured his soul into his vision. Designer Jeremy Scott recalled that Kanye was "so passionate about design that we can have conversations about fashion for five or six hours." His second collection launched in March 2012, during spring Fashion Week, in front of a star-studded audience that included Sean Combs, Alicia Keys, Anna Wintour, and André Talley. This collection was much better received than the first and, although critics still had reservations, it appeared that Kanye the designer had finally achieved grudging respect.

"In our humble opinion, this sophomore showing proved to be bigger and better than his first," wrote the *Huffington Post*.

Sitting prominently in the first row at the launch of his spring collection was his rumored new romance, Kim Kardashian. In interviews, Kanye was beginning to articulate his vision in the kind of soaring rhetoric that he had previously reserved for his music, and he was fond of comparing the two worlds. "Before the Internet, music was really expensive," he told *T* magazine.

> *People would use a rack of CDs to show class, to show they had made it. Right now, people use clothes to telegraph that. I want to destroy that. The very thing that supposedly made me special— the jacket that no one could get, the direct communications with the designers—I want to give that to the world.*
>
> *I think high fashion is about elitism and separation, and I am completely opposed to that. If someone was to say, "Hey, do*

you want to go to a high-end house now?" I'd absolutely say
no. Because I'm only concerned with making beautiful products
available to as many people as possible. The least I could do is
spend my time trying to give other people a piece of the so-called
good life. Everyone should have the good life.

His frequent discussion of making high-end fashion affordable
to everyone sounded remarkably similar to another celebrity who
had launched her own fashion line vowing to help her fans dress like
the rich and famous but without the high price tag. When Kim Kardashian launched her inaugural line for Bebe in 2010, she had promised to make fashion "affordable for everyone."

And although most observers had dismissed the unlikely pairing at first or believed that "Kimye" was merely a publicity stunt, it
appeared that the new couple were actually kindred spirits.

Still, in the world of the Kardashians, it's impossible to take anything at face value. The relationship with Kanye came along at the
low point of Kim's career, precisely when she desperately needed
to change the subject of her failed marriage to Kris Humphries and
appeal to a new demographic. It was quickly apparent from the media
focus on the new couple that she had accomplished this in spades. For
Kanye, he was obsessed with reaching a new market for his affordable
but somewhat mediocre fashion lines, preferably a demographic not
known for their sophisticated tastes. Kim's fan base offered millions
of new consumers and a direct pipeline to middle America.

Yet marketing executives were not convinced at first that the relationship could help either one of them. "We are starting out with two
individuals with the deck stacked against them, and when you put
the two of them together, they will be a turn-off to the majority of
the audience," Steven Levitt, the president of Marketing Evaluations,
told Fox News in 2012. Citing their "Q ratings," which measures the
likability of celebrities, Levitt noted that Kanye had a negative rating

of fifty-eight. "While his positive rating isn't dreadful, his negative is way beyond the average for the category," Levitt said. His company had not run the numbers on Kim since the Humphries divorce, but in August, around the time of the wedding, her numbers had been even worse than Kanye's, with a positive score of twelve (compared to Kanye's eighteen) and a negative of fifty-three. "When you look at Kim and Kanye together you see that the audience does not favor either of them," Levitt said. "For the most part they turn off the general audience."

Similarly, when the first rumors of their relationship surfaced, *In Touch* senior editor Dorothy Casterceri told Fox that such a relationship would not help Kim win back the hearts and minds of America after the divorce backlash. "Right now Kim needs to focus on repairing her image and winning back the public's approval and their trust in her," she said. "Kanye West is a horrible choice. Those two would be the most hated couple in America if they started dating. He's extremely outspoken to the point of self-absorbed and conceited in the eyes of many. She needs to go with someone who the public already loves."

There were certainly enough good reasons for the cynical to dismiss the relationship. Apart from the fish-out-of-water elements on both sides, Kanye was not known for monogamy. I met up with a woman named Alicia Banton, who dated Kanye's cousin Tony Williams, his longtime collaborator and backup singer. Banton, who was also one of Kanye's dancers at the Brit Awards in 2004, claims the Kanye she knew was something of a womanizer. "He was engaged at the time and was having affairs on the side, including an affair with his stylist. I saw her go to Kanye's hotel room several times and not come out until the next morning. Back in the day, Kanye would like to go out to clubs and would always be around beautiful, young women. I hope his marriage to Kim lasts, but with Kanye you never know. He has a very big ego." But, despite almost weekly tabloid headlines predicting the demise of the relationship, it is still going strong four years later. Whether or not they are using each other for their own reasons, it is very clear that Kanye West is no Kris Humphries.

In a profile entitled "American Mozart," the *Atlantic Monthly* perfectly captured the many facets of the Kanye of old. "He is a petulant, adolescent, blanked-out, pained emotional mess who toggles between songs about walking with Jesus and songs about luxury brands and porn stars."

He had once been dubbed "the most hated man in show business." But by the time he started dating Kim, there were already indications that he had softened his image and shed some of the old bombast. Using a parable, he would later reveal to *T* magazine that this was no mirage. He had consciously vowed to rein in his once massive ego. "I have this table in my new house," he said. "They put this table in without asking. It was some weird nouveau riche marble table, and I hated it. But it was literally so heavy that it took a crane to move it. We would try to set up different things around it, but it never really worked. I realized that table was my ego. No matter what you put around it, under it, no matter who photographed it, the douchebaggery would always come through."

Indeed, Kanye seemed to have mellowed considerably by the time he was introduced on *Keeping Up with the Kardashians*. In 2012, viewers got to see Kanye show his sensitive side, when he arrived to give Kim a "style makeover."

Kim gushes about how much her new boyfriend inspires her to be more of an individual. "He's a fashion designer and he loves clothes," she tells the viewers, noting the irony that she's the one who once made her living doing closet makeovers, and now the roles are reversed. With his personal stylist, Kanye proceeds to discard massive amounts of clothes—almost the entire collection, including more than a hundred pairs of shoes—into what is dubbed the "donation pile," so that Kanye can fill her closet with new clothes that he has picked out for her. By the time the episode aired in July 2012, it had become apparent that rather than simply a closet makeover, the purging of Kim's wardrobe was merely a part of the image makeover that Kris had been engineering for months.

The public quickly learned that the thousands of dollars' worth of designer clothes and high-end shoes would be going to a good cause when Kim Tweeted, "The clothes I got rid of will be up on EBay next month for a charity auction! Going to Life Change Community Church."

This was the beginning of the new altruistic Kim Kardashian, who believed in giving back some of her millions in earnings to the community. The eBay charity auctions would be a crucial part of her publicity machine in the months and years to come. Like many celebrities who choose to align themselves with a charitable cause to defuse negative publicity, Kim publicly announced herself as a spiritual person who would bathe herself in the goodwill of religious work. What most of her millions of followers didn't know when she announced the recipient of her first charitable endeavor was that the church with which she chose to align herself was one her own mother had founded—an institution that would later uncharitably be dubbed the "Kult of Kardashian."

From the time she married Robert Kardashian, Kris Jenner had embraced the evangelical Protestantism that his family had long practiced since their ancestors rejected the tenets of the more traditional Armenian Orthodox Church. In those days, they attended weekly prayer sessions at the house of the strictly fundamentalist Pat Boone and others of a similar religious bent. When Kris moved with Bruce to Calabasas, they soon discovered the evangelical Calvary Community Church just down the Ventura Freeway from their Hidden Hills home. They were especially taken with its charismatic pastor, Brad Johnson, who had built a congregation of a massive 4,000 members with his hip, irreverent style. The minister and occasional surfer, with his long hair and tattoos, had the congregation eating out of his hand during his fiery sermons. "You went to church and you felt like he was talking to you," Kris later told the Ventura County *Star*.

But in 2007, Johnson and the church were rocked by scandal when it was discovered that he was cheating on his wife of twenty-eight years, Kimberley. The revelation forced him from his ministry, resulting in a huge drop in church attendance and even staff layoffs. A year later, Johnson took to his blog to apologize to his former congregation, whom he felt he had betrayed along with his wife.

"I am sorry for the pain and emotional upheaval my actions have caused you and the precious bride of Christ," he wrote. "I'm sorry for the deceptions, the irresponsibility, and the sin of adultery that came from my life and infected others. I assume full responsibility for my actions with no excuses and no rationalizations."

His wife left him when the scandal erupted, and Johnson tried to kill himself three times, including once with an overdose of pills that forced paramedics to break down the door to resuscitate him. He had hit rock bottom. "The shame was suffocating," he recalled. Since Johnson's resignation from Calvary, Kris had missed the inspiration that she had always found in his sermons. She had heard that Johnson had taken a job at a Starbucks, but she had no idea where. Bruce Jenner was dispatched on a mission to find him. "I felt God was saying to me, 'Go get him. Go find him,' " Kris recalled. Finally, Bruce found Johnson working at a Starbucks in Westlake Village, not far from his old church. Kris met with him and proposed starting a new place of worship near Calabasas. She agreed to finance the startup of the new venture—the Life Change Community Church—which would be dedicated to giving people second chances. Her own mega-empire, after all, had been built on her daughter's sex tape and America's seeming willingness to see past it.

"It's not about me. It's just about God's word," she told the *Star*. "I don't think anyone has the right to tell anyone else they don't have a right to a second chance."

At the time, Johnson said his church services might seem more like an Alcoholics Anonymous meeting than traditional worship. "People won't have to meet a standard or even change their behavior to become part of the congregation. Acceptance will be automatic and if change comes, it will happen naturally. God loves you just the way you are, but he loves you too much to leave you that way," he said.

They scouted locations and decided to hold Sunday services in the rented ballroom of a Sheraton hotel in Agoura Hills, about fifteen minutes from Kris's Calabasas home. Agoura Hills just happened to be the location of another church built and financed by a celebrity. In 2003, Mel Gibson had built the Church of the Holy Family, a seventeen-acre compound dedicated to Gibson's extremist interpretation of Roman Catholic doctrine, which rejects most of the reforms of Vatican II.

Although Kris was undeniably sincere about her religious beliefs, the church became a convenient prop whenever she or the family needed to burnish their image. After her divorce from Kris Humphries and the subsequent backlash, Kim started Tweeting regularly about her church attendance.

"Early morning workout done now off to church with the family," she Tweeted in 2011. Around the same time, she Tweeted, "On my way to church with the girls! I want to start a Bible study group with my friends!" On another occasion, she included a photo of herself and Kris in the parking lot of the church. "Perfect day so far! Church and family brunch."

She also took to re-Tweeting messages from Pastor Johnson. "RT @brad_s_johnson: When Jesus died on the cross, He was judged for the sins of the world . . . court is no longer in session. Stop Judging." Kris took an increasingly active role in the church that she had founded and even acted as an officiator at the 2011 remarriage of Johnson.

So when Kim publicized the fact that she was donating her discarded clothes to charity, the family's new church was a logical choice. What neither Kim nor Kris ever trumpeted in the myriad press coverage about this new charitable bent—Kim also occasionally donated to an organization benefitting adults with life-threatening illnesses—was the fact that Kim donated only 10 percent of the proceeds to these charities. After subtracting administrative expenses, including Kris's managerial fee, the rest of the money was pure profit, estimated at millions of dollars.

When Kim announced that she was directing the proceeds of her eBay auction to typhoon relief in the Philippines, Radar Online discovered that in fact only 10 percent would be donated. The revelations sparked something of a backlash. "Most of the profits from Kim Kardashian's charity eBay auctions appear to have gone to her favorite cause: herself," reported *Gawker*. But Kim defended the practice, explaining that she tithes 10 percent of her income, not just the eBay auctions, to various causes.

"The problem comes in when I get attacked for giving and trying to help people," she wrote on her blog. "My dad always taught me the importance of giving back. I don't publicize everything I do to help charities and people all over the world. I do it because I want to. I do it because my dad taught me to. I do it because it's the right thing to do. So for people to attack me for giving 10 percent of my eBay auction sales to the people of the Philippines, that hurts."

Despite PR setbacks such as these, Kim had largely succeeded in erasing her negative public image by the time she started dating Kanye in 2012. And despite the cynicism of the so-called image experts, who predicted the relationship would be a disaster, it was soon evident that the opposite was true. Their relationship became a mainstay of both the tabloid press and more serious magazines, which quickly anointed the couple as the high priest and priestess of the fashion world.

And while Kris Jenner was always ambivalent about her daughter's relationship with Kris Humphries, she appears to have embraced Kanye from the start. "A lot of people don't see the real, soft, wonderful side of Kanye," she told *Rolling Stone*. "We fell in love with who Kim fell in love with. I will never be able to replace the relationship he had with his mom, but I sure can make him know he's loved, unconditionally, and we would do anything for him."

Contrary to those who predicted the Humphries divorce would put an end to the Kardashian phenomenon, figures soon showed that the family was more popular than ever. Bruno Sciavi, president of the Kardashian Kollection fashion line, revealed that sales of family-branded items had actually increased since the split. "These girls have grown up in front of a camera and Kim's fans are loyal fans," he told *TheWrap*. "From a brand perspective, I think [the divorce] will only reiterate to fans that they are human."

Through it all, Kris Jenner was deftly maneuvering her daughter's image through a series of carefully controlled photo ops and events, many featuring the new couple. Only two months after Kim and Kanye started dating, for example, a number of media outlets reported that she had dropped a whopping $750,000 on a present for her new boyfriend's thirty-fifth birthday. Because he was in Ireland at the time, Kim took a video of the car to send him, which just happened to make its way into the media, along with breathless reports of the "surprise" gift. My own sources informed me that it was Kris who arranged for the "surprise" and negotiated the purchase of the car for a fraction of its book value. Indeed, Kris appeared enamored of her daughter's new love and gushed endlessly about him, making sure to leak the news that she liked Kanye much more than her former son-in-law Kris Humphries.

By the time Kanye announced to his fans that Kim was pregnant six months later, the media appeared to have forgotten all about the Humphries backlash. Now it was all about Kim and Kanye. In an essay for *Rolling Stone*, entitled "The Kardashians: The Egos That Ate America," essayist Rob Sheffield attempted to explain the lasting appeal of the family and why nothing seems to diminish the brand.

"The Kardashians are the last ladies standing in reality TV because they've simply always believed they were celebrities—endlessly amused with themselves, endlessly oblivious to one another," he writes.

> *Their vanity is impervious to the outside world, which is how many of us often wish our own personal vanity worked. Their gargantuan egos, their petty jealousies, their catty feuds, the effort-vs.-eye-roll they put into reciting their lines, their commitment to frivolity at all costs—these are seductive qualities in a reality-TV star, however repugnant they might be in real life. Whatever it is you watch reality TV for, the Kardashians just have a lot more of it. . . . You might loathe the Kardashians, and that's more than understandable. But there are hardly any ex-fans of the Kardashians, because all they ever promised is what they keep delivering: a journey into the American ego at its most luridly monstrous, with lots of shopping. The ongoing Kardashian saga has turned into the rise and where-the-hell-is-that-fall of an American-family empire, bigger than U.S. Steel.*

Indeed, his comparison to a business giant may not have been much of an exaggeration. In 2011, a rep for the family's lifestyle brands had revealed an eye-popping estimate of the family's earning power. "The Kardashians could easily be a billion-dollar business worldwide in the next two years," Brian Dow told *Women's Wear Daily*.

Indeed, the revenues seemed to be coming from every direction. In 2012, for example, Kris signed a three-year deal with E!—worth upward of $40 million—to continue producing the show, making it the most lucrative deal in TV history and ensuring distribution of the show to more than a hundred markets around the planet. Of course, as the family members regularly acknowledge, the show is merely a vehicle to hawk the many lucrative products in their empire. Kris had struck a deal with Sears back in 2011 to market the Kardashian Kollection of affordable clothing and accessories. In 2013, according to *Forbes*, the collection had raked in a staggering $600 million in sales, which would have netted the family at least $30 million. Add to that proceeds from the Kardashian Beauty Cosmetics line, appearance fees, book royalties, and countless other endorsements. Kim's take? At least $28 million, according to *Forbes*.

Through it all, Kris Jenner spent twelve to sixteen hours a day wheeling and dealing and earning every penny of her 10 percent. The *Hollywood Reporter* got hold of Kris's calendar from one February day to illustrate a typical schedule for Kris when the show is not filming:

- 3:30 a.m. Satellite media tour with Khloé for T-Mobile.
- 7–8 a.m. Workout with Gunnar Peterson.
- 8–8:30 a.m. Return East Coast business phone calls from the car.
- 8:30–9 a.m. Shower and dress.
- 9–9:30 a.m. E-mail correspondence from office.
- 10 a.m. Meeting with Leonard Armato about filming an upcoming Skechers commercial with Kim.
- 10:30 a.m. Phoner with *Seventeen* magazine about Kendall and Kylie.
- 10:45 a.m. Phone interview with writer for *Redbook* magazine article.
- 11 a.m. Meeting with QVC about new Kris Jenner clothing line.
- Noon. Lunch with Lighthouse Beauty regarding fragrance

launch for Khloé and Lamar's Unbreakable for Valentine's Day at the Beverly Hills Hotel.

- 1 p.m. Phoner with Keith Frankel to review spring ads for QuickTrim line.
- 1:30 p.m. Meeting with Jupi and Sears for creative approvals for new Kardashian collection.
- 3 p.m. Creative meeting with Ryan Seacrest Productions at E! about new series.
- 5 p.m. Drop by Khloé and Kourtney's *Kardashian Konfidential* book signing at Barnes & Noble in Santa Monica.
- 6 p.m. Finalize and approve photos for Robert's new OP campaign.
- 7 p.m. Dinner at home with Bruce, Kendall and Kylie, Scott, Kourtney and Mason.
- 8 p.m. Watch *American Idol*.

Given the sheer size of the family's empire and the never-ending endorsement deals, the paper asked Kris whether she ever actually says no to any proposed business venture. She gave an example of one such veto involving a sex-toy company that wanted to sign Khloé and Lamar.

"The company wanted to know why I was turning them down," she recalled. "I said, 'It's just not the look we're going for at this moment, but thank you.' They said, 'It's not hardcore, just vibrating panties, nipple rings and vibrators.' I was like, 'Hell to the no!'"

Still, there was no shortage of other opportunities. "Kim has shown up to cut a ribbon on a public toilet!" notes Bonnie Fuller, editor of Hollywoodlife.com. "They've really shown though that you can extend far and associate yourself with all types of companies without killing your brand. The Kardashian philosophy is 'let's take advantage of everything we can while the iron is hot.' They're less concerned with a 20-year brand and more about the moment."

"The Kardashians get the big picture," agrees marketing consultant David Caplan. "They've branded the entire family and make use
of each one as their own economy and as joint brands—mother and
daughter, daughters—they cover a large demographic of people who
aspire to their kind of imperfection and will buy anything related
to it."

From the beginning of the show's run in 2007, Kris had been
content to let her children, especially Kim, be the public face of
the marketing efforts that had brought the family countless millions.
But as she became a personality in her own right—her antics were
undeniably the highlight of most shows—she appeared to believe
that she could cash in on her increasing notoriety. In 2011, the matriarch published a memoir, *Kris Jenner . . . And All Things Kardashian*,
which failed to shoot to the top of the *New York Times* bestseller list
as her publisher had hoped but still enjoyed decent sales. The same
year, she launched the Kris Jenner Kollection on QVC, with a tagline
that attempted to build on the success of her show.

"Kris Jenner, self-titled 'momager' of the Kardashians, manages
the careers of seven of her family members & always looks great while
doing so! Who better to trust for comfy, yet fabulous fashions? Her
Kollection of blazers, knits, outerwear & more will take any wardrobe
to wow."

With a modicum of success in her own solo endeavors, Kris
apparently believed that it was time for her turn in the spotlight. The
woman who was once described as a narcissist by her therapist had
evidently decided to embrace this description rather than run from
it. She convinced Fox to grant her a daytime talk show, which would
focus on pop culture. Not entirely convinced she could carry her own
show without her husband and children to provide the drama, the
network agreed to a trial six-week run. With considerable hype in the
weeks leading up to the launch—"Kreative, Kaptivating, Karing, Kos-
mopolitan," previews trumpeted—there was much speculation about

whether Kim would appear to show off her baby bump. She had married Kanye two months earlier in Florence, Italy, and the birth of the couple's first child was generating much media buzz. Kris had been hinting that her soon-to-be-born granddaughter might even receive her first public exposure on the new show.

In preshow publicity, Kris revealed that she had often played talk-show host while driving her children to school when they were little. "They were stuck back there in seat belts and they had to listen to me because they had no choice. So I interviewed them. I would banter and they would listen and pretend like they were on a talk show."

When the show, *Kris*, finally debuted in July 2013, it was an unmitigated disaster, as viewers failed to tune in. There was a slight bump for the last show of the run, when Kanye appeared to unveil the first photos of the couple's baby girl, North West, but it wasn't enough to salvage the show, which was unceremoniously canceled by Fox in a curt press release. The network's programming VP, Frank Cicha, later revealed that he had known the show wasn't going to work almost from the beginning, hinting that the network's corporate bosses thought they could piggyback on E!'s notable success with the Kardashian franchise.

"I think she was pretty uninteresting," he told the *Hollywood Reporter*. "That was one where 20th Television tried to capitalize on a name. When the camera was on she looked not just like a deer in the headlights, but like a deer that already got hit."

A year later, Kris would publish a cookbook, *In the Kitchen with Kris*, which also proved something of a failure on both a commercial and culinary level.

"The recipes in here are bland and tasteless," one reviewer wrote on Amazon.com. "I made the macaroni and cheese, and you would think with all the different varieties of cheese used, it would be flavorful, but instead I got a very expensive, unedible mass of oily noodles."

Despite these setbacks in her personal ventures, Kris had managed to deftly maintain the family brand and the Kardashian retail empire, thanks in no small part to America's fascination with Kimye and Kris's knack for reinventing the brand when necessary. Indeed, Kim proved that her appeal was stronger than ever when she launched a mobile video game, *Kim Kardashian: Hollywood*, that would allow players to interact with her as they maneuvered the glamorous world of celebrity. "Join KIM KARDASHIAN on a red carpet adventure in Kim Kardashian: Hollywood!" trumpeted the app's description. "Create your own aspiring celebrity and rise to fame and fortune!" The app was downloaded almost twenty-three million times—resulting in 5.7 billion minutes of game play—in the first few months of its release, and the company that developed it predicted that the app could produce a staggering $200 million in sales in its first year alone.

Its success proved that the loyal base of support had not abandoned Kim or her family as many had predicted. Yet while the family's core fans remained undaunted, the rest of America now seemed to regard the Kardashians as the living embodiment of the dumbing down of American society. It now appeared to be open season on the family. While Michelle Obama, for example, had once hinted that her husband feared the influence of the family's show on his daughters, the president now spoke for himself.

In an interview with Amazon in 2013, Obama talked about how America had changed since he was a child. "I don't think people went around saying to themselves: 'I need to have a 10,000 square-foot house.' . . . We weren't exposed to things we didn't have in the same way kids these days are. There was not that window into the lifestyles of the rich and famous. Kids weren't monitoring every day what Kim Kardashian was wearing, or where Kanye West was going on vacation, and thinking that somehow that was the mark of success."

In addition, tabloids and entertainment websites appeared to be falling all over themselves to declare that the TV series was—gasp!—

scripted. Indeed, Kris's former lover Todd Waterman had revealed that Kris had confided in him that the shows were fake. "There's no truth to the shows," he said in 2012. "They're all preconceived. Kris shared that with me once, that they make it up. It's mindless, it's nonsense, like *Jersey Shore*."

Now TMZ purported to have obtained new proof. While the *Keeping Up with the Kardashians* executive producer Russell Jay had already confirmed that some scenes were staged, the site claimed that they had gotten hold of an actual production outline for an episode of the show's upcoming tenth season, which proves that the premise of shows are actually planned in advance.

The site revealed that, according to the outline, after Kim and Kanye move into their new home, Kim returns to Kris's house and takes some silverware and cookware. The script has Kris storming over to the couple's new house to confront her daughter.

According to the site's production sources, "In one scene, after Kim and Kanye move into their new home, Kim goes back to Kris' home and takes a bunch of cookware and silverware.

"And through a crack in the door Kris screams, 'I gave you life and you stole my cookware!,' " the script reveals. "Kim fires back that if Kris doesn't back off she'll have her removed from the premises."

Kim then slams the door, at which point "Kris goes crazy. She picks up a rock and throws it at an upstairs window, shattering the glass as she screams, 'You won't get rid of me this easily.' "

According to a woman I know in Los Angeles who once worked on the technical side of the Kardashian TV empire in its early years, the shows are not in fact "scripted" per se. Rather, she explained, they are closer to what she called "improv comedy." She compared the Kardashian shows and their spinoffs to Larry David's popular HBO series, *Curb Your Enthusiasm*, and Christopher Guest's mockumentaries such as *Best in Show*, where the participants are given scenarios in advance and urged to improvise the dialogue.

In each episode, she explained, there is a rough outline of the premise produced in advance—including a "main plot and a subplot"—with ideas sometimes contributed by Kris Jenner, sometimes by other family members, and other times by the producers. Then the cameras are turned on, the family performs, some scenes are reshot, and hours of footage are condensed in the editing room to produce each show.

Does this fit the definition of scripted deception? When I came across accusations such as these while researching the rise of the Kardashians, and witnessed the ensuing outrage on social media and pop culture websites, I wondered two things. First, why would anybody care? Second, why is anybody surprised? It's patently obvious that the producers of all so-called reality shows manipulate the premise for entertainment value, whether in the editing suite or with pre-conceived show outlines designed to maximize the entertainment value. Otherwise, "reality" can be exceedingly tedious. It's not a federal crime, and nobody gets hurt, just entertained. For the millions of Kardashian followers, the shows are a simple escape from their own humdrum lives. Is that not the purpose of the so-called Hollywood dream factory?

CHAPTER THIRTEEN

When I set out to chronicle the family's unique place in popular culture, I had vowed not to let myself get caught up in these type of controversies, nor treat any such revelation as an exposé that would confirm *Rolling Stone*'s description of the Kardashians as the "vapid, vain and banal American dream." I couldn't be less interested in the drunken revelry of Scott Disick, nor could I give a rat's ass about Kim's alleged surgical enhancements. My goal was to determine what lies behind the remarkable cultural and business phenomenon that the family has come to represent. If I were to focus on the myriad tabloid rumors or the foibles of the Kardashians and their assorted hangers-on, I would have enough material for a trilogy.

A chance encounter in the spring of 2015, however, threw me briefly off course. While I was on a media tour promoting my book about the circumstances behind the death of Bobbi Kristina Brown, I found myself appearing on a radio show hosted by my old friend Greg "Opie" Hughes, whom I first met when he was one half of the popular radio duo Opie and Anthony, on whose program I had appeared multiple times. When I happened to mention to Opie that I was working on a new book about the Kardashians, he asked me whether I planned to reveal who Khloé's real father was. "Who's that?" I asked. With a straight face, he answered, "O.J." The London *Mirror* reported O.J. confided to a prison guard that he is not Khloé's father. Jeffrey Felix claimed O.J. confided to him some of his deepest personal secrets, including the rumors about his affair with Kris. Felix told the *Mirror*, "I would never do that to my friend Bob. I would never tap Kris".

One of O.J.'s closest friends for more than twenty years didn't buy Felix's story. "I know how O.J.'s mind works," said the friend, who wanted to be referred to as Gary. "O.J. was with a lot of women throughout the years. He was good friends with Bob so of course he would try to deny it. But I never put anything past O.J., especially when it comes to his dealings with women. Women loved O.J. back then and would do anything to sleep with him. They loved his charm, his fame and his all-American persona. I reserve judgment on this one, the truth would come out only if Khloé submitted to a DNA test. Until then, the jury is out."

On its surface, it's a story on par with Elvis spotted working at a 7-11. The genesis appears to be claims by both women who married Robert Kardashian after he divorced Kris. Both women have separately stated that Robert told them Khloé was not his biological daughter. "Khloé is not his kid—he told me that after we got married," Jan Ashley told a magazine in 2012. "He just kind of looked at me and said [it] like it was a matter of fact. He said, 'Well, you know that Khloé's not really a Kardashian, don't you?' And I said, 'OK,' and that was it."

In 2013, Ellen Pierson, who married Robert weeks before his 2003 death, told *In Touch*, "He never would have considered a DNA test. He loved her very much. Robert did question the fact that Khloé was his."

Neither ever mentioned the Juice. The genesis of that rumor appears to lie in November 2013, when O.J.'s former manager, Norman Pardo, told *In Touch*, "It's all going to come out sooner or later. Khloé could be O.J.'s kid. They all took their vacations together. There was a lot of partying going on back then. Kris cheated on Robert—she was known for having a good time." Pardo said he believes that Khloé was conceived during a "drunken hookup." While he offered no proof, Pardo claimed that he had brought up the question of Khloé's paternity with O.J. "Whenever I bring it up, he giggles," he said.

The story gained traction when O.J.'s good friend Thomas Scotto told Radar Online that even O.J. believed it could be true. "O.J. shared with me on a few occasions that it is a possibility, so it's time to find the truth," he said. "That would end all speculation and rumors, then the truth can be revealed once and for all." Scotto, in fact, was the reason that O.J. had traveled to Las Vegas in September 2007—to be the best man at his longtime friend's wedding. While he was there, the notoriously acquitted murderer learned that some men were trying to sell mementos of his football career and organized a group of friends to confront the sellers. When they arrived at the hotel room where the merchandise was allegedly being housed, O.J. physically stopped the men from leaving. One of them later called the police and accused the Juice of kidnapping, which resulted in his subsequent conviction and thirty-three-year prison sentence.

Could the stories be true? In the book she wrote with her sisters, *Kardashian Konfidential*, Khloé noted that when she was a child, "I just didn't look like my sisters. I was little and petite and this big curly afro. . . . Everyone would say, 'Oh my god. You're a Karadashian sister? You look nothing like them.' And it was true, I looked nothing like them." In a 2009 episode of *Keeping Up with the Kardashians*, Khloé wondered if she had been adopted because she looked so different from her sisters. Kris agreed to take a maternity test to prove that she was in fact Khloé's biological mother. Conspicuously, however, Khloé's DNA was never compared to her other siblings to determine whether they all had the same father.

When the O.J. rumors surfaced, Kris Jenner characterized them as "blatant lies." On *Good Morning America*, she said, "I have never heard such crap in my life. . . . I mean, I was there. I gave birth. I know who the dad was. Everything is good."

In a long-standing Twitter feud with the Kardashian siblings, model and hip-hop artist Amber Rose—a former girlfriend of Kanye West—Tweeted at Khloé, "U think because ur dad was a professional football player that got away with murder ur better than me girl? Haaaaannn?"

The family chose to dismiss the stories with humor. Kim Tweeted, "Now we have all the answers! It makes sense now! Khloé u are so tan!" Khloé went on the *Insider* to address the allegations. "I would hope if I'm half black and [half] white, I would be a little tanner than [my siblings]. I don't know where these stories come from. But, hey, you never know," she said. She was a little crasser while hosting Chelsea Handler's late-night talk show in 2014. Discussing the rumor, she said, "I really hope that's not the case because I did fuck him once."

In a 2012 episode of the spinoff *Khloé and Lamar*—before the O.J. Simpson story surfaced—we see Kim phoning Khloé and bringing up the rumor. "Have you been paying attention to this stupid story that's been running in the tabloids?" she asks. Khloé says she hasn't heard about it. "Well, you need to pay attention," Kim scolds her. "Dad's exes claim that Dad told them right before he died that you are not his biological daughter."

Khloé uses the episode to accuse them of being "desperate for money" and calls it "disturbing." Rob then tells her that Kris had recently called a family meeting, where she revealed that she had "made a mistake as a mother" but urged the siblings not to tell Khloé the truth, which is that she's "not related to us." When Khloé calls Kim to ask about it, Rob confesses that he has been playing a prank because the whole story is "ridiculous." Later, Kourtney says that she and Kim are suggesting that "we get a DNA test" to prove the story isn't true. "Wouldn't you just want to know?" she asks her sister, revealing that Kris thinks it's a great idea and "you'd never have to hear about this rumor again."

Khloé refuses, saying, "I don't really care. . . . I appreciate you and Kim offering your DNA services to me but this whole thing weirds me out, it makes me uncomfortable." Later, we see Kris herself urging her daughter to take the test, but Khloé calls her a "psychopath." When Kris later asks whether it's upsetting Khloé to hear all these rumors, she admits that it is. "Of course," replies Khloé, "because I know you had an affair on my dad who knows how many times, so who knows?"

"It was one time," Kris assures her. "It's not okay."

When Khloé again says she doesn't care, Kris tells her that's not true. "There's got to be a part of you that wants some resolution in your heart."

"I don't care either way, because my dad is my dad, and my step-dad is my stepdad," she says, leaving Kris emotional.

In her final confessional, Khloé says, "I think I've been going back and forth on whether to get a DNA test and, you know what? I'm one million percent comfortable with not getting a DNA test and knowing that my father's my father. I'm more than happy to live with that for the rest of my life."

It's fairly obvious that the entire episode has been stage-managed to do damage control after the claims of Robert's exes received considerable media play. Suspicious about why Khloé had readily submitted to take a DNA test to prove that Kris was her mother but refused to take a similar test to determine paternity, Opie Hughes, who at the time had a radio show on Sirius XM radio, publicly offered $250,000 if Khloé would take a DNA test and prove that Robert Kardashian was her father. Hughes offered to donate the money to a charity of her choice.

Scotto also challenged Khloé to take a DNA test to clear up the matter. "That would end all speculation and rumors, then the truth can be revealed once and for all," he said. "Simple, if she wants everyone to know that he is not the father, otherwise she wants to hide the results."

When I heard the rumors, I immediately dismissed them out of hand. While it's true that Khloé looked nothing like her sisters, I thought she was too light-skinned to have been fathered by O.J., notwithstanding the fact that he is a light-skinned African American with significant white blood in his ancestry. Still, Kourtney and Kim were darker than she was. They'd be more likely candidates, I assumed.

Then I saw a photo of O.J.'s daughter Sydney when she was young and a photo of Khloé at a similar age. They were the spitting image of each other. Maybe there's something to this after all, I thought. But I had determined not to stray onto the path of tabloid trash, and this issue certainly appeared to qualify.

When I heard that Opie's offer of $250,000 applied to anybody who could conversely prove that O.J. was indeed Khloé's father, however, I had a change of heart and an idea. By this time, I had watched nearly two hundred hours of soul-destroying episodes of *Keeping Up with the Kardashians* and its assorted spinoffs. I had seen things that made me want to have my eyeballs sewed shut. I had watched the sisters engage in what they called a "vagina smell-off" in which—hearing that pineapple juice makes everything sweeter—Kourtney and Kim decided to drink vast quantities of the juice and then have Khloé judge whose nether regions smelled better. And then there is the episode where Kim decides on a dare from her sisters to have her butt x-rayed to disprove the rampant speculation that she has had her derriere enhanced with implants.

Surely even I couldn't get any more distasteful than that. If it's true that most people watch the Kardashians as their "guilty pleasure," I decided my guilty pleasure would be to pursue one of the countless tabloid reports to its logical end. I decided to write to O.J. at the Lovelock Correctional Center in Nevada, where he is serving his sentence for kidnapping and armed robbery. Because he had lost a civil suit filed by Ron Goldman's family and been ordered to pay more than $33 million in damages, I knew that O.J. was in dire financial straits and would be looking for sources of revenue after he was eventually released. I was also aware that any official income would immediately be seized to pay what he owed Goldman.

With this in mind, I crafted a letter that I hoped would pique the

Juice's interest. My goal was simply to get a face-to-face meeting with the wife-killing maniac. If I could establish his trust, my goal would be to have him at least admit that he had had an affair with Kris Jenner back in the day. That would at minimum attract enough headlines to send my book soaring up the bestseller lists. I had a vague notion that perhaps I could also convince him to take a DNA test if it ever came to that. In the unlikely event that I could win Opie's challenge, I figured I'd donate the $250,000 to a charity that benefits battered women, which would both accomplish a good deed and get me some positive publicity. But first I had to simply get my foot in the door—or in this case, the cell.

In the letter, I told O.J. I'd be interested in having him document his time behind bars for a film that I planned to produce. I had enough credibility as a *New York Times* bestselling author and an award-winning filmmaker to pull it off, I reasoned. As an incentive, I implied that a creative arrangement could be worked out to siphon the proceeds offshore beyond the purview of the authorities or perhaps into a trust for his children if he so chose.

I was hoping that he would at least be intrigued enough to ask for a meeting. If nothing else, it would be an excuse to spend a weekend in Las Vegas, located a few hours' drive from the prison where he was being held.

Alas, I never received a response from the charismatic killer. I should have known that anybody smart enough to get away with murder is too smart to fall for a transparent ploy by a desperate writer hoping for a diversion from Kardashian watching. Just as well.

Although I had little interest by this point in the family's vapid day-to-day lives as chronicled onscreen, I had to my surprise developed a fascination and grudging respect for the behind-the-scenes machinations of its matriarch. In 1987, long before he became better known as a xenophobic Republican blowhard, Donald Trump published a memoir, *The Art of the Deal*, that rocketed to the top of the *New York Times* bestseller list and stayed on it for nearly a year. The book chronicled the rise of Trump's business empire and quickly became a Bible of sorts for budding entrepreneurs hoping to duplicate the Donald's success. However, I never drank the Kool-Aid regarding Trump's supposed business genius. The fact is that he was hardly a rags-to-riches success story. He was born with a silver spoon in his mouth to a millionaire tycoon father whose business and real-estate empire he merely expanded to impressive proportions.

In contrast, I found myself considerably more impressed with how Kris Jenner—the middle-class daughter of a small-business owner married to a nearly bankrupt former athlete—managed to parlay the notoriety of her daughter's sex tape into a billion-dollar empire. In her memoir, Kris Jenner quotes one of her producers, who says, "Fame may come and go but family is forever."

It's been said that Kris sold her soul to the devil to achieve her success or that she is a monster who whores out her family as a vanity exercise for the sake of her narcissistic ego. That's the Kris Jenner whom I assumed I would encounter when I probed deeply into the Kardashian phenomenon. Instead, I discovered that Kris is a loving but controlling mother who cares deeply about her family, and it is for them that she devotes the grueling hours and nonstop wheeling and dealing. Indeed, her children have become rich beyond their wildest dreams and appear to be living a lifestyle that most people can only envy. She is also an undeniable business genius who serves as a genuine inspiration to female entrepreneurs.

Beyond the fairy tale, however, there lies a cautionary tale. In Kris Jenner's single-minded pursuit of success, the telling fate of young Rob Kardashian reminds us that such an outcome may not be possible without unintended consequences.

CHAPTER FOURTEEN

When Bob Kardashian died in 2003 from esophageal cancer, his only son, sixteen at the time, was living with him and Bob's new wife, Ellen. His father's death hit him hard, which is perhaps why he would establish such a strong bond with his sister Khloé, who was also profoundly affected by Robert's passing.

According to Kris, Robert's dream had been for his son to attend his alma mater, the University of Southern California. Bruce had reportedly promised Robert on his deathbed that he would take care of his children. To keep that promise, he embarked with Kris on what they called the "Get Rob into USC" campaign. Rob's high school marks were not stellar and did not guarantee acceptance. But when Bruce met personally with the dean of admissions, a letter of acceptance soon followed, and Rob was admitted into the school's Marshall School of Business.

Rob wouldn't graduate from USC until 2009, a full two years after his family exploded to stratospheric success and his sisters struck gold in their various enterprises. On his *Keeping Up with the Kardashians* appearances, Rob never really made much of an impression during the early years, except in episodes where his sisters got involved in his flailing love life while he was dating the actor and singer Adrienne Bailon, whom he ended up cheating on. A recurrent theme in those years was Rob's desire to launch a menswear line or open up a men's version of his sisters' D-A-S-H boutiques. After graduating from USC, he had started his own skin-care company, Perfect Skin, but it never really seemed to go anywhere. Eventually he settled on the idea of launching a line of high-end socks, but for a long time it never got off the ground because, as we see him repeatedly stew, nobody is interested in helping him out. It's all about his sisters.

The high point perhaps of Rob's career came in 2011, when he appeared on season 7 of the hugely popular TV show *Dancing with the Stars*, on which his sister Kim had flamed out in spectacular fashion three years earlier. Unlike her, he displayed a surprising grace, paired with Cheryl Burke, and ended up in the finals, coming in in second place against the eventual winners, J. R. Martinez and Karina Smirnoff. He also did some modeling for the agency Nous Model Management.

In 2011, Khloé and her husband, Lamar, were given their own spinoff and, as it turns out, *Khloé and Lamar* finally offered Rob his turn in the spotlight. He ended up moving in with his sister and brother-in-law during the first season, and we quickly discover that Rob and Lamar have bonded in a significant way.

"Having Lamar as a brother now, it definitely makes me realize how much I miss not growing up with a brother," Rob says in an early confessional. The bromance plays a significant part during the spinoff's first season, and it is soon evident that the bond with Lamar is an important emotional anchor for Rob.

By season 2, Rob has moved out but he still ends up featured prominently, as we discover that he has obsessive-compulsive disorder and that Khloé is very concerned about it. "I really am worried about Rob," she says. "I definitely think he has a bigger problem than what he's willing to admit that he has." She believes that he developed the disorder around the time that his father died and notes that the siblings have commented on his tendencies for years. Among these is an obsession with the number seven, which is the number he counts to as he obsessively cleans the phone, every area of the bathroom, and other areas with which he comes into frequent contact.

"I'm just super-organized and clean and it's just about me feeling comfortable," he says. "It doesn't really affect my life." He rationalizes that he is merely "super-anal" but explains that everybody in the family is like that. "We just don't talk about it." But after Khloé and other family members call him out on this behavior, it becomes apparent that the problem runs deeper than just a compulsion to clean.

"My brother has always had, you know, levels of OCD," Khloé says. "I think he has a bigger problem than he's willing to admit and I believe he needs to speak to someone, but I know that's not going to happen, because in Rob's head there's nothing wrong with him."

After a worrisome incident while driving, however, Khloé finally convinces him to seek help. We see him call a psychotherapist to find out what's triggering his issues. "I think I have some type of, I don't know, OCD or something," he tells the shrink.

After he explains what's going on, the therapist tells him that it sounds like "pretty classic OCD." He believes the problem is fairly mild but tells Rob that it "can escalate if you're stressed out" and recommends treatment.

It's unclear whether Rob ever followed up on the suggestion, but within a few months, it was clear that his problems had indeed escalated. In December 2011, the New York *Daily News* had reported that Rob was launching a line of dress socks with "funky, colorful, cool designs." But months later, there was still no sign of the venture. While his sisters seemed to launch a new scent or clothing line every month, Rob's socks were nowhere to be seen. He had made it clear that he wasn't planning to launch the enterprise as part of the Kardashian brand but that he wanted to keep them separate.

By the time season 7 of *Keeping Up with the Kardashians* aired, however, we discover that he is bitter about the fact that his mom and sisters are not doing enough to help him launch his sock line. His frustration comes to a head in an episode aired in August, when Oprah Winfrey is scheduled to interview the family. In the van on the way to the interview, he tells his sisters, "I don't have anything coming in. I mean, I have the sock thing." He mentions that he wants to open up a menswear shop with Lamar but nobody will support him. Kim dismisses his whining. "Rob, you've proved you're flaky, so they're not going to work with you," she says. "I literally have no income," he replies.

When the queen of talk shows arrives, Rob is asked to wait while Oprah interviews Kim solo and then his other sisters. He is told by a producer that they will interview him at "the end." Finally, Oprah asks him if he ever feels like he is "living in their shadow." He admits it's "tough" but assures her that he couldn't be happier for their success. "My dad was an entrepreneur and that's something I want to be," he says. "Everything they're doing is, right, because of my mom—but also more importantly because of my dad, because he was the one who taught everybody." Khloé pipes in, annoyed, protesting that "we work hard."

In her confessional, Khloé says she thinks it's hard for Rob to be compared to his sisters but says he doesn't realize how much work she and her sisters have put into their businesses. "I don't think Rob remembers the struggles that we had and how long it took for things to get going," she says.

Afterward, Kim is at Kourtney and Scott's house, where she reveals to her sisters that she has an opportunity to do her own lingerie line in the Philippines. She assures them it won't conflict with their Sears Kardashian Kollection or other family ventures. When the girls express concern, Kim gets annoyed. "What's wrong with me doing that? What's wrong with me doing something on my own?"

Visibly upset, Khloé tells her that they have a long-term plan to promote things as a family. "Why are you going to taint our water by diluting it?" she asks.

Kim wonders why her sisters feel threatened by the idea of her doing something without them. She assures them it won't affect any project she does with them. She notes that Kris will often agree to stick the other girls in with Kim's endorsements because "she's not paying attention half the time." Kourtney believes it's more rewarding if they're all together to experience it.

Afterward, the tension from the exchange is still simmering. "I know my dad would be disgusted if he ever knew that business deals came between my sisters and I," Khloé says. "I feel like we have a lot to say and we need a mediator and we need someone who can, like, volleyball it and make it fine." Talking to Kourtney after their blowup with Kim, Khloé believes that the only way to deal with the "issues" is to arrange a therapy session with Kris, the three sisters, and Rob.

"We just need someone to help us get through everything," Khloé says. "[Kim's baby] is coming. The baby can't be brought into all this negative energy."

Khloé calls Kim and tells her "it's time for an intervention." When Kim asks her what she's referring to, she says, "All you guys are majorly obnoxious and Robert might be OCD among other problems . . . so I think we should have a family intervention."

Kim isn't buying the idea. "I think that sounds like the most ridiculous idea, and I'm so not into it." Khloé tells her that Kris agreed to go, which leaves Kim skeptical because "she's so not into therapy." Finally, after calling Kris, Kim reluctantly agrees to attend a family-therapy session. Like countless other episodes of *Keeping Up with the Kardashians*, the premise is clearly staged—one of those ideas that Kris or a producer undoubtedly conceived to ramp up the drama for the cameras. Indeed, the argument about Kim's solo lingerie line may very well have been an infomercial to pave the way for Kim to launch a line of products separate from the family.

But when it comes time for the therapy session, it sets the stage for some rare genuine insights into the family and, more important, offers a seemingly candid glimpse of the angst and emotional dysfunction plaguing the family's only son. While the girls are having their hair and makeup done to prepare for an interview on *Jimmy Kimmel* later in the day, Kourtney tells Kim that Rob wants to open up a menswear store in London.

"Is that okay with you?" Rob snaps.

When his sister asks why he's always fighting, he continues in the same vein. "I'm asking Princess Kim. Princess Kimberly." Kris wonders why he's so angry all the time. "Because Kim is literally the most selfish person here and doesn't give a fuck if I have a career!" he shouts. "All she cares about is herself. I told you this for years. Kim is selfish, obviously. She doesn't ever want to include me in anything."

Kim rises. "My job is to help you out? You're not a charity case. Get a job."

Rob fires back. "The point is you would rather hook yourself in and take me out of it because you want all the attention. 'I want to do Oprah by myself.' I get it; you want to separate yourself. You're your own person."

Kim ignores him, looking very uncomfortable.

"You can just look at her, right there—a picture is worth a thousand words. Right there, selfish," Rob says.

"You sound like a fucking idiot," Kim retorts.

Kris intervenes, asking everybody to take a deep breath. "I really don't believe in therapy but seeing them fight like this, it's probably a really good idea that we're here," she says in her confessional.

Soon the therapist arrives, a Los Angeles psychotherapist named Nicki J. Monti, who has appeared on a number of TV shows to help people deal with personal issues, including *Millionaire Matchmaker* and *Love Handles: Couples in Crisis.*

Kim immediately tells her that she is not crazy about therapy. "It's just not for me," she says. "I get it. I'm a very logical person, so if I'm acting crazy, I know all the reasons why." Afterward, she says in her confessional, "I feel, like, after having this huge fight right before we walk into our therapy, I'm not in the mood for this and I don't really want to talk to a stranger about my family problems."

They tell the doctor what went on before she arrived. "Robert has a lot of deep-rooted issues," says Khloé, "because Robert doesn't talk to a lot of people. He shares certain things with Kourtney, certain things with Kim, and certain things with me."

Rob says he's not antisocial, just very private. "The only people in my life that matter is my family," he says. "I don't have many friends."

"I think we as women don't even give him time to talk," Khloé explains.

When it's Kris's turn, she says she wants to come away with a "line that we learn not to cross." She feels that they all take each other for granted. "Appreciation I think would be really cool." Kourtney notes that appreciation goes both ways, prompting Dr. Monti to ask whether she feels that her mom favors Kim. "I think all three of us could say that," Khloé says.

The doctor asks Kim whether she agrees.

"I feel that my mom and I have a close relationship, and I can understand her more, so I think she's more comfortable communicating with me," she replies.

Kris tells Khloé that she thinks she takes things too personally, protesting that she doesn't mean any harm but that she's very busy and it often takes a long time to get back to her kids and tell them they've done a good job with something.

"I don't know why our mom finds it such a shock to learn that we think [she] favors Kim," Khloé says afterward. "It's just facts. And I'm obviously hurt. And to tell us that she's just too busy—we're not just our mom's clients, we're her children."

Eventually attention turns back to Rob.

"Are they right that you're kind of like a simmering volcano waiting to erupt?" Dr. Monti asks him. He says he speaks his mind if it's something he's passionate about. Kim pipes up, reminding him he does it with a "screaming voice." Only if he's speaking the truth about something, he insists. Kourtney tells him he reminds her of the way she used to be when she had "this anger inside." Sometimes it's impossible for the others to know what's going to set him off.

"My whole thing," he explains, "is that my anger stems from the working environment, because they all kind of put this cloud on me like I'm a loser."

KIM: But then you blow up later.
ROB: I blow up later because when there's a business opportunity all my mom cares about is the three girls, and whenever I say I want to open up a men's store . . .
KIM: But mom never helped us with that.

When Dr. Monti asks him how he feels, Rob says he's frustrated.

"You look sad," she observes. "Am I misreading you?"

At this, he breaks down sobbing, then rises and walks away.

"Robert don't leave," Kris says.

Dr. Monti repeats the plea. "Please don't leave. Stay and talk about this. Things don't get better when you walk out."

Kim remains silent while Khloé goes after her brother.

"It's just sad to see him cry, because he never does," Kourtney observes.

From the back of the room, we hear Khloé say, "It's okay; you're allowed to cry. I can help you. You just have to tell me what you need help with."

The therapist joins them to find Rob still sobbing and tells him he obviously doesn't feel "safe." When she asks him what he wants to have happen, he says, "I just want my family happy. All I care about is saying yes to my mom, making her happy, doing whatever my sisters want to make them happy, and I feel like when it comes to the easiest things, they won't help me."

Meanwhile, Kim appears unmoved by her brother's anguish.

"Nobody ever gave me anything," she says. "When I wanted something, I worked and I made it happen. When Kourtney wants something, she makes it happen. When Khloé wants something, she makes it happen."

When Rob continues to blame Kris for favoring the girls over him, Kim rises to her mother's defense, saying that Kris is doing the best she can. "I feel bad for her that all of us are really mean to her (crying). I think she's doing the best that she can, which is why I have her back because I don't think it's her fault. I just don't think she knows how to raise a son that well. That was, like, Dad's thing, and now that Dad's not here, it's, like no one's fault, you know, so I don't think any of us know what we're doing. With our career, I think Mom and I were just lucky and made it happen. . . . I feel bad that everybody is so mean to Mom. She does what she can with the girls. That's her thing . . . girls."

The topic then turns to Robert's death. Dr. Monti asks Kim what it was like at the end. "I think I handled it very well," Kim says. "I worked in his office. I was the last one working there."

Khloé reminds her that she worked there, too. This prompts a tense exchange between the two, with Kim suggesting that Khloé is lying.

After watching episodes of the show for weeks, the therapy session felt like the first genuine raw human emotion that I had witnessed among the family. It also left the impression that Kim was somewhat insensitive to her brother's pain, which is at odds with the picture painted of her by others who know her. Contrary to what I had expected when I set out to chronicle the family, I found very few people who knew her who were willing to speak badly of Kim. The word most often used to describe her, in fact, was *nice*. My longtime friend Hardy Hill—best known as a contestant on season 2 of *Big Brother*—was also a longtime ambassador for Miami's Opium Group of nightclubs. He recalls the first time he met Kim, when she was hired to work an event by the South Beach nightclub Privé around 2007, and she arrived with Kourtney and Khloé.

"I didn't realize that they were all sisters immediately because I didn't realize that Kim had sisters at the time," Hardy recalls. "She was just new on the scene. She was very nice, very down to earth." He called all three sisters very "sweet." They were very kind to anybody who approached, he recalled. "They were not standoffish at all." The same can't be said for all celebrities, he notes. When he hosted Kourtney and Scott for a New Year's Eve party years later, he said he found Kourtney once again "lovely" but that Scott was "a dick. Very unapproachable, very arrogant, very cocky and aloof and, to be honest with you, a not-all-around-good guy."

Although I had started this book assuming Kim was a diva or a spoiled princess like her old friend Paris Hilton, I was soon disabused of the idea by just about everybody I met who had come into contact with her. Her pleasant demeanor is also an assessment echoed in a 2015 *Rolling Stone* article, "Kim Kardashian: American Woman."

After Kim notes that many fans find the family's success "aspirational," the magazine observes, "That someone might not find the Kardashians aspirational is simply something she would not consider. She's not conflicted about the point of life: It's to be happy and make money, and she's doing both. Kardashian is a nice person—there's no way to spend time with her and not come away with that impression."

So when we see Kim being mean to her brother, it's likely more an example of complicated sibling dynamics than a reflection of her true personality. In 2014, she would tell talk show host Andy Cohen, "My brother and I are so close, he's one of my best friends. I'm definitely a tough-love kind of person. If I don't like something that's going on in my life, I change it, and I don't sit and complain about it for a year."

Whatever the case, things only seemed to go downhill from there. At the end of 2012, Rob finally managed to launch his sock line, Arthur George—combining his and his father's middle names. The high-end department store Neiman Marcus struck a deal to sell the line exclusively for $30 a pair, although the line never seemed to enjoy the success of his sisters' more affordable clothing lines and has seen only fair-to-middling sales over the years.

The year 2013 saw Rob, once a buff male model, gain significant weight, which would become a recurring theme on *Keeping Up with the Kardashians*. In one episode, Rob receives the results of a blood test that has Kris openly chastising him about his weight gain.

"Your liver is shutting down," she tells the twenty-six-year-old. "This is life-threatening at this point. You can only sustain this level of being unhealthy for so long."

If it's possible to pinpoint the nadir of Rob's struggles, it would have to be the breakdown of Khloé's marriage to Lamar Odom in 2012 and 2013, reportedly over his heavy use of alcohol and drugs and his cheating on her with other women. Although Lamar, whose father was a heroin addict, had reportedly binged on crack, Rob was, by most accounts, content with smoking pot and listening to rap music when the two hung out. According to a buddy of Rob's named Craig Long, Lamar's departure from the scene is the reason Rob "went wild high on drugs." Long told me he believes Rob was lost without Lamar.

"They became best friends. They were brothers. When Lamar's marriage to Khloé fell apart, Rob lost the only man he was close to since his dad died. He felt alone, somewhat abandoned. He got heavy into drugs and let himself completely go. I know Lamar for years, and him, too—he's always been up and down. But the marriage to Khloé was long over before anybody really knew. That's why Lamar also went into a tailspin, abusing drugs and alcohol like you can't imagine. It got messy."

When Kim married Kanye in May 2014, Rob was a conspicuous no-show at the wedding, despite the fact that he had flown to Italy with the rest of the family to attend. After rumors of a blowup with his sister surfaced, Kim set the record straight. "He sent me a long email the morning of, that he was going to leave," she explained. "There was no fight."

A few months later, it appeared as if they were anything but best friends after he notoriously posted a photo to Instagram of Rosamund Pike's blood-soaked psychopathic character from the movie *Gone Girl* and labeled it: "This is my sister Kim, the bitch from *Gone Girl*."

Although it was widely reported that Rob had checked in to rehab in May 2015, Kris slammed the reports, telling *Entertainment Tonight* that the claims were "completely fabricated." Several people close to the family said Kris was trying to do damage control. "Rob needed help and he got it," a family friend said. "He was desperate and sought help to change his atrocious habits." Soon he stopped appearing in episodes of the show altogether, reportedly because of anxiety over his severe weight gain. He even disappeared for an extended time from social media, which, as with the other siblings, is an important source of income for him. In a 2015 episode of *Keeping Up with the Kardashians*—in which he is shown only in flashbacks—Khloé takes note of Rob's retreat from public life.

"If you're out and photographed and people rag on you and talk about you, it only gets you into this deeper, darker hole and you just don't want to be seen anymore," she explains. Later, Kris expresses her own anguish. "As a mom, it breaks my heart to see him go through what he's going through. He's kind of stuck in a really bad place and I just want to help him get out of it."

In the episode, we see her talk on the phone to somebody to

whom she hints that Rob has a serious problem. "I just think that as a family we have to do something immediately," she says.

It emerges that she has contacted a "life coach," who has an entire team to deal with people in crisis. She wants to bring him in to work with Rob, she tells Kim. "I feel that if I don't do something drastic, then he's going to die," she says ominously. We see the family meet with the coach, but without Khloé, who Kris explains has been excluded because she's a little too protective of her brother and might not think it's a good idea.

"He was always someone who was very athletic growing up, and he's gained over a hundred pounds in the last year," she tells the life coach, before breaking down in tears. "He doesn't want to participate. He doesn't go out of the house. He's missed Christmas, he's missed Kim's wedding."

Kim interrupts. "He obviously has some kind of depression." When Kris explains that he keeps procrastinating about getting anything done, Kim puts in, "He is the king of excuses." Kourtney explains that everybody has been overcompensating for him since Robert died when he was sixteen. "I don't know if it's because he has it so easy, but then also at the same time with what he's going through, I don't want him to feel even more alone."

Kim adds, "I'm the only one that's really tough with him, so he probably avoids me the most."

The coach suggests bringing somebody to the house to make sure he's stabilized, "bring meds in and make sure he's comfortable." Sounding as though they are considering committing him, or the equivalent, Kris says, "It's like you're just waiting for this horrible thing to happen and there's nothing you can do about it."

When Khloé eventually discovers what has been happening, she accuses her family of "ambushing" both Rob and herself. Rob has been living with her, so she believes she knows what he is going through better than Kris or her sisters. She notes that they haven't bothered to visit him for days. "Do you even know his daily routine?" she asks, noting that there are other things they can do before taking such a "drastic" step. She predicts the intervention will simply leave her brother agitated.

Kris protests that she calls him on a daily basis and gets "rejection on a daily basis. We're all trying in our own way," she tells Khloé, who finally agrees to allow the intervention at her house.

When the time comes, Khloé reveals that Rob has announced he is locking himself in his room and doesn't need any help. "He said this isn't the right way." Kim is visibly annoyed. "You just need to say, 'You're kicked out of the house, you're cut off, your bank accounts and your credit cards are closed. You do not have a dime,'" she tells her younger sister.

KHLOÉ: I can't kick him out of my house.
KIM: Yeah, you can. That's what you have to do.

Later, when Kris invites Rob to stay with her, Kim gets annoyed again: "Now, what we have to do is everyone back off. Everyone licks Rob's ass and does whatever he says and at some point you just have to give it up. . . .We all make his life so easy. 'Okay, we'll drive you around with the chauffeur so no one has to look at you. We have a chef on standby, a trainer; we have someone to run out and buy you socks and underwear.' This is pathetic. We are not going to cater to him anymore, but it has to be all of us."

The episode ends with no resolution, and Rob has continued to stay for the most part out of the public eye. It's fairly obvious to me that this isn't the usual Kardashian family drama designed for publicity or TV ratings. Yet it's easy to trot out clichés to explain Rob's emotional spiral as the price of fame. In the Miami Beach complex where I live, one of my neighbors happens to be Eva Ritvo, a psychiatrist and TV personality in her own right who has treated many celebrity clients. I asked her to give me a sense of Rob's issues, notwithstanding the fact that she has never met him.

"The Kardashian family is female-centric," she explained.

Although both Robert Kardashian and Bruce Jenner were powerful figures, it appears that Kris is more powerful when it comes to family dynamics. Kris has run a multimillion-dollar operation successfully for the last decade. Although some criticized her for monetizing her family members, she has certainly been successful in her mission. Her daughters and grandchildren will not have to worry about money, and how many women can say they achieved that? Rob seems to be the family member having the most difficult time with the unusual family lifestyle. He has struggled with weight, depression, and substance abuse. The constant scrutiny of the public eye is a strain, and it is remarkable how well the girls seem to handle the stress. They have leveraged their fame to date and marry high-status men and to create professional success via modeling, book writing, and retail businesses. Rob too has tried to monetize his success with a sock company but seems to have succumbed to the stress, as evidenced by overeating and turning to drugs to alter his mood. Many celebrities fall victim to drugs and alcohol as a way to cope with the chronic cortisol released by the stress of being in the public eye. Depression, obesity, and substance abuse are all medical conditions that should be treated by mental health professionals. With access to the best of everything, I hope that Rob can tap into the proper resources and overcome the obstacles he has faced. Family support is often vital to combating mental health issues, and it would be important that the family stay close and aid him in his recovery. Monica Lewinsky beautifully describes the role of her family in helping her overcome the shame of cyberbullying. Rob's family must similarly bond together to assist their seemingly weakest family member. As my dear mentor, Robert Michels, once said, "A family is held hostage to its sickest member." We often hear, "A mother is only as happy as her least happiest child," and in Kris's case, I imagine that this rings true.

As it would turn out, Rob's emotional turmoil wasn't the only family crisis Kris was dealing with.

CHAPTER FIFTEEN

In early 2010, I found myself in Los Angeles working on a documentary about Michael Jackson. On Valentine's Day, I happened to be sharing a romantic dinner with my girlfriend at Mastro's steakhouse in Beverly Hills. Midway through the meal, my date nudged me and pointed out that Kris Jenner was dining a few tables down. I had barely kept up with the Kardashians and was only vaguely familiar at the time with Kris but, as an avid sports fan, I was acutely aware of whom she was married to. I found it odd, then, that on Valentine's Day, she wasn't with Bruce Jenner, but rather a female companion.

After dinner, as we were waiting for the valet to bring the car, Kris stepped out with her friend, a middle-aged woman whom I didn't recognize. She was immediately ambushed by a cameraman from TMZ. "Where's Bruce?" he shouted. "He's golfing," Kris replied. I thought nothing more about the incident until 2012, when the first bizarre reports began to surface. In January of that year, Robert's widow, Ellen, claimed that Bruce's first wife, Chrystie Crownover, had confided to her over drinks one day that Bruce had a penchant for cross-dressing.

"Of course Bruce was every woman's heartthrob when he was that age, right?" Ellen claimed that she asked Chrystie about their marriage. The answer surprised her. "Yeah, until I went on a trip and I came back and he had gone through all my clothes. And I found my bras. . . . He'd clip them together and wear them. I couldn't live with that."

Crownover denied the bizarre report at the time, and most people assumed it was simply more tabloid trash. A year later, stories surfaced that Bruce had moved out of the family's home in June 2013 and was living in Malibu. By then, his face was beginning to take on a decidedly feminine appearance, but most assumed that his unusual facial features were merely the result of one of the numerous plastic surgeries that Bruce was fond of. The whole family, in fact, were fans of surgical enhancement. A friend of Kris's once told me that "the Kardashians live by the knife." Kris, in fact, had gone through a televised facelift on a 2011 episode of *Keeping Up with the Kardashians* so that she could look good for Kim's wedding to Kris Humphries and had bragged about undergoing at least two boob jobs.

The family's former nanny Pam Behan later recalled that Bruce had once suggested that she have a procedure done, even though she was only a teenager. "Bruce told me one time that I was a cross between Farrah Fawcett and Goldie Hawn, which put a big smile on my face," she wrote. "Despite this, the subject of plastic surgery came up one day in an unexpected way. Bruce was looking at me funny," she wrote. "'What?' I asked as he stared at my face. 'You should probably have a little taken off your nose.' Huh? I'm nineteen. It had never, ever occurred to me that I might need a nose job. . . . I guess in the land of the beautiful and perfect people, there was always some 'work' that could be done." Indeed, Bruce had talked often about undergoing a botched facelift and nose job in the mid-'80s, which he claimed had effected his self-esteem. He later underwent another procedure to correct the first one, which was featured on an episode of *Keeping Up with the Kardashians.*

"If you Google my name, 'the worst plastic surgeries of all time' or whatever it is . . . they've compared me to Michael Jackson," he said on the show. So his changing facial features weren't necessarily indicative of anything unusual.

By the fall, the reports of a separation had gained traction and were already an open secret. Finally, on October 8, the couple made it official. "We are living separately and we are much happier this way," they said in a joint statement issued to *E! News*. "But we will always have much love and respect for each other. Even though we are separated, we will always remain best friends and, as always, our family will remain our number one priority."

Bruce could barely disguise his jubilation at a Virginia speedway event that weekend when he announced, "I'm finally free to do what I want and live life the way I want." For her part, Kris delivered what appeared to be a low blow when she told *New You* magazine, "The one regret, if I had to do it over, would be divorcing Robert Kardashian."

Before long, the newly single sixty-three-year-old Jenner had grown his hair out into a ponytail, and was spotted sporting earrings and lip gloss. The long-dormant rumors started anew, especially after he was seen leaving the office of a Beverly Hills plastic surgeon. He confirmed that he was planning to undergo a "tracheal shave," which in effect removes the Adam's apple and is a common procedure among transgender women before they undergo gender-reassignment surgery, better known as a sex-change operation.

At the time, however, Bruce denied he was transitioning. "I just never liked my trachea," he claimed. The transgender community wasn't buying it. Dr. Marci Bowers, the first transsexual woman to perform gender reassignment surgery on others, told *Radar*, "The real hallmark of being male is the presence of an Adam's apple. Someone choosing to have that reduced is pretty much making a statement that when they're going to be dressed as a woman, they're hoping to pass as a female in public. . . . That could be the step that Bruce is making. It's complicated, but it would be very surprising if it was just a final step for doing something about a feature he didn't like, and not the beginning of a slippery slope [to gender reassignment surgery]."

In January 2014, he was photographed leaving the same clinic, the Beverly Hills Surgical Center, with a bandaged throat, having undergone the procedure. The news only escalated the rumors. A month later, TMZ asked Kris about the reports and whether she would support Bruce if he was indeed transitioning. Laughing, she merely said, "You're crazy," before ducking into her car. Soon afterward, she told the *Daily Mail* that "99 per cent of the rumors are made up." While promoting her cookbook a few months later, she was once again asked about the rumors. "It's silly! [The tabloids have] been saying that since the '70s, so you think he'd be cooked by now. . . . They just keep regurgitating the same old stuff."

In December, Chrystie Crownover had denied that Bruce was a cross-dresser when she was married to him, as Ellen had alleged the previous year. She believed she knew who had been spreading the rumors. "This is a plan by Kris to destroy his life, she's not a pleasant woman. . . . She's out to get him. She doesn't want him to be happy," Chrystie said. "There was no suggestion of cross-dressing when I was with him. He's a man's man."

But the idea that Kris was behind the reports was clearly preposterous. As we would soon learn, Bruce's ex-wife had no interest in exposing his secret. On the contrary, Kris Jenner was getting nervous.

In 1975, a tennis player and opthamologist named Richard Raskind underwent gender-reassignment surgery and emerged as a woman under her new name, Renée Richards. Raskind had served as a doctor in the United States Navy where he played tennis for the Navy Team and won both the singles and doubles all-Navy championships, thanks to a ferocious serve that regularly stymied opponents. By 1974, he was ranked thirteenth in the nation in the men's thirty-five-and-over tennis standings.

A year after her sex change, Richards applied to play in the US Women's Open but was denied the opportunity after she refused to take the sex-verification chromosome test required of all women competitors. A year later, seeking to enter the US Open once again, she filed an injunction under New York State human rights law and the Fourteenth Amendment of the Constitution to prohibit the US Tennis Association from subjecting her to the sex-verification test. The judge determined that the test was initially designed to "prevent fraud"—specifically to weed out men masquerading as women, which was not the case with Richards. The judge ruled that USTA had employed the test specifically to prevent her from competing in the tournament, knowing she would have failed it. "This person is now a female," the judge ruled. Requiring her to take the test was "grossly unfair, discriminatory and inequitable, and a violation of her rights."

At the time, she was widely mocked for her efforts, with *Sports Illustrated* describing her as an "extraordinary spectacle." But with the court victory, she was free to play professional tennis. In her very first US Open, in 1977, she reached the doubles finals, losing a close match to Martina Navratilova and Betty Stöve. Two years later, she won the US Open singles title in the thirty-five-and-over category.

Around the time that Richards emerged as a pioneer for transsexual rights, Bruce Jenner was emerging as the world's greatest athlete at the Montreal Olympics. He would later reveal that he was watching her battle closely at the time and that Richards would serve as his "inspiration."

When I was attending university in Montreal during the eighties, I organized a human-rights lecture series. One of the speakers happened to be Harry Edwards, who in 1968 had organized the Olympic Project for Human Rights, in which two black athletes, Tommie Smith and John Carlos, had given the black power salute, fists raised, on the podium at the Mexico City Olympics. In the years since, he had emerged as an influential sports sociologist who focused primarily on race relations in sports. When I picked up Edwards at the airport, he told me he had just come from mediating a crisis at a Los Angeles university that I believe was UCLA. It seemed that the US Olympic track team had been using the university facilities to train but that the athletes were in open revolt because they were refusing to use the same locker room as the US team's star athlete, Carl Lewis. The mostly black athletes, Edwards told me, believed that Lewis was gay and therefore wanted nothing to do with him. He had been called in to try to resolve the conflict.

A few years earlier, Jenner's successor as Olympic decathlon champion, Britain's Daley Thompson, had sported a T-shirt during an ABC news interview bearing the words, "The world's second greatest athlete is gay." It was an obvious reference to Lewis. The winner of the Olympic 100 meters is informally dubbed the "world's second greatest athlete," with the decathlon winner considered the greatest.

It is a reminder that track and field—a sport dominated by black athletes who hold deeply religious views—is rife with homophobia, and we can assume that a transgender athlete would have been welcomed with no less hostility than Lewis had been. And yet it's still unclear whether Jenner was struggling with his gender identity at the time he started out in track and field or whether in fact the process started later, perhaps even as a result of his athletic training.

The question first arose when Bruce's former Olympic teammate Ken Patera gave an interview claiming that Bruce had used anabolic steroids in his training regimen before they were banned. After a mediocre showing in the 1972 Munich Olympics, Jenner had turned to Patera—the reigning Pan Am Games champion—for help in strength training. Both used steroids legally to pump themselves up, he claims, until they were added to the banned-substances lists by the International Olympic Committee in 1975.

Patera believes the chemicals could have played a role in Jenner's eventual transition. "Maybe that flipped a switch in his brain," he said in May 2015.

Although the claim seems far-fetched, it is not entirely without precedent. Heidi Krieger was a world-champion East German shot putter who had taken massive doses of steroids since she was sixteen as part of the notorious East German doping program. In 1997, she underwent gender-reassignment surgery to become a man and became known as Andreas Krieger. He later claimed that the androgenic effects of steroids altered his body chemistry and exacerbated his existing gender dysphoria, contributing to his gender transition.

It is an intriguing theory, but when Bruce Jenner finally decided to end all speculation and go public with his transition in the spring of 2015, he revealed that he had been struggling with gender-identity issues long before his athletic career took off, and that he secretly wore dresses as a young boy growing up in Tarrytown, New York.

The interview—broadcast by ABC's Diane Sawyer during a two-hour *20/20* special—was teased in advance by the network with a number of provocative quotes from the pretaped interview. "My whole life has been getting me ready for this. . . . My family members are the only ones I'm concerned with. . . . It's going to be an emotional roller coaster but somehow I'm going to get through it. . . . It made me who I am. . . . I want to know how this story ends. How does my story end?"

But until viewers heard Sawyer ask him the question on the April 24 broadcast, few people knew for sure. "Are you a woman?" Sawyer asks the sixty-five-year-old former Olympian early in the interview. "I've always been very confused with my gender identity. For all intents and purposes, I am a woman," Jenner replies.

The show achieved its highest Friday-night ratings in more than fifteen years, as almost 17 million viewers tuned in to hear Jenner's dramatic revelation. There was no shortage of intriguing details during the two-hour special. He revealed that he had been struggling with his gender identity for decades and had even contemplated suicide after his Adam's apple–removal surgery was made public. "I thought, wouldn't the easiest thing to do right now—and I could see where people get to that—is go in the room, get a gun, boom? Pain's over, it's done, go to a better place. And I thought, nah. I can't do something like that. I mean, I want to know how this story ends."

He disclosed that his first wife, Chrystie Crownover, was the first person he had told about his cross-dressing, despite her recent denials. Three days later on *Good Morning America*, Chrystie confirmed that he had indeed shared his feelings early on in their marriage, telling her "he wished to be a woman."

She recalled, "It was this type of shock in my experience, but he opened up his heart and revealed it. [He said] he had to share with you this dark secret that is strong, and he told me he always desired to be a female and, understandably, I was speechless. I didn't actually know what to say."

More surprisingly, Jenner revealed to Sawyer that he had actually started to transition in the '80s, before he met Kris. "I had been on hormones for five years and I was a really solid 36B-something and you really can't hide those things," he laughed. "And [Kris] goes, 'Well, okay, you like to wear women's clothes.' And I kind of downplayed it some. I feel in a lot of ways that when you love somebody you don't want to hurt them."

At one point, Sawyer asks him whether he's sorry he participated on *Keeping Up with the Kardashians*. He provides a revealing answer, appearing to confirm years of accusations that the reality show bears no resemblance to reality. "*I* had the story," he says. "We've done four hundred twenty-five episodes, I think, over almost eight years now, and the entire run, I kept thinking to myself, 'Oh my God. This whole thing, the one real, true story in the family was the one I was hiding, and nobody knew about it.'"

Asked about his relationship with Kris, he seems to imply that she was less than supportive. "It was tough on her. I understand that. Kris is a good woman, I've got no complaints with her. She's a good person. Honestly, if she would've been really good with it, and understanding, we'd probably still be together."

He then reveals an unexpected detail about their time together, especially after months of denials by Kris. He claims that during their relationship, she had actually seen him dressed in women's clothing. "She didn't say much," he recalled. "Just, like, 'Okay, you gonna change now?' I probably was not as good at saying that this was down deep in my soul and 'I don't know if I can go any farther like this.'"

By the next day, the reverberations of the interview were being felt around the world, but nowhere more so than in the Kardashian family, where Bruce's revelations were already wreaking havoc. The first controversy erupted when the media descended on Kris for comment and wondered why she had not participated in the special, even though Jenner's other two wives, Chrystie Crownover and Linda Thompson, had provided supportive comments. At the end of the broadcast, Sawyer claimed that Kris had declined to comment. That prompted blogger Perez Hilton to report on her refusal, at which point Kris Tweeted, "@PerezHilton fuck you Perez no one asked me to comment. . . . and I'm sitting with Bruce now watching this show so let's keep it real."

But the network was quick to set the record straight. "ABC News sent an email to her publicity team more than once," they said in a statement. "They called and said no comment."

Finally, Kris backtracked slightly on her previous claim. "Kris does not have official representation but a message was left at her office and she was asked for fact checking. Kris said she was unable to respond because she had not seen the special. She did not say, 'No comment,'" her publicist told *People*.

In the days leading up to the special, reports were circulating that Kris was petrified about what Bruce might disclose. Two days before her ex-husband was scheduled to sit down with Sawyer, it was alleged that she had dispatched one of her daughters to remind him he has a financial stake in the empire they created and not to say anything to jeopardize it. In April, the New York *Daily News* reported that Kris "is so nervous about the tell-all that she tried to talk the former Olympian out of doing it."

Of course, true to form, no matter what reservations she had about her ex-husband's transition, Kris was not about to pass up an opportunity to cash in on the publicity. At least that's how cynics interpreted the two-part *Keeping Up with the Kardashians* special, "About Bruce," which aired in May. In it, Bruce discusses his transition with his family, revealing the truth for the first time.

A year earlier, the transgender surgeon, Dr. Marci Bowers, had predicted that if Bruce did decide to transition into a woman, the process could be harder on his family than on him. "It's very cathartic and liberating to go through, but it's much more difficult for the people around you," she said at the time. "His family's going to feel all sorts of reactions: shame, betrayal. They're going to end up discussing it and he's going to need to be patient with that."

Sure enough, in the special, we see the reactions of each member of the family, except for Rob, who was still lying low. Surprisingly, the usually confident Khloé—who had brought along as a present a stack of size-13 high-heeled shoes—appears to be the most nervous before he arrives. She tells her siblings, "I don't know if I'm saying the right thing, if I'm using the right terminology. I don't want to offend anyone. I'm fine with him dressing as a woman. I want Bruce to be happy." But when they get together, she accuses him of lying to them. "I didn't lie to you, Khloé, I just didn't tell you," he responds. She demands to know when he plans to actually transition into a woman, telling him he owes it to them to reveal the truth.

"Are you planning on not being Bruce anytime soon?" she asks. When he confirms that's the plan, she fires back, "You have children! You don't have to answer to us, but you need to tell us! I don't care that you want to do it, I support you, I have always supported you, but I don't think it's fair that you won't tell us how close this is in the near future. We're still your kids!"

It is clear that the most accepting sibling is Kim, who not only offers her full support but offers to help Bruce with his new female wardrobe. "Girl, you gotta rock it and you gotta look good. If you're doing this thing, I'm helping you," she tells him. At one point, she asks the question that is on everybody's mind. "Are you going to fully become a woman?"

"I see myself in the future that way," he says.

When Diane Sawyer had asked him about his sexual orientation, Bruce had been adamant. "No! I am not gay! I am not gay. I am—as far as I know—I am heterosexual. I've never been with a guy. Sexuality is who you're personally attracted to, who turns you on, male or female. But gender identity has to do with who you are as a person, and your soul, and who you identify with inside."

When he tells Kim that he is still attracted to women, but considered himself to be "totally heterosexual," she called him on the glaring contradiction. "If you're a woman, then aren't you a lesbian?" Rather than address the question head on, he offers a vague reply. Many wondered whether his Republican leanings and long-held religious beliefs prevented him from acknowledging Kim's logical conclusion.

But despite the fact that she appeared to be asking uncomfortable questions, Bruce has long maintained that Kim has been the most supportive of his transition. "Kimberly has been by far the most accepting and the easiest to talk to about it," he told Sawyer. It's hardly surprising, considering her long history of opposing homophobic bigotry. As far back as 2009, Kim issued a strong statement when the California Supreme Court upheld the homophobic referendum, Proposition 8, in which Californians had voted to ban gay marriage in their state. In response to the regressive decision, Kim wrote on her blog, "This really makes me sad. I thought we were more forward thinking than this, and I'm disappointed in the Supreme Court for being so closed minded. Everyone . . . gay, straight, bisexual, transgendered, EVERY-ONE should have equal rights to marry who they want to."

She had also been a strong supporter of Barack Obama as well as the Occupy Wall Street movement, in contrast to both her mother and stepfather, whose own political views were far less enlightened. "My household is really split up," she told a red-carpet interviewer in 2009. "The parents are Republicans and the children are Democrats. So it's like a political warfare in our household when we talk about politics." Indeed, Kris once told a reporter that she and Bruce were "complete Republicans" and that every TV in their house was tuned to Fox News. Kim would later credit Kanye with helping her accept and support Bruce's transition—a marked contrast to the numerous rappers who reacted with homophobic disdain after the news surfaced. Snoop Dogg referred to Caitlyn Jenner as a "science project," while Timbaland Tweeted, "His Momma Named Him Bruce, I'mma Call Him Bruce."

In the end, all the children end up offering their support to Bruce in his transition, despite any initial misgivings or apprehension about meeting "her" for the first time. The *Huffington Post*, like many media, would shift from its usual disdain for all things Kardashian to an appreciation for the family's role in helping shift society's values on an important social issue.

"Yes, it would have been a big deal for a former Olympian to come out as transgender no matter what, but couple that with Caitlyn Jenner doing it on the heels of a very public divorce in a family that documents every waking moment of their lives, and it's a whole

new ballgame," the site observed. "The support of each of her family members has gone a long way to showing the public exactly how
to react to this kind of change." Suddenly, the family were no longer
responsible for the decline of Western civilization but rather a force
for good. Who would have thunk it?

The emotional high point of the "About Bruce" special is undeniably Bruce's on-air reunion with Kris. Publicly, Kris had professed to
support her ex, Tweeting, "Not only was I able to call him my husband
for 25 years and father of my children, I am now able to call him
my hero." Privately, reports were swirling that she was feeling humiliated and deeply resentful. In the episode, the estranged spouses have
clearly not spoken in a long time and Kris is reeling at the recent string
of revelations about his new life, even though the *Keeping Up with
the Kardashians* special was allegedly filmed before he went public
to Diane Sawyer. When the two sit down together, Kris appears dis-
traught, breaking down in seemingly genuine tears. It is clear that she
hasn't been using the "tear stick" that her daughter is said to employ on
occasion when she wants to display emotion on the show. Bruce tells
Kris he doesn't want to hurt the family, especially her. "We've raised
amazing children and those memories will live inside forever," he says.

"Being honest is something we all would have appreciated," Kris
tells him. "The truth in your head is different than your actions. I
always knew that you struggled with wanting to dress differently and
that was something you did when you got that urge. I don't know
when you went from, 'This isn't working for me anymore and I'm
going to start taking hormones.' You never told me you were taking
hormones. . . . You never said this was going to be the end result, ever."
After she accuses him of being dishonest, Bruce refuses to be put on
the defensive. "You know you treated me badly those last four or five
years of our marriage."

During their encounter, Kris admits that she knew he had been
taking hormones before he met her but denied knowing he wanted to

be a woman. She concludes by telling him, "I miss Bruce and it's going to take me a minute to mourn that relationship. You think you're going to grow old with someone. . . . I have to mourn Bruce Jenner because I miss Bruce, I'll never be able to have Bruce, and all I have are my memories. I feel like Bruce died, and it's really hard for me to wrap my head around that."

On February 7, 2015, Bruce was driving a Cadillac Escalade when he rear-ended a Lexus, pushing it into oncoming traffic where it crashed head-on with a Hummer, killing the Lexus's driver, sixty-nine-year-old Kim Howe.

The question Jenner dodged for months was whether or not he would be charged with reckless driving. In August 2015, there were reports, quickly denied by the LA County Sheriff's Department, that the department would recommend that Jenner be charged with vehicular manslaughter, which carries a potential sentence of up to one year in jail.

Then, on September 30, 2015, the Los Angeles district attorney decided against charging Caitlyn.

"We believed from the start that a thorough and objective investigation would clear Caitlyn of any criminal wrongdoing," Jenner's attorney Blair Berk said in a statement. "We are heartened the District Attorney has agreed that even a misdemeanor charge would be inappropriate. A traffic accident, however devastating and heartbreaking when a life is lost, is not necessarily a criminal matter."

Although she was acquitted, Caitlyn was facing multiple multimillion-dollar lawsuits for negligence by victims, and their family members, of the deadly crash. Jessica Steindorff, a twenty-nine-year-old woman who was driving a Prius involved in the crash, sued Caitlyn in June 2015 for property damage and personal injury, and Kim Howe's stepchildren hit the transgender reality star with a wrongful death lawsuit.

A longtime friend of Jenner's accused him of misdirecting the serious offense by promoting his transition.

"Before Bruce got into the accident, he gave the world hints about his true sexuality," the friend who only agreed to be referred to as "Dan" said. "After the accident, he went full steam ahead. I truly believe he was trying to misdirect the negative publicity he received after the car crash. I don't think he would have gone so fast if he hadn't been in an accident. And it was clear he was worried about being charged in some way related to the death of the elderly woman. The Diane Sawyer interview was a great way to derail the whole thing and to turn the attention to his transgender. To this day I remain skeptical about Bruce's true motives."

By the time the special aired, Bruce had still not officially come out as a woman. He had told Sawyer, in fact, that he still wanted to be referred to as "he." It was around this time that I was put in contact with an NCAA coach who had known Jenner for years. He told me that he had been in contact with his old friend since the separation and that Bruce had confided what finally led to his decision to go public.

"I couldn't be part of the Kardashian circus anymore," he said. "I have to be real." It's similar to the language that he used on the Diane Sawyer special when he said, "This whole thing, the one real, true story in the family was the one I was hiding, and nobody knew about it."

The coach also told me that Bruce had revealed that Kris had influenced him to suppress his desire to be a woman for all those years. "She told him he should pray," he reveals, "that church would help heal him."

This sounded to me suspiciously like conversion therapy, though I'm not entirely sure whether the word *heal* was used by Kris or by the coach. Still, the idea of using religion to suppress homosexuality has a troubling history associated with evangelical Christianity, especially during the '80s and '90s, when the idea gained momentum in various Christian ministries throughout the United States.

In a 2015 article about the practice, the *Atlantic Monthly* cites the example of a girl named Julie Rodgers to illustrate how such therapy typically works.

"After she came out as a lesbian in high school, [Rogers's] conservative Christian parents urged her to join a ministry in Texas to help make her straight. Ministry leaders promised her that if she continued praying, reading the Bible, attending meetings, and of course, refusing to identify as gay, her sexual orientation would eventually change and she could even marry a man."

Evangelical Christians were fond of citing the supposed successes in which homosexuals underwent conversion or "reparative" therapy and thereafter labeled themselves "ex-gays." Kris Jenner was of course an early adherent of evangelical Christianity and attended prayer sessions led by Pat Boone, who has been regularly accused of homophobia. In the 2008 Kentucky election, for example, he recorded a robocall for Senator Ernie Fletcher, who was facing a tough Democratic opponent:

"Now, as an American and a Christian I am very conservative about the upcoming governor's election," Boone said on the calls. "Ernie Fletcher is a typical Kentuckian; he's worked long and hard for the state, its people, and its traditions. And, of course, he has come under attack by political opponents and now he faces a man who wants his job, who has consistently supported every homosexual cause: same-sex marriage, gay adoption, special rights to gay, lesbian, bisexual, even transgender individuals."

Before she founded her own church, Kris was a regular attendee of the Calvary Community Church in Westlake, California. The church has long been associated with homophobic positions. As recently as 2012, the church leadership fired a member of Calvary's executive team, Kevin McCloskey, when he came out as gay. He later wrote an essay for the *Advocate* about what happened when he revealed that he was dating a man.

"They were shocked to learn about my sexual orientation and were genuinely concerned for my family and me and all we were going through," he wrote. "'Even if I wanted to keep you,' my senior pastor said, 'you know it would never be accepted by the congregation.' I knew he was right. Our church is located in a very conservative, family-oriented enclave of Southern California, with very few openly gay people."

When Kris Jenner sought a pastor to run her new church, she chose a former pastor from that same church, Pastor Brad Johnson. Before he served at Calvary, Johnson received his training under another evangelical minister, Rick Warren, when Johnson served as a teaching pastor at Saddleback Church in Orange County.

Warren came under fire when he gave the invocation at President Obama's 2009 inauguration, and it was later revealed that he had posted a YouTube video supporting California's Proposition 8, the referendum to outlaw gay marriage in that state. More controversially, he was said to have been an early supporter of Uganda's infamous bill to make homosexuality a capital crime, and in March 2008, he was reported to have traveled to the country and told the Ugandan Church that gay rights is "not a civil rights issue," because homosexuality is not to be tolerated. "We shall not tolerate this aspect at all," he allegedly said. While he would maintain that he never supported the Ugandan bill and would call it "un-Christian," his earlier statements gave a fairly good idea of his views on homosexuality.

Apart from her religious affiliations with a virulently homophobic church, there is no evidence of Kris Jenner herself ever taking a stand on gay rights. A woman who knew her and Bruce for more than twenty years recently told me that she doubts Kris is homophobic.

It's not so much a question of Kris having a problem with gay people. She knows plenty. But you have to understand the circles that she and Bruce traveled in. Neither of them, let's face it, are

*very sophisticated. She was never comfortable with the liberal,
secular Hollywood crowd. She had lots of opportunities to hobnob with those people but she preferred the Giffords [talk show
host Kathie Lee and her late broadcaster husband Frank] and
the Garveys. Quite conservative, not very well educated. She and
Bruce were Republicans but not the right-wing, fire-breathing,
bigot variety. This was California, after all. So I think she just
didn't really understand it, even if she really knew that Bruce
had those tendencies way back when. She couldn't wrap her
head around that kind of thing. Gay people, maybe, but trans-
sexuals? They may as well have been aliens. She wouldn't have
been comfortable with it. I really don't know if her religious views
entered into it. Bruce actually went to church more than she did.*

I approached the advocacy group PFLAG to get their take on any
attempt by Kris to suppress her husband's trans feelings by encouraging
Bruce to heal himself through prayer when he still lived as a man. The
group's northeast regional president Amy Mesirow was troubled by
the allegation. "I share PFLAG's stance that people's sexual orientation
and gender identity are natural, and cannot be 'prayed away,'" she said.
"I imagine that any effort by Kris Jenner to have Caitlyn pray to cure
herself would only serve to damage her emotional and mental health,
as it has other LGBTQ people who have been asked to do this. When
transgender people of faith are told that God sees them as being sick,
this only compounds the harmful messages society sends them every
day about who they know themselves to be."

Another longtime advocate told me how concerned she was in
the days after Bruce first went public about his desire to become a
woman. "Word in the community was that Kris tried to get Bruce to
suppress his true desires and to cure himself by prayer and to remain
a man," the respected advocate who asked to go by the name of Sheila
told me. "That would have been very hard on Bruce. And from what

I've heard Kris was not the only person doing that. There were others before her. Bruce wanted to transgender for a long time. The world would have seen Caitlyn a long time ago if there were not people like Kris trying to get him to heal himself through prayer and to suppress his true path in life."

Before the dust had even settled on the Diane Sawyer interview, *Vanity Fair* announced that it would feature Jenner on the cover of its July issue. When it was announced that famed photographer Annie Leibovitz was shooting a "special" cover, speculation began to mount that the issue would be his official coming out as a woman. In the Sawyer interview, he had referred to his female identity as "her" but had declined to dress as a woman and had asked that he still be called Bruce. The New York *Daily News* had secretly captured a photo of Bruce in a dress back in April, but there had been no official appearance as a woman to date.

Now it appeared that he was going to use the respected magazine to unveil his new self. Sure enough, in advance of publication, the magazine leaked a stunning cover photo, taken by Leibovitz, featuring Jenner dressed in lingerie—a low-cut corset—and full glamorous hair and makeup. Days later, the issue hit newsstands with the headline, "Call Me Caitlyn."

"He says goodbye, she says hello," read the caption announcing that Bruce Jenner was now a woman named Caitlyn. It's hard to imagine that anything could have topped the dramatic coming out of the Diane Sawyer interview, but this appeared to create even more buzz as the world marveled at the new look.

By the time Caitlyn sat down with Buzz Bissinger for her first interview as a woman, it was clear that her taped reunion with Kris a few weeks earlier had not cleared the air between them. If Bruce had subtly implied to Diane Sawyer that his ex-wife was less than supportive, Caitlyn now added more detail.

"The first 15 years I felt she needed me more because I was the breadwinner," she explains of Kris.

Then really around the show, when that hit and she was running this whole show and getting credit for it and she had her own money, she didn't need me as much from that standpoint. The relationship was different.

I think in a lot of ways she became less tolerant of me. Then I'd get upset and the whole relationship kind of fizzled. One has to watch only a sampling of the show to see the interaction. A lot of times she wasn't very nice. People would see how I got mistreated. She controlled the money . . . all that kind of stuff.

When the reporter asked Kris for her side of the story, she told him that she couldn't understand how her husband, after a strong marriage, could just say "I'm done now" without explaining his gender-identity issues to her until after they had separated. "It was, like, the most passive-aggressive thing I think I've ever experienced," she said.

Within hours after Caitlyn's unveiling, she was being hailed as a hero—by the 700,000-strong transgender community; by her fellow celebrities, who were falling all over themselves to Tweet their support; and by the media, who praised Caitlyn's "brave" and "courageous" coming out.

"I'm so happy after living such a long struggle to be living my true self," she posted in her inaugural Tweet as Caitlyn. "Can't wait for you to get to know her/me." Within twenty-four hours, she had amassed one million followers, the fastest in history to achieve that milestone.

Instead of rushing to cash in on her new popularity, she let it be known that she planned to dedicate her new position to advocacy for the trans community and to help end discrimination against this marginalized group. A 2013 report released by the Human Rights Campaign, among other groups, had found that transgender workers had an unemployment rate double that of the general population. More troubling was a study that showed the attempted-suicide rate for transgender women and men was an eye-popping 41 percent, compared to 1.6 percent in the general population.

Caitlyn went out of her way to stress that she didn't consider herself a leader just because of her celebrity. "I would like to work with this community to get this message out," she said. "They know a lot more than I know. I am not a spokesman for this community. I believe we can save some lives here."

I was curious myself to know how grassroots trans people viewed Caitlyn's coming out and whether they thought it genuinely benefitted their community. Although reaction from community leaders had been largely positive since she'd announced her transition, there had been some backlash as well. The most glaring criticism surrounded the stunning *Vanity Fair* cover in which Caitlyn had widely been described as beautiful and glamorous for her lingerie shot.

"Caitlyn Jenner is just Kardashian 2.0," complained Zoey Tur, the trans correspondent for *Inside Edition* and host of the radio talk show *He Said, She Said*. "I've received well over 100 messages from trans women who said they didn't want to transition anymore because they feel that they can never live up to the Caitlyn Jenner ideal."

I wasn't particularly interested in hearing what so-called community spokespeople thought of Caitlyn. I wanted a grassroots perspective. I had once gone undercover as a gay actor to infiltrate Scientology, but this was definitely different. Now I resolved to pose as a man wishing to transition into a woman. With a little research, I found out about a trans support group that holds bimonthly meetings in Miami. I decided to attend a session. Posing as a gay person had been easy. Gay men look like everybody else. But if I were pretending to be trans, would I need to dress like a woman or at least put on some makeup or jewelry? It didn't take me long to discard that idea. I didn't want to go over the top and maybe give myself away. Besides, after a little research, I discovered that many trans people live their lives undetected before they fully transition, especially at work.

The group didn't publicize their meeting location, perhaps out of fear of harassment. But after making indirect contact, I was finally emailed a location.

I was greeted warmly by a trans man with short hair who appeared to be the facilitator. When I arrived there were only two other people, including an older woman, and I kept expecting more people to show, but it soon became obvious that we were the entire meeting. I introduced myself, using the pseudonym I always use when I go undercover, Al Newman (short for *Mad* magazine's Alfred E. Newman, my childhood inspiration.)

The facilitator, E.R., kicked off the meeting by answering a question that somebody had asked him earlier: how a person typically knows when they're trans.

"Not every trans person knows very early but many do when they're little, as little kids. Some of us have that memory of 'I knew then' and some don't, and I don't ever condemn people for not knowing when they were little, but I knew. I didn't know I was trans, because there's no words for that when you're a little kid, but you just know that you're different." He then asks me to introduce myself.

I tell the group that I've known for a long time about my gender identity but I never had the guts to come forward. "I think what convinced me finally was the Caitlyn Jenner stuff," I tell them.

E.R. nods knowingly. "You're not the only one I heard that from," he said. "That's made a big difference for a lot of people, not just on an internal and personal level, but societally. I've seen changes in the last month that are big. People on Facebook, Twitter, saying, 'I would have thought this person was a freak if I hadn't watched the Diane Sawyer interview. It must be so hard, what she's been through.' People who before only thought of trans people as crazy or freaks or whatever got to see this whole other side of somebody being very authentic, very honest, and somebody who they can relate to as a very famous athlete, as a man, and all of a sudden it gave credibility to the issue, it gave weight to our feelings; it's just been tremendous. Certainly there's been plenty of haters as well, but I prefer to look at what's positive and what's come out as positive for the movement."

He then congratulated me on "taking a big step." The other man introduced himself as Enrique. He introduced the woman beside him as his mother. I told him I thought it was cool that he brought his mother along. The middle-aged Latina woman said that it wasn't easy at first when her son told her he wanted to be a woman. "I was a little homophobic," she admitted. "I'm from Haiti and I had a Catholic grandma and my priest and the nuns at school taught me that being gay is wrong."

"You were very homophobic," Enrique tells her. "Thank you for coming. It means a lot."

"You're my baby," she replies.

"Don't call me that," he protests.

"I don't know whether to call you my little boy or my little girl," she says sweetly.

"She's also my ride," he notes. "I don't currently have a driver's license."

"Because I love you, I'm really trying to be supportive," his mother adds.

Enrique turns to E.R. and asks, "How does the process go of obtaining hormones and all that?"

"That's the easy stuff," E.R. responds. "People think that's the hard stuff. The hardest part is getting to your own internal acceptance, feeling you're going to be safe. That's much harder. Some places make you get a letter certifying you're trans, which I find very oppressive. Some places just make you sign a letter which they call 'informed consent,' where you say you're aware of the risks of the medications and you agree to the risks. Some regular doctors will do it but I recommend going to someone who has experience. They do a very basic psycho-social, which is how you get a letter. There are challenges."

He says that he went to a regular OB/GYN when he wanted to transition. "And for transitioning male to female, it's actually a very inexpensive prescription. It doesn't cost a lot. Hormones are easy; surgery is a little more complicated. Breast augmentation is comparable to what any other woman would pay. Thirty-five thousand dollars. But surgery is more complicated; you want to put some thought into it."

I asked the facilitator how he worked up the courage to come out as a man.

"I was part of a sorority and I had nothing in common with them," he recalled. "They were always like, 'Let's do our hair, our nails, and what about my boyfriend?' and I couldn't identify. I mean, I love men. I've always been attracted to men, so my orientation and gender are not necessarily tied in together in that way. A lot of people think trans men must date women but I never have. So I've always been attracted to the guys and always had that conversation with them, but that's all we had in common. And then when they found out I was trans, they'd ask, 'Well, don't you like women? You're a lesbian, right?'"

He said he recommends taking everything in small steps.

"First I cut my hair, then I started wearing boy's underwear. Then I started wearing ties," he explained, but he pointed out that he has a very close friend who just went "balls in."

After we finished laughing, he recalled, "She dived in. She didn't test the water at all. She dove in and couldn't be more happy. Starting hormones when you're transitioning from male to female is slower. For us, within a month, our voice starts to change, but for you all, the changes are a little bit less physical, unfortunately, and a little bit slower, so you could start hormones and for months nobody would even know anything is happening. If that's something you want to do; some people don't want hormones, they don't want surgery."

I asked whether he had any recommendations for a clinic where

I could get the procedure done. He told me he had simply gone to an OB/GYN but noted that there are a number of clinics in South Florida that specialize in the procedure. He offered to refer me. The group had been very helpful in providing perspective, so much so that I felt a little guilty about deceiving them. When I left the meeting, however, I decided that if I were to gain any insight into how Bruce became Caitlyn, I would have to head to her backyard.

Just days after the *Vanity Fair* issue hit the stands, I decided to go undercover at the same Beverly Hills clinic where Bruce had his Adam's apple removed back in 2014. When I landed in Los Angeles, I had my assistant Grace call the clinic on a Tuesday to try to book an appointment. But my plan hit a snag almost immediately. She told the receptionist that I was only in town for a few days, but she was informed that I couldn't just waltz in the same day and make an appointment. She said I'd have to fill out some forms before receiving a consultation. The usual wait time was several weeks. When Grace informed me that she was rebuffed, I told her to call back and demand an appointment for the next day. She was instructed to say I was a Middle Eastern prince with unlimited financial resources and that money was no object. That seemed to do the trick. The receptionist informed Grace that I could come in the following day.

When I arrived at the Beverly Hills Surgery Centre of Excellence on La Cienega Boulevard, I noted that it was just a few doors away from both Larry Flynt's towering *Hustler* building and the former offices of private investigator Tom Grant, with whom I had collaborated on my first book, about Kurt Cobain, almost two decades earlier.

The first thing that struck me upon entering the elegant clinic offices was a copy of the Caitlyn Jenner *Vanity Fair* issue lying out in the open on the receptionist's desk. I told her that I grew up in Canada but had moved to Israel when I was young because I had ancestors who were part of the Israeli royal family. I took a deep breath, hoping she wouldn't realize that there is no Israeli royal family. She didn't.

She informed me that Dr. Malek, the surgeon whom my sources told me treated Caitlyn Jenner, was out for the day. His assistant, Rozeta Avetisyan, a late-twentysomething attractive woman, came out to greet me and informed me that she would perform the consultation. When I discovered that she was Armenian, I wondered whether there was a Kardashian connection, but I hesitated to ask. After some small talk with Grace, we stepped into the examination room. I told Rozeta that I wanted to be "just like Caitlyn Jenner" and asked her if she knew anything about her surgery.

"We never talk about clients," she curtly replies. I take that as an admission that Caitlyn was treated by Dr. Malek. I tell her I had noticed the *Vanity Fair* cover on the reception desk and ask her how she thought Caitlyn looked on the cover. "I prefer not talking about it," she says. "But the cover looks very good."

She reveals that Dr. Malek is a world-class painter and she is eager to show me his work, but his paintings are located on the second floor, which is closed off for a few days for renovation. "Dr. Malek is an artist; he and his family are very serious in painting and creativity," she tells me. "That's why he is so good at surgery. He's very specific and detailed. He takes his time with every procedure. If you go online and type Malek Masoud, you'll see all his paintings. Him, his daughter—they're all painters."

Rozeta seats me in a small room and starts examining my face and neck. After only a few moments, she tells me it is "essential" to get some work done. Pointing to my neck area to the left and right of the Adam's apple, she says I need liposuction there.

"See this part and this part you can get this done. They'll clean it very nicely. As for the Adam's apple, he [Dr. Malek] needs to see it. He can shave it and do everything because he's a plastic and reconstructive surgeon."

Excusing myself for a moment, I fetch the *Vanity Fair* and point to the photo of Caitlyn on the cover, asking if he can shave it like that. "You want it like that?" she asks. I nod in the affirmative. "Yes, if you talk to him, he can do that for you."

She tells me the procedure will likely take between three and five hours and the recuperation would be around five to six months. "It varies from patient to patient," she explains. "Everybody recovers completely differently. You have to come in three days after the surgery and after that every week so we can follow up and see that everything is right."

Next, I inquire about the price. She tells me liposuction would be two thousand dollars and that the Adam's apple shave will be "substantially more" but will not commit to a figure. "When you see Dr. Malek, he will give you the exact price."

Next I tell her I want breast augmentation. She examines my chest area and tells me it won't be a problem. I ask her the price for this procedure and this time she has no hesitation replying. "It goes from six, seven, eight thousand. It depends on the size."

Meanwhile, Grace asks Rozeta if she can video some of the consultation so we can go back to the hotel and make a decision. I tell her I'm staying in the penthouse of the Four Seasons Hotel in Beverly Hills. In actuality, I'm staying at a $180-per-night hotel on the seedy part of Third Avenue in lower Beverly Hills. Grace tells her that I am willing to pay the maximum price.

"He, or, may I call her 'she,' wants the best in the world," Grace assures her. "Price is no object." Rozeta has no objection to us filming. As Grace trains her video camera, Rozeta also takes out a camera and starts taking digital photos of my neck from different angles. I ask her if I can get the surgery performed the next day. "No, not tomorrow," she said. "You need to get your blood work done and after that I can put you in for next week."

She tells me that before the surgery she'd show me pictures of people they've worked on. I ask her if there were any celebrities. "We do but it's very confidential," she replies. "It's very safe. You have nothing to worry about. He's been in business for over forty years. He knows his stuff."

Before we leave, she tells me she is optimistic they can help me on my "journey" and that surgery will help turn me into a beautiful woman.

CHAPTER SIXTEEN

During all those years on *Keeping Up with the Kardashians*, Bruce never really emerged as his own fully formed character, even though Kris had initially used his fame to pitch the show. Rather, he always came across as the mild-mannered, henpecked husband and father. Publicly, Kris liked to sing his praises.

"The best part is how much the kids adore Bruce," she told an interviewer. "He's the best daddy in the world. We get up at 5:30 and that's my only time to myself, when I can go to the gym. That's my ice cream for the day, working out. Bruce does the car-pool, the breakfast, feeds the baby, changes the diapers. Then he takes off for forty-seven cities in four days, or whatever. Thank God for phones and faxes. If only somebody would invent fax sex, we'd be all set."

But it never appeared that he was an important player either in the show or in the family, where Kris clearly dominated both personally and professionally. For the younger generation that made up the show's target demographic, it would have been difficult to guess that Bruce was once a ubiquitous personality in his own right. When the *New York Times* reviewed the very first show in 2007, Ginia Bellafante wrote, "Acting as patriarch of the family now is Bruce Jenner, the 1976 Olympic gold medalist whose emasculation would seem to begin with the absence of his name from the show's title, even though he is the only person in his household to have actually accomplished anything. Mr. Jenner seems to function now more or less as a domestic and weak-willed disciplinarian."

For all that time, people assumed that Bruce was okay with the way he came across. Now the world learned from Caitlyn that he had resented his treatment and found Kris controlling and manipulative. It appeared to confirm people's worst suspicions about the matriarch. It also appeared to coincide with a noticeable decline in the Kardashian brand. The first signs came when Sears announced that it was dropping the Kardashian Kollection of clothes and accessories, which had been a staple at the retail chain for years and had once sold as much as $600 million in a single year. Sales had been plummeting, and the retailer had been forced to deeply discount many of the family's line of affordable low-end merchandise. A $59 lace crop top, for example, was being offered for $9.99 on the company's website only two weeks after the Diane Sawyer interview.

Although Kim's personal brand appeared to remain strong, with a slew of endorsements and an ever-increasing presence on social media, a controversy in 2015 provided a telling insight into just how she and her family still used social media for questionable financial gain. When Kim became pregnant with her second child, America soon learned that she was enduring terrible morning sickness. It was hard to escape the news as she shared her agony on Facebook, Twitter, and her hugely popular blog. Imagine her relief when she appeared to discover a drug, Diclegis, that could relieve the awful symptoms.

"OMG," she wrote. "Have you heard about this? As you know my #morningsickness has been pretty bad. I tried changing things about my lifestyle, like my diet, but nothing helped, so I talked to my doctor. He prescribed me #Diclegis, I felt a lot better and most importantly, it's been studied and there are no increased risk to the baby. I'm so

excited and happy with my results that I'm partnering with Duchesnay USA to raise awareness about treating morning sickness. If you
have morning sickness, be safe and sure to ask your doctor about the
pill with the pregnant woman on it and find out more."

But as Kim reaped untold sums from posts like these, it appeared
that she might have been unwittingly jeopardizing the health of her
followers. In August 2015, the US Food and Drug Administration
slammed the company with which Kim had contracted to hawk the
drug and singled out her paid postings in particular. "The social media
post is false or misleading," it warned Duchesnay, "in that it presents
efficacy claims for Diclegis, but fails to communicate any risk information associated with its use and it omits material facts. Thus, the
social media post misbrands Diclegis within the meaning of the Federal Food, Drug, and Cosmetic Act and makes its distribution viola-
tive." Stories like these only reinforced the idea that the Kardashians
had become corporate shills—an image that Kim had been working
hard to shed since she married Kanye.

Keeping Up with the Kardashians ratings for season 10 had also
plummeted, with the series dropping viewers in droves. The premiere
of season 10 had drawn only 2.54 million viewers, beaten by another
reality show in its time slot, *The Real Housewives of Atlanta*, which
was watched by 3.2 million Americans.

Only a few months earlier, Kris had negotiated an incredible $100
million deal with E! to renew the series for four more seasons. Now the
network must have been wondering if they had thrown good money
after bad. Meanwhile, Caitlyn had announced that she would be par-
ticipating in a new reality series of her own that would be known as
I Am Cait, following her new life as a woman. It was widely reported
that she had demanded and received the same lucrative $100 million
deal that Kris had won to renew *Keeping Up with the Kardashians*.
When the new show premiered in July 2015, its debut episode drew
a healthy 4.7 million viewers over three showings. On that first epi-

sode, Kim appears and again shows public support for her stepfather but also delivers an ominous warning, apparently referring to Caitlyn's comments about Kris in *Vanity Fair*. "You look amazing; it's your time," Kim tells her. "But you don't have to bash us on your way up."

It appeared that while Caitlyn was indeed on her way up, the Kardashians might have been heading in the opposite direction. Or at least that's what the family feared. And it soon emerged that while Bruce Jenner had seethed with resentment all those years as he watched Kris control his life, he had also learned a thing or two from her savvy business techniques.

With considerable fanfare in June 2015, it was announced that Caitlyn had been chosen to receive the ESPY Arthur Ashe Courage Award, presented every year to an individual who "transcends sports." And although her initial coming out was widely praised in the sports world, there was now a significant backlash surrounding the news that Caitlyn Jenner was being presented with the award instead of "more worthy" candidates such as Lauren Hill, who had received widespread coverage playing college basketball for months despite suffering from terminal brain cancer that resulted in her death two months earlier.

Broadcaster Bob Costas called the decision to give Caitlyn the award a "crass exploitation play." *Friday Night Lights* producer Peter Berg posted a photo on Instagram of the amputee war veteran Gregory Gadson, who had been featured in Berg's 2012 film *Battleship*. Beside it was a photo of Caitlyn. The caption read, "One Man traded 2 legs for the freedom of the other to trade 2 balls for 2 boobs. Guess which Man made the cover of *Vanity Fair*, was praised for his courage by President Obama and is to be honored with the 'Arthur Ashe Courage Award' by ESPN?"

Responding to the criticism, the network immediately defended its decision to give Caitlyn the award. "I think Caitlyn's decision to publicly come out as a transgender woman and live as Caitlyn Jenner displayed enormous courage and self-acceptance," ESPY executive producer Maura Mandt told *Sports Illustrated*. "Bruce Jenner could have easily gone off into the sunset as this American hero and never have dealt with this publicly. Doing so took enormous courage. He was one of the greatest athletes of our time."

But it soon emerged that there was more to the decision. Behind the scenes, Caitlyn and her people had allegedly pulled off a ploy right out of the Kris Jenner playbook. Radar Online reported that the idea to present Caitlyn with the award originated from her own camp, which pitched the idea to the sports network in exchange for public relation plugs on her upcoming reality series.

"It was a brilliant move because the executives at ESPN loved the idea, and immediately began making sure it got done. Caitlyn's journey to accepting the award will also be featured on her upcoming reality show, *I Am Cait*," a source told the site. "There was a hiccup during the talks about Caitlyn receiving the award, and her reps were prepared to pull her interview with Diane Sawyer if she didn't get it. It was ironed out and ABC [the parent company of ESPN] owns one of the biggest stories of the year."

Meanwhile, Kim Kardashian appears to have gone out of her way to distance herself from the family brand as she forges a separate identity largely tied to her marriage with Kanye rather than as a reality-TV star. This would seem to leave her sisters and former business partners out in the cold, as they had long feared, watching her ascendancy. In April 2015, the couple achieved a significant coup in their joint quest to be taken seriously in the world of fashion when they appeared on the cover of the world's most prestigious fashion Bible, *Vogue*, photographed by the same photographer who had shot Caitlyn for *Vanity Fair*.

As yet another indication that she is consciously trying to shed her widely caricatured reality-TV image, it was announced that Kim would deliver a lecture on the "Objectification of Women in the

Media"—no small irony from the woman who only a few months earlier had posed for full frontal nude photos in the edgy lifestyle magazine *Paper*. To her credit, Kim had long associated herself with serious causes, especially her crusade to have the 1915 Turkish massacre of Armenians recognized as genocide. She had even volunteered to act as a UN ambassador like her purported role model, Angelina Jolie, but that sounds as much like a PR ploy designed to burnish her image as a realistic idea. After all, Jolie had successfully transformed herself from a widely disdained junkie bisexual into her present-day incarnation as "Saint Angelina" through a shrewd image reinvention worthy of Kris Jenner. But Jolie was also an Oscar-winning actor and had some bona fides to work with before her transformation.

While Kim has never been known for her political astuteness—she urged her followers to support Barack Obama in the US midterm elections even though he wasn't running for anything—she appears to be genuinely committed to using her influence for social change. She has also emerged as a strong supporter of Hillary Clinton's presidential candidacy and, in contrast to many of her mind-numbingly vapid peers, she hasn't been afraid to call herself a "feminist."

There have even been unconfirmed reports that Kim has been in discussions to extricate herself from the family brand and terminate her management agreement with Kris Jenner so that she can "move in a different direction." This seems exceedingly unlikely, given their close bond and the fact that Kim could never hope to find somebody as capable and business savvy as Kris whom she can trust. More likely it is a rumor deliberately designed to distance her personal brand from Kris's own tarnished reputation, at least until Kris concocts a way to make the public forget the story of the moment and once again pull the spotlight back onto her own family.

More credible are reports that Kris has been using alcohol to get over her apparent humiliation from Caitlyn's public revelations and the fact that her ex has been hogging the spotlight that had once been reserved for Kardashians. Kris's younger sister Karen Houghton had in fact implied as far back as the spring of 2014 that Kris was hitting the bottle heavily after her separation from Bruce.

"Pray for Kris Jenner she needs it . . . crazy. Shes a nutcase. She doesn't need prayers she needs sky vodka hahaha hahaha hahaha," Karen posted on Facebook in April 2014. Their father, Robert, was in fact an alcoholic whose death in Mexico years before was reportedly the result of drunk driving.

"Back in the day Kris was quite the party girl," a Los Angeles hair stylist named Stella Fagan told me, recalling that she had styled Kris's hair a number of times while she was still married to Robert. "Sometimes she reeked of alcohol when she came in to get her hair done. She was young, she was wild. Nothing like the all-American mom Kris Jenner we see on TV today."

Even after she emerged in the public spotlight, issues with Kris's drinking surfaced a number of times. In 2012, Kourtney Tweeted during a family vacation in the Dominican Republic after Kris fell into the pool. "I think my mom is definitely drunk already," she posted. "She is just such a freak." A year later, Khloé announced on video while attending a basketball game with Kris, "We're at a Clipper game. My mom is fucking drunk; what's new?" In 2013, Robert's widow, Ellen Kardashian, told *In Touch*, "I know her partying and drinking was a big issue in their marriage. I thought she had a problem with alcohol because she would drink in such excess. He worried about the children."

It's difficult to determine from these comments whether Kris genuinely has a problem or if, like many people, she likes to tie one on from time to time. She has undoubtedly kept a lower profile in the months following Caitlyn's unveiling, emerging occasionally to grant an interview. She seemed especially determined to counter Caitlyn's charge that she had "controlled" Bruce throughout their marriage.

"I guess if I get a little weird about something that isn't the way I want it, and I complain, then it's called controlling," she told the *New*

York Times. "I like everything a certain way. I'm not somebody who can just lay back and let it happen. That's never going to happen for me. And I think that's what's gotten me to where I am in life, at the same time. I can't turn it on and off."

In the summer of 2015, I spoke to a sixty-one-year-old Los Angeles fund-raiser who has known Kris since the '80s. I wondered if she could share some insight about her current frame of mind and the truth of Caitlyn's allegations.

"Everyone who goes to Kris's house has to sign a confidentiality agreement," she told me.

It's very annoying. Not even the Queen of England is as controlling as Kris. I knew her years ago from her days with Robert Kardashian and still bump into her today. They were good friends of mine. They were not together a lot. Kris used to show up at functions often alone. She was wild back in the day, lived very carefree. There were rumors about her having extramarital affairs and lots of stories about how she liked to party. Robert once told me she scared him, and that he had never met a more domineering woman in his life. She lived very similarly to the way her daughters live today—always in the spotlight, always needing to have a man in her life. With Bruce, I truly believe they went their separate ways years ago. They would rarely be seen together in public, only on the TV show, which I believe a lot of it was staged for ratings. The one thing I remember is that whenever I saw them together, they never showed any affection to each other. They looked more like business partners than a couple who were in love. Kris wanted the Kardashians to be a modern-day version of the Brady Bunch when she met Bruce. Two families coming together, living as one big happy family. But it never really happened. The Kardashian kids and the Jenner kids never really were very close. It was obvious there was a rivalry between them.

And I think that's one of the main reasons why Kris and Bruce's marriage didn't last. Too much tension, too much rivalry between the kids. The Jenner kids weren't pleased with how much attention Bruce gave Kris's kids. It got on their nerves. They confronted Bruce numerous times about this, especially Brody Jenner, who was furious that Kris wouldn't do anything to try to boost his music career. She had a lot of connections in music and could have done more to make Brody the star he wanted to be.

Kris's personality has always been up and down. I've known her for decades and she has never been consistent. She always seems stressed out. I do give her credit, though; she works harder than anyone I know. She's always been determined to make it big, and she was never shy to work for it. I can tell you for sure that without Kris, the Kardashians would never have made it remotely to where they are today. Kris is a shrewd woman, despite her dominating personality. The last time I saw her was a couple months ago at a restaurant. We talked for a few minutes. She was dining with that new alleged boyfriend of hers, Corey Gamble. She didn't look happy at all. I was worried something was wrong with her. I gave her a hug but didn't want to ask her what's wrong because her boyfriend was right there. I think despite all the fame and fortune, Kris is more sad and lonely than she lets on. The Kris I saw that night was not the Kris of old, who would light up a room when entering and would be the person everyone thought didn't have a care in her life.

And yet some things never change. When Khloé's ex Lamar Odom was found unconscious in a Nevada brothel in October 2015, the obvious conclusion was that he had been indulging in more than just the pleasures of the flesh. Considering his long-standing problems with drugs—which derailed both his NBA career and his marriage to Khloé—it didn't take much imagination to speculate what may have caused the troubled Odom to lapse into the coma that kept him unconscious for four days before he finally woke and was taken off life support. Indeed, *People* magazine eventually reported that he had cocaine and opiates in his system when he was brought into a Vegas hospital. But during the interval when the cause of Odom's condition remained a mystery, *TMZ* carried an "exclusive" report about what had caused the thirty-five-year-old to go "off the rails." According to "sources," Odom had been having a perfectly normal time at the Love Ranch until an episode of *Keeping Up with the Kardashians* aired on Sunday night in which he was featured. In the episode, Khloé recived a call from Lamar inform-ing her that his best friend, Jamie Sangouthai, had died of an apparent heroin OD. In another scene, Khloé was seen fleeing a nightclub after she heard Lamar was on his way in. "My heart dropped to my stomach" at the news, Khloé informed the cameras. *TMZ* reported that before the episode, Lamar was "chill" and there was no evidence he had been high on drugs or alcohol. Afterward, he was "irate" and "inconsolable." The leaks were not confined to *TMZ*. Even *People* participated. "It's hard for Khloé. He is on his last leg," a family friend told the magazine. For their part, the Kardashians wasted no time letting it be known that they "dropped everything" when they heard of Lamar's state. Kim even cancelled a baby shower she had planned.

Radar quoted a source describing the arrival of family members who came to visit while Lamar was still unconscious. "It's a shit show," the source said. "The Kardashians are trying to run every-thing. They walked into the hospital with cameras rolling. It was shocking, but hardly a surprise. . . . They are all crying and pretend-ing like they care."

The family denied the report but the brothel owner, Dennis Hof, let it be known that he had been contacted by Khloé's publicist order-ing him to stop talking to the media about Lamar. "That's Khloé's job," he was informed. Hof was not impressed. "I told her to pass on a message," he told CNN. "Go to hell."

The *Post* ran a feature detailing the family's questionable behavior during the ordeal. The headline spoke for itself, "How the Kardashians Exploit and Destroy for Reality Ratings."

Would Kris Jenner really go so far as to exploit her daughter's family tragedy for the sake of ratings? It's telling that more than one media outlet was even asking the question.

Even if the Kardashian brand is irreparably shattered, Kris still has an ace in the hole. Since the launch of the series in 2007, her daughters Kylie and Kendall have grown up in front of the camera, evolving from cute children into gorgeous teenagers before the viewers' eyes. In the process, they have embraced the family business in impressive fashion. In 2013, the sisters launched the Kendall and Kylie Collection with the youth-oriented clothing brand PacSun. Soon after, they launched their own jewelry line, followed by a shoe and handbag line and another clothing line with the British retailer TopShop. They also have separate product lines under their own names. Together, they have earned millions of dollars and are already far more successful than their older sisters, Khloé and Kourtney. Both have been modeling since they were young teenagers, and Kendall has emerged as a full-fledged supermodel, fronting campaigns for Marc Jacobs and Karl Lagerfeld and appearing on the covers of countless fashion magazines. It's widely predicted, in fact, that Kendall will eclipse even her sister Kim before long.

Meanwhile, like Kim, Kylie has been romantically involved with a world class hip-hop artist, Tyga, who publicly declared his love for the seventeen-year-old in the summer of 2015, even though Kylie denied at the time that they were dating. For her eighteenth birthday, Tyga, twenty-five, bought Kylie a luxury red Mercedes SUV. And, like her parents, Kylie appears to be a fan of facial augmentation, having developed a set of lips and a "resulting pout" nearly as distinctive as Kim's posterior. After denying for months that she had her lips enhanced, she finally came clean on an episode of *Keeping Up with the Kardashians*, on which she and her sister have emerged as the new stars and will undoubtedly help to keep up the ratings in the three years left on their E! contract. "I have temporary lip fillers," she confessed on the show. "It's just an insecurity of mine and it's what I wanted to do. I'm just not ready to talk to reporters about my lips yet because everyone always picks us apart. I want to admit to the lips, but people are so quick to judge me on everything. So I might have tiptoed around the truth, but I didn't lie."

Manufactured controversies and the girls' modeling careers have shifted them into the spotlight at a very convenient time. And while Kris may have been keeping a lower profile since Caitlyn's emergence, she is working as hard as ever behind the scenes to manage her youngest daughters' burgeoning careers and, of course, collecting her 10 percent. It may just help that Kendall and Kylie have a last name that is not Kardashian but one that aligns them with the hottest story of the year. It would surprise no one, in fact, if the name of the TV show is one day changed to *Keeping Up with the Jenners*.

Whatever the name of the show, the financially savvy matriarch seems to have predicted as far back as 2011 that the younger generation would be her secret weapon in prolonging her entertainment dynasty. In fact, she appears to have only one regret.

"My fantasy is to have *Keeping Up with the Kardashians*, Season 26. Who knew it would be this profitable? I should have had more kids."

ACKNOWLEDGMENTS

The making of a book is a collective effort. With that in mind, I want to express my deep gratitude to the following people who contributed to the making of *Kardashian Dynasty*.

I would like to thank the incredible team at Gallery Books and Simon & Schuster for enabling me to publish this book. Jeremie Ruby-Strauss who acquired and edited the book is brilliant. Jennifer Bergstrom is sterling, the most incredible publisher an author can ever dream of working with. The same goes for her incredible team, Jennifer Robinson, Nina Cordes, Elisa Rivlin, and the entire staff at Gallery Books.

Chris Casuccio and John Pearce at WCA worked tirelessly to make this book come to fruition.

Max Wallace is the consummate pro when it comes to selection and suggesting content.

I beg forgiveness of all those who contributed or inspired this book and whose names I have failed to mention.

Cassandra Simon, Ron Deckelbaum, Manny Pollock, Martin Rouillard, Johnny Tiegen, Autumn Stone, Whitney Penelas, Jarred Weisfeld, Eric Clark, Nadia Solmon, Dr. Charles Small, Dr. Eva Ritvo,

Judith Regan, Dylan Howard, Mancow Muller, Clover Sky, Al Zoltan, Roosevelt Hotel, Hardy Hill, Trey Newman, Jay Jackson, Rob Dolinski, David Gavrilchuk, Uber, Anthony Sabin, Ronnie Tochman, Alex Doyan, Emmanuel Wilcox, Les Weitzman, Michael Friedlieb, Irving Jacobson, Chaim Leibovitz, Sirius XM, Opie & Jimmy, Travis Tefft, Sam Roberts, Edward Santiago, James Doligan, Nikita Rooney, Cheryl Lapierre, Dany Houle, Martine Albert, Carol Lagace, Marc Andre Lord, Gabriel Auclair, Atalier, Stephane Fiset, Claude Lussier, Donna Block Taran, Mike Cohen, Stuart Nulman, Tony Bingham, Matthew Hould, Fred Cabrera, Althea Munger, Timothy Klein, Alexandria Benson, Bertha Carrasaco, Rudy Virag, Jamie Brewer, The Detroit Cast, American Airlines, Gabriel Tyner, Candice Fishman, Roger Winchester, Leona Scott, Angela Joyner, Emma Segal, Taylor Roman, Laurent Medelgi, Esmond Choueke, Kris Kostov, Rory and Diana Conforti, Barbara Baker, Harry Unger, Margot Montpezat, Ratep Cirag, Tony Gadd, Ellen Vaynerchuk, Bridget Fox, Emmanuel Kuhn, Tori Dalton, Mark Williams, Yaniv Yanckovich, Roberto Dia, Carmen Mia, Teemu Aaltonen, Luke Milovanski, Tess Ryan, Trixie Dupont, Vince Cauchon, Sando Williams, Jason Turcotte, Ruth and Helen, Barry Weinstein, Byron Adams, Blake Harper, Jeff Moriarty, Summer Logan, Enya Rose, Mark Stinson, Jake Lieberman, Marcy Stein, Alberto Rodriguez, David Mindel, Herm Vinson, the late Joe Franklin, Kaira Jones, Giana Richardson, Mina Guerrero, Moishe Rabinovitch, Tova Waxman, Gavin Solomon, Alannah Shechter, Regan Weiss, Phebian Markus, Glenn West, Yuri Mandel, Javier Santos, Alissa Grant, Joanna White, Harry Cohen, Abby Taran, Lawrence B. Benenson, Lina Blumberg, Joseph Del Vecchio, Al Perlmutter, Patricia Fourcand, Elza Carlos, Tommi Aaltonen, Margot Montpezat, Vivaldi Jean-Marie, Steven Uran, Susanne Birbragher, Glenn Feder, Yanko Horvath, Vanesa Curutchet, Dov Shapiro, Jonathan Ollat, Eric Dulac Graeme Dunne, Jennifer Cechetti, DJ Frank Delour, Michelle Richardson, Xin Rassinoux, Nola Perez, Dragana Chang, Albert Faur, and all my loyal readers at IUC.